Derek Jarman – Moving Pictures of a Painter

Derek Jarman – Moving Pictures of a Painter

Home Movies, Super 8 Films and Other Small Gestures

Martin Frey
Translated by Michael Wetzel

Ingram Content Group Inc.
LA VERGNE, TENNESSEE

First English edition:
Copyright © 2016 by Martin Frey, Vienna

Title of the original German edition:
Derek Jarman - Bewegte Bilder eines Malers
Home Movies, Super-8-Filme und andere kleine Gesten
First published edition:
Copyright © 2008 by Martin Frey, Vienna

Cover design and typesetting:
Copyright © 2016 by freyprojects, Vienna

Book interior layout:
© 2016 by freyprojects, Vienna / Joel Friedlander, San Francisco

Translation into English:
Michael Wetzel, Berlin

Printed and published by
Ingram Content Group Inc. – La Vergne, Tennessee

Cover illustrations:
Derek Jarman, *Sightless*, 1993
© Estate of Derek Jarman. Photo: Prudence Cuming Associates
Stills from the film JOURNEY TO AVEBURY, Derek Jarman, 1973
Derek Jarman 1992 courtesy. © LUMA Foundation

Photo page 2:
Derek Jarman, Berlin, 1988. © Photo: Ekko von Schwichow

A CIP catalogue record for this book is available from the British Library.

Library of Congress Control Number: 2016904674

Derek Jarman – Moving Pictures of a Painter / Martin Frey. —1st Engl. ed.

ISBN 978-3-200-04494-4

Contents

[1]

Introduction

DEREK JARMAN, WHO COMPLETED a degree in painting and stage design at London's Slade School of Art, became known to a broader public primarily through the medium of film. However, he never saw himself as a film-maker and *also* a painter but always as *primarily* a painter. Painting was his most important and direct medium of expression, his 'lifeline': the filmic images are the moving pictures of a painter. The first edition of *Derek Jarman – Moving Pictures of a Painter* was published in German in 2008. It was the first work in German to deal in depth with the works of Jarman. In terms of content, it is primarily an examination of Jarman's lesser known and – at first glance – not readily accessible work in the area of home movies and Super 8 films as well as the 'cinema of small gestures' he developed out of them. The English translation is based on the unaltered original text. Only the bibliography and filmography have been expanded and supplemented.

In 1987 I saw THE ANGELIC CONVERSATION for the first time, at Amsterdam's Desmet cinema: I was impressed and fascinated by the extraordinary intensity of the film's images. THE ANGELIC CONVERSATION provided the decisive impulse for my gradually becoming interested in the – at that time, little-known – British artist and his work during the years that followed. However, until the early nineties, the search for informative material resembled the proverbial hunt for a needle in a haystack. Aside from Jarman's first autobiographical works, *Dancing Ledge* (1984) and *The Last of England* (1987), a few thin volumes were the source of all the information available in the realm of secondary literature: *After Image 12: Derek Jarman ... of Angels & Apocalypse* (1985), *De Jonge Romantici en Derek Jarman in de Britse Film* (1986, published on the occasion of an Amsterdam film festival on the Romantic Aesthetics) and *The Complete Derek Jarman* (1989, edited by the Kommunales Kino Stuttgart). These publications already contain detailed filmographies and initial theoretical approaches towards Jarman's work. His feature films and some of his Super 8 films were gradually released on video and later on DVD. Until the mid-nineties, however, the area of secondary literature – with the exception of a few exhibition catalogues – consisted solely of various magazine and journal articles, which vary greatly in terms of quality and approach. Noteworthy publications about Jarman appeared only after his death in February of 1994. However, in addition to his films and artworks, Jarman himself continued to tirelessly publish further texts, which were always very autobiographical in nature.

For Jarman, life and work represented an indivisible unity that immediately and directly manifested itself in every area of his work as an artist, by way of autobiographical elements and points of reference. His numerous texts and publications are thus among the central and most important sources for this book – with their subjective mode of expression always taken into account. In particular his two books *Dancing Ledge* and *The Last of England*, which were published in the mid-eighties, provide a great number of valuable details about the history of his Super 8 films' creation and their background. However, along with *Modern Nature* (1991) and *At Your Own Risk* (1992), these books primarily provide very personal information about his childhood and adolescence in post-war England, which he experienced as repressive, and his coming out during his studies as well as the liberated life of the seventies. They also provide detailed information about his struggle against the permanent repression and unequal treatment of homosexuals during the Thatcher era, about how he dealt with his own HIV infection and later illness and about his personal commitment to combating discrimination against people infected with HIV or suffering from Aids.

The direct presence of autobiographical elements in his works therefore stands at the centre of my examination of his work. Thus, an initial attempt to more closely grasp Jarman's individual understanding of the home movie in connection with the concept of 'home' is carried out in the chapter 'Somewhere over the Rainbow – Images of Childhood'. He integrated numerous sequences from the store of his parents' and grandparents' 8 mm films into his film THE LAST OF ENGLAND; in this way, he provides us with very personal glimpses into his own (family) history. In an environment constantly experienced as hostile, Jarman himself gradually developed isolated islands of individual strategies, which I refer to as the 'strategy of the autobiographical' and the 'strategy of naming'. In this context painting became the first form that he explored, and it was originally primarily an opportunity to withdraw into a free space created by himself. Chapter 3 explores the question of influences from the fields of painting and literature on his work. The Beat Generation, Allen Ginsberg, Robert Rauschenberg, David Hockney and Yves Klein – above all, however, his first journeys to America – produced a lasting resonance. A multilayered dissolution of boundaries becomes manifest in every area of Jarman's work: collage techniques, associative elements of the fragmentary and the open narrative forms inherent to them become elemental means of communication in his paintings, films and texts.

Throughout his life Jarman nonetheless vehemently resisted the attempts made to categorise him, particularly with regard to his filmic work. He was always focused on his desire to visually realise a message; the appropriate medium was selected during the search for the form of realisation corresponding to the given case. Classifications by means of keywords, such as 'avant-garde film' or 'experimental film' lead to a dead end in approaching his work – as does a polarisation into 'narrative' or 'non-narrative', with its implicit evocation of diverse approaches from film theory or aesthetics. In the chapter 'Beware of Definitions', this issue is discussed in greater detail and – in direct connection with the autobiographical elements inherent to his films and his self-image as a painter – an attempt is made to position his work in an individual fashion.

Jarman, who grew up with the tradition of the classic home movie, extended this tradition while modifying it. In the early seventies, when he attempted to liberate himself from the outwardly imposed conventions of painting in that period, the Super 8 camera seemed to him like the ideal means to do so. Thus the images of his first Super 8 films displaced the impersonal, geometrical surfaces of his paintings. His camera became his brush, and light took the place of colour. Chapter 5 analyses the shooting techniques he explored in connection with the process-oriented form of working that he developed – a practice which originated in the spontaneous and improvisational recordings of his first home movies and Super 8 films. His filming without a screenplay, which also originated in the early home movies, additionally demanded an extreme openness to chance elements and their unpredictable results: the camera became a part of everyday life. Finally, an exemplary exploration of the most representative films for each of five thematically grouped areas follows. The aesthetic results that Jarman was able to achieve with his Super 8 films – but also the freedoms he enjoyed during the film-making process and his independence in terms of production – led him to continue to pursue the idea of developing the Super 8 format into a professional and recognised medium in the field of film. He called this the 'cinema of small gestures', and his films IN THE SHADOW OF THE SUN, THE ANGELIC CONVERSATION and IMAGINING OCTOBER belong in this context. The first two are discussed in detail in Chapter 6.

In December of 1986, one year after completing THE ANGELIC CONVERSATION, Jarman learned that he was HIV-positive. The topic of Aids had been omnipresent to him for years on account of numerous infections and deaths among his circle of friends and acquaintances. Nonetheless, the knowledge of his own infection brought about fundamental changes, for example, the direct politicisation in the themes of his remaining films or his direct and active political commitment to the gay rights movement. However, 1986 was to become a decisive year not only because of his all-defining diagnosis with HIV, but for other reasons as well. Jarman was finally able to complete CAR-AVAGGIO, his first film on 35 mm, after spending years working on it. And it was also in the same year that he began with THE LAST OF ENGLAND, the film with which he would bid farewell to the 8 mm format. Only a few years before, Jarman had still been determined to professionalise the use of the Super 8 format in feature films, but after THE LAST OF ENGLAND he intensively turned his attention to working with 35 mm film; from then on, he used Super 8 only selectively. Years later, he explained this turning away from 8 mm film through precisely that shift in content from the 'documentation' of private events or associative sequences of images to 'concrete' themes, whose appropriate formal realisation was now the focus of his interest. However, parting with Super 8 did not mean parting with the home movie and the ideas of the 'cinema of small gestures'. On the contrary: for Jarman, work on 35 mm productions still meant the collective realisation of a project, and it meant working with friends – perhaps more so than ever.

At this point I would like to thank Michael Wetzel for his very thoughtful and perceptive translation of my work into English and Igor Hlavati for his dedicated support in finalising the English edition.

I would additionally like to thank all of my friends who have assisted me in searching for material and have engaged in very valuable discussions dealing directly with the works of Derek Jarman. I would like to express my special gratitude to Andreas Brunner, MA, Holger Reichert, MA, and Wolfgang Wilhelm, MA, who provided decisive assistance with their readiness to engage in discussion and their critical view from the outside. I also thank Prof. Wolfgang Greisenegger and Prof. Ulf Birbaumer, of the Institute for Theatre, Film and Media Studies at the University of Vienna, for supervising my work and for the valuable impulses they offered over all the years.

I would furthermore like to thank the following individuals and institutions who provided valuable assistance to me while I conducted my research: Janet Moat, Special Materials Librarian at the British Film Institute, London, who helped me greatly while looking through the original material on site; Tim Highstead and the team from ICA – Insitute of Contemporary Arts, London, for their support in looking through the Super 8 films by Derek Jarman; James Mackay, of Basilisk Ltd, London, for granting his permission to produce these copies; Susanna Goodson, of the Museum of the Moving Image, London, who provided me with help in my search for literature; Aino-Astrid

Gaedtke, of Premiere Medien GmbH, Hamburg, Redaktion Kino, who sent me a VHS copy of Corny Littmann's portrait of Derek Jarman, which had been broadcast on Premiere in 1993; and Henny Brandhorst, of Homodok in Amsterdam, which repeatedly provided me with copies of recent magazine and newspaper articles about Derek Jarman.

I thank the following individuals and institutions for their assistance in searching for reproductions, sending me images for the reproductions in my text and granting permission to print them:

Keith Collins (The Estate of Derek Jarman) and James Mackay, and additionally Dennis Bell (Bob Mizer Foundation), Prudence Cuming Associates, Jeannine Guido (The Eli and Edythe L. Broad Collection, Los Angeles), Désirée Hailzl (Bildrecht, Vienna), David Hockney, Mike Laye and Katja Lehmann (The Museum of Modern Art, New York/Scala, Florence), Margaret C. McKee (The Menil Collection, Houston, Texas), Thomas Matyk (MAK – Museum für angewandte Kunst/Gegenwartskunst), Domniki Papadimitriou (Birmingham Museums & Art Gallery), Ekko von Schwichow, Howard Sooley and Laura Whitton (Tate Gallery, London).

[2]

Somewhere Over the Rainbow
– Childhood Images

'Oh rainbow colour
please wash away
the grey in my life
the grey of the day.'[1]

IN THE BEGINNING THERE was a rainbow. Jarman's first film experience, whose impressions were to accompany and influence him throughout his life, lies a long way back. It was Victor Fleming's THE WIZARD OF OZ, which Jarman saw at the age of five – with his parents on a cold winter day in Rome in the year 1947, at a matinee for the children of members of the air force. Fascinated by the breathtaking scenes, the house whirling through the air and the adventures that Dorothy Gale experienced in that dreamland over the rainbow, this film was to fill his childhood with dreams and nightmares: 'The lights were dimmed and we were transported to Kansas. It started happily enough with Dorothy singing "Somewhere Over the Rainbow". She was magical and I wished the other kids in the cinema – my schoolfriends – could have sung like her. But then it began to go wrong. A terrible storm blew up. I hung on to my seat, desperately, as the menacing dust devil bore down on us. No one else in the cinema seemed to be taking the danger seriously, and then, pure horror, we were blown into the sky. [...] I bolted and was captured by the usherette and handed back along the row to my embarrassed parents. I took part in the rest of THE WIZARD OF OZ, rather than merely watched it, and am grateful to this day that it had a happy ending.'[2]

Over the rainbow a wondrous dreamworld shines in glaring Technicolor; at first glance it corresponds to that 'place where there isn't any trouble [...] far away, behind the moon', which Dorothy dreams of on her farm in Kansas. Victor Fleming's 1939 film permits its viewers to escape from their realities and invites them on a journey to a perfectly staged fantasy world, where evil is conquered through seemingly magical powers. At the end, with the conciliatory words 'There's no place like home', they are released 'home' once more into their own worlds. This first cinematic experience of his childhood impressed Jarman so much that it still continued to fascinate him many years later. In his autobiographical texts *Dancing Ledge*, *The Last of England*, *Modern Nature* and *Chroma*,[3] he repeatedly refers to the film and to its conscious or unconscious influence, which left its mark – among other things – on the scenery of THE DEVILS, which he had developed for Ken Russell in 1970, and a short scene in THE TEMPEST, which actually displays astounding similarities to THE WIZARD OF OZ: '[...] Stephano, Trinculo and Caliban danced along the Bamburgh sands and I realized I'd directed them as if they too were on the road to the wicked witch's castle.'[4]

As in the case of the film, we find a world in black and white on this side of the rainbow: Michael Derek Elworthy Jarman was born during the Second World War, on 31 January 1942, in the small suburb of Northwood in north-western London. In multiple ways his family history seems to be directly interwoven with the history of British colonialism in the nineteenth and early twentieth centuries. His mother was born in Calcutta, studied at the Harrow School of Art and later worked as an assistant to the British couturier Norman Hartnell. Her parents worked in the tea and timber trade in India and retired to Northwood when they became older. Jarman's father was from the second generation of a family that had left its farm in southern England (Uplowman, Devon) in the late nineteenth century and immigrated to New Zealand to work in agriculture near Christchurch, on the southern island. The 'Elworthy' added to Jarman's name refers to a distant connection with a community of the same name in the English county of Somerset: 'My father told me that the Jarmans linked names with the Elworthys early in the eighteenth century when they married the last of the line. When he arrived here in 1928 he still had relatives in Exeter. Jarman is a fairly common West Country name.'[5]

Jarman's father came to England in the late twenties, originally intending to remain only a few years; he enlisted in the Royal Air Force in London, where his career as a military pilot, officer, commander and bomber pilot began.[6] His return to New Zealand was prevented by the Depression years that followed and the beginning of the war in 1939. That was the year when Jarman's parents met at a dance at the Northolt airfield; they married in March of 1940. They were able to announce the birth of their son two years later: 'My parents sent out a card, a drawing of me in a spitfire. Welcome Pilot Officer Derek Jarman and congratulations.'⁷ The Spitfire, which had already attained mythical status during the war and epitomised the victorious British warplane, became a cradle and announced the joyous event while also expressing the desired choice of career.

War and Disciplining

In later years Jarman himself reconstructed and filled out the trail of memories leading back to his early childhood with the help of the extensive photographic and film material of his parents and grandparents. From the last four years of the war, which were simultaneously the first four years of his life, it is primarily the din of warplanes, bombs and sirens howling in the ruins of the war that were still present in his memory: 'The bomb dropped in this child's eye.'⁸ However, it was not only the outside world but also the inner world of the family that was becoming dominated by a more and more extreme militarisation: in the years that followed, Jarman's father – who had flown numerous missions against Nazi Germany as an RAF pilot – developed into an almost tyrannical, strictly patriarchal and authoritarian father figure for Jarman, who later mentioned him as a substantial cause of his extreme aversion against every form of authority and patriotism. Jarman experienced his father in ambivalent terms. The father of the family – whom he experienced on a real level as 'bad', authoritarian and violent and who forced him to put on a uniform and join the cadets – stood in contrast to an abstract, ideological notion. The figure of the 'bad' father was simultaneously also the figure of a 'good' father, who had fought heroically against the enemy: 'Old RAF flying jackets, loaded pistols, medals and wartime souvenirs. They became my inheritance. I have never been anti-military in the way that some are, how could I be? My father fought a hard war. He fought Hitler, prosecuting the war with a violence that proved uncontainable. I don't know how to solve that, but without men like my father the war would not have been won! After it was over, he carried on the war.'⁹

Jarman linked memories of pleasant moments in the first years of his life almost exclusively with life at the Northwood home of his grandmother Mimosa – who repeatedly protected him from the violent attacks of his father – and with his mother, whose 'life was as open as my father's was closed' and whose warm-heartedness and love of life likewise stood in contrast to his father.¹⁰ The house in Northwood was synonymous with a feeling of 'home', which lasted only a short while – very much like that place where Dorothy is so happy to return at the end of THE WIZARD OF OZ. Directly after the end of the war, however, this safe and well-defined world fell apart. For Jarman the actual militarisation of his surroundings, of his immediate 'life-world', began only after 1945 and would become substantially more intensive and extensive in the years that followed. Because of his father's profession Jarman did not live the life of the classic 'nuclear family' of the fifties, settled down in a terrace house; instead, an unsettled period of a nomadic existence began and went on for years, leading the family through the bleak landscapes of countless RAF stations and military barracks: to Rome in 1946, Cambridge in 1947, Abingdon in 1948, Long Hanborough in 1949, Kidlington in 1950–51, Yorkshire in 1952, Somerset in 1953 and Karachi (Pakistan) in 1954.[11]

The themes of militarisation and war would later also be directly or indirectly present in many of his works – not in the form of abstractly condemnatory metaphors for violence and inhumanity but, instead, in a form often traceable back to personal experiences and impressions from the past or present. References of this kind emerge in varying degrees of clarity in several of his films. On the one hand IMAGINING OCTOBER, which is based on material from a journey to the Soviet Union, reflects different forms of repression in two political systems as different as those of the Soviet Union and the United Kingdom. On the other hand, in addition to the societal state of war in THE LAST OF ENGLAND (see pp. 25 ff.), SEBASTIANE also thematises and deals ironically with power structures in a wider sense among soldiers – entirely in Jarman's pacifist sense and according to the motto: 'If we must have troops let's have them in bed.'[12]

In this context only the cinematic conversion of Benjamin Britten's WAR REQUIEM, as a reworking of existing material, takes the form of a thematically adapted condemnation of the senselessness of war or the violent pursuit of conflicts:[13] 'War, the most celebrated of institutions, has many memorials, but where are the memorials to peace?'[14] In his oratorio, Britten had musically and thematically interwoven the texts of the Latin requiem with poems from the front by Wilfred Owen, a young soldier of the First World War, who was shot and killed by a German soldier one week before the end of the war. In 1989, two years before the Gulf War and before fighting began in the former Yugoslavia, Jarman completed his film WAR REQUIEM. He had integrated historical film and propaganda material from both world wars – but also from war zones of recent decades, such as Cambodia or Afghanistan – into the film and thus visually situated the theme at the level of a general condemnation. The images of the film involve no speech and are associatively arranged relative to Britten's composition. By using numerous flashbacks (in Super 8) to thematise the life of Owen and make it into the plot structure of the film, Jarman counters the danger of seemingly abstract generalisations at the level of content. The condemnation, which is kept general, is personalised and rendered directly intelligible and tangible. In the script for WAR REQUIEM, which contains numerous comments and personal notes, Jarman once again makes the link to his own history clear: 'My father was congratulated by George VI for his small part in winning the war; he flew one of the very first missions from Lossiemouth, against the German advance in Norway. He remained on active service until 1944; he retired in 1957 when I was fifteen. It seemed to me he lost everything in the numbing destruction to which he was party; it drove him into some far-off region from which he never returned. A world distant from everything and everyone around him. He stared in disbelief at the society he had helped to save. In 1939, he was young, handsome and artistic, but unlike Owen unable to release his inner feelings. Owen's poems scream off the page, my father embraced silence. He never spoke of what had happened. He stopped playing the piano.

'I missed the National Service by two years, but Dad made up for my loss: he put me into uniform, and barracks, in Gibraltar, and taught me how to fly in a dual-trainer Chipmunk. But the nearest I came to the horror of war was at the age of six, in RAF Halton, when I had my tonsils removed. I was put quite alone in a ward full of young men, who had been dreadfully maimed by the war. One of them, surrounded by screens, coughed up blood continuous-ly; others had lost limbs. Alone for the first time in my life, and feeling very poorly, the few days I spent there left an indelible memory on me.'[15]

However, this environment of his youth defined by drill, discipline and disciplining was only briefly limited to his life in the monotone brick housing estates secured behind the barbed wire of the military camps. Very soon it had expanded to include a further very personal area of experience characterised by his attending constantly changing boarding schools, which were also organ-ised along strictly hierarchical-authoritarian lines. In these schools discipline and order were taught and experienced in terms of desirable ideals and it was not rare for the cane, which was seen as a suitable pedagogical instrument, to be put to use. Both the permanent repression of individual personality devel-opment and the prohibition against experiencing a self-determined sexuality became a lived reality in this closed system. Jarman recalls this situation in several of his autobiographical texts: 'There were bells for lessons, bells for in-spections of shoe polish, trouser crease, clean collar, combed hair. Punishment and beatings. [...] Bells for PT, the cadet corps, marching on the spot, field days, cross country running, rugby. There were character building bells, bells for fagging, above all there was the chapel bell. Could all of this be conceivably thought "a normal upbringing"?'[16]

Teaching, exercising, living and praying were all done to the rhythm of the school bell. Mental and physical fortification were accompanied by cor-poral punishment and repression. Jarman ironically cites this traditional, hier-archically authoritarian educational system in a scene in THE GARDEN. Nine scholars attempt to funnel their knowledge into their pupil to the rhythm of the crushing descent of a cane. Before the projected background of a high-voltage power line and the Dungeness (see p. 67) nuclear power station, the scholars visibly enter into a state of ecstatic rapture and the schoolboy rotates an old globe more and more quickly:[17] a world which – precisely through the rationalism of science and education – is increasingly spinning out of control.

Sexuality was a blind spot on the 24-hour schedule of the boarding schools, and nonetheless – precisely for this reason – it was secretly and covertly omnipresent. When a nine-year-old Jarman revealed his fondness for a fellow pupil in the dormitory of the Hordle House School in Milford and was caught in his bed one night, he had perpetrated an 'act' that was strictly punished within this system and would have serious consequences for him. Punished more harshly by the school's director than any other offence, Jarman and his friend were publicly caned in front of the entire school and threatened with expulsion. Jarman wrote extensively about this experience that had been so formative for him in both *Dancing Ledge* and, under the title 'Child Abuse', in *The Last of England*: 'This public exposure gave me an incredible shock and opened wounds that will never heal. The violence of the attack drove my heart into shadows, where it remained buried. I became detached and dreamy, spent hours alone painting or watching the flowers grow, had a physical aversion to chumminess and sexual innuendo, organised games and school showers. [...] From thirteen to eighteen I had no form of sexual expression at all.'[18] The boarding school students had begun to develop their own, 'internal' rules and hierarchical systems within these school structures; in this way they countered their feeling of powerlessness through their own rituals of power.

It was not until the eighties, that is, decades later, that a series of films set in boarding schools, such as MAURICE (UK, 1987, dir. by James Ivory), ANOTHER COUNTRY (UK, 1984, dir. by Marek Kanievska) or DEAD POETS SOCIETY (USA, 1989, dir. by Peter Weir), undertook attempts of varying merit to deal with these taboo themes from different perspectives. Both MAURICE (the film version of a novel by Edward Morgan Forster) and ANOTHER COUNTRY (based on a play of the same name by Julian Mitchell) produce a more or less clichéd and romantically idealised image of life and gay love affairs at turn-of-the-century or 1930s British boarding schools. Sexuality between the students, which was to be kept secret and repressed, and the hierarchical structures of life at the boarding schools are thematised in a marginal way and thus seem primarily to take the form of a thematic veneer, a means to a (cinematic) end: the protagonists themselves make their way through the scenery with a dandy-like nonchalance. In MAURICE, rudimentary solutions are found in attempts at upper-class repression and the sexual fulfilment provided through a lower-class servant. By contrast, in ANOTHER COUNTRY, an enemy of the system confronts the hostile system. Along with its superficial systemic critique with the help of boarding school pupils citing Marx, this film also makes use of the equation 'homosexuality – communism' in trying to deal with the topic of the homosexual British diplomat Guy Burgess. Burgess was exposed as a Soviet spy in England in 1951, and he fled to the Soviet Union together with his colleague Donald Maclean. This was that phase of the 'Cold War' in which the UK, under pressure from the US and Senator Joseph McCarthy's hunt for communists, had also launched a campaign against homosexuals in government institutions and classified homosexuals as a security risk.

In Peter Weir's DEAD POETS SOCIETY, on the other hand, the structure of an American elite school – with its corresponding rituals of obedience and the individuals acting and seemingly trapped within them – forms the thematic focus, and becomes a metaphor for the structures of life or, alternatively, society in general. The school's four fundamental principles of tradition, honour, discipline and excellence are countered through the figure of the dedicated teacher and freethinker John Keating, a personified plea for self-determination and taking responsibility for one's own actions – even (and particularly) within a system that seems almost totalitarian. Poetry is freed from its ivory tower of being an end in itself, written into reality and made fruitful through the well-known saying 'carpe diem' (seize [lit. 'pluck'] the day), from Horace's *Odes*. It becomes a key that opens the way to a concrete experience of knowledge previously only abstractly transmitted, and it also renders concealed mechanisms of power transparent.

Nonetheless, the British director Terence Davies has created the most personal – and simultaneously also the most convincing – exploration of the topic with his autobiographically influenced TERENCE DAVIES TRILOGY (UK, 1976/1980/1983), which features the character of Joseph Tucker living in Liverpool. Unlike the other films already mentioned here, it depicts the violence of the regulations, threats and scrutiny just as directly and authentically as the pressure of a tabooed sexuality not lived out and that feeling of being an outsider which is caused by an environment based strictly on heterosexual norms. The personalised experiences here are immediate and direct. Particularly in the first two parts, 'Children' and 'Madonna and Child', direct connections are revealed between a highly masochistic homosexuality necessarily lived out in secret, the tortures of his daily life as a schoolboy and the regimentation of the Church, founded on commandments and proscriptions, punishment and atonement. Jarman wrote of the character Joseph Tucker in Terence Davies's film: 'Like Kafka's prisoner, Tucker is eternally on the run – in waiting rooms, in the corridors of the school, at the hospital, at the office – always running away from the reality of his homosexuality, forced into any number of costumes meant to conceal the spiritual poverty of the life of the petite bourgeoisie: during the day, the efficiently working and repressed office employee in his suit – at night, in the leather and chains of the sado-masochist.'[19]

Tabooed Sexuality

The reality of childhood and adolescence sketched in Terence Davies's trilogy was largely also that of Jarman: alongside the coincidental parallel of a strict and violent father, it primarily shows the personal experience of repression in almost every area of post-war society. Jarman had felt himself to be 'queer', to not fit in, to exist outside the norm since the ninth year of his life, as he describes in detail in *At Your Own Risk*: 'I was aware of my sexuality at nine, which makes a nonsense of an age of consent of twenty-one and of the ideas of CONVERSION, PERVERSION and CORRUPTION of youth.'[20] His homosexual orientation was entirely clear to him at the age of sixteen; however, at that time – in the late fifties – there were neither positive social patterns nor were there people leading openly gay lives. Instead, the opposite was the case: 'There is no accepted pattern to growing up, you are at the mercy of chance. In my childhood there were no accessible patterns that were positive, everything was negative. It affected me deeply, I became a very backward kid, uncertain, terribly shy. I knew I was "queer", and I knew that was totally unacceptable.'[21] The topic of homosexuality was discussed neither openly nor in public, and the homosexual orientation of friends and acquaintances or public figures was discussed (if at all) in a discreet and disparaging tone.

'[...] everything was negative' – and wanting to take up a position outside of the predefined roles was absolutely unbearable. The social and societal framework of the UK in the forties and fifties was, as in many other countries at that time, filled with countless negative notions, restrictive regulations and behavioural patterns that left either no space at all or only an extremely marginal space for self-determined developments. Gay identification figures, gay ways of life and gay life strategies were non-existent. Homosexuality could be lived only in concealment, within a rigorously staged double life feigning heterosexuality. 'Queer' was a pejorative term of exclusion with exclusively negative connotations. However, the term – which has been used in this context in the UK since the early 1920s – had already repeatedly been used as a term of self-reference within the gay subculture before the establishment of a self-liberating and radical gay-and-lesbian movement and its use in the sense of 'queer culture' and 'queer politics' in the early nineties.

A public and open discourse on sexuality, even corporeality in the widest sense, was problematic, taboo and – even in the field of medicine – considered wholly inappropriate for the general public. In the forties, for example, in the course of the public health and information campaigns about venereal diseases carried out because of the strong increase in the number of infections among the general population during the war years, it was impossible to refer to terms related to sexuality directly by name or to find even remotely clear words to describe them. From today's perspective this could lead to very curious situations, and for the audiences of that time it meant that they were provided more with disinformation, based on questionable moral views and principles, than with the intended information: 'Journalistic prudery remained an obstacle to effective public health campaigns of any sort. In 1942 a national effort to convince people to wash their hands after defecating was abandoned because newspapers could not bring themselves to print the word "water-closet". [...] Their bowdlerization of another sentence – "The first sign of syphilis is a small ulcer on or near the sex organs" – by deleting any reference to sex organs caused grotesque misery as people all over Britain with ulcers on other parts of their body feared they had VD [venereal diseases] and appealed to doctors or the Ministry of Health for advice.'[22]

In the face of avoidance strategies and efforts of this kind, the laboured and tabooed treatment of forms of homosexual desire is hardly surprising. If homosexuality was thematised in the public sphere, then it was almost exclusively in a negative light: as a crime and pathological phenomenon that was said to spread by way of seduction, in the manner of an infectious disease. The centuries-old tradition of punishing same-sex desire was joined by the ever-increasing numbers of the conventional medical establishment's 'attempts at a cure' – such as hormonal treatment, psychiatric care or aversion therapy – which likewise represent the theoretical camps of a genetically determined versus a socially acquired homosexuality. While sex researchers like Magnus Hirschfeld had already been making efforts within the field of medicine to depathologise homosexuality during the first half of the twentieth century, the first concrete beginnings of a real and successful depatholigisation were achieved only through the efforts of gay-and-lesbian interest groups in the US. Through the pressure they applied, the categorisation of homosexuality as a mental illness was successfully revoked within the American Psychiatric Association in 1973: it was replaced by the classification 'egodystonic homosexuality' (which describes homosexuals as suffering from their orientation). In 1984 the recommendation that homosexuality no longer be seen as a mental illness was adopted by the European Parliament. In 1987 the American Psychiatric Association finally removed the classification 'egodystonic homosexuality'. It was not until 1992 that the World Health Organization revoked its classification of homosexuality as an illness!

The tables of figures and the statistics of the Kinsey Reports, published by Alfred C. Kinsey in 1948 and 1953, represent an exception within this discourse of prejudice and condemnation.[23] With his studies on male and female sexual behaviour, the American biologist – who had initially specialised in the study of gall wasps – strove to summarise the results of personal interviews with over 11,000 men and women in a normatively objective manner in the form of descriptive statistics. Here the area of homosexuality was one among many, and it was not the focus in the manner of those medical 'problem studies' that had been so popular and published in such great numbers since the late nineteenth century; instead, the figures were partial results from the overarching question regarding the sexual behaviour of humans. As open to criticism as numerous methodological and analytical elements of Kinsey and his team's studies may be, the meticulous classification and quantification of various sexual practices established the scientific basis for an objective handling of the topic and thus for removing the taboos surrounding sexuality at that time. Nonetheless, the foreword of a 1951 brochure about the Kinsey Reports leaves no doubt as to their emotional effect on the general public: 'The figures and facts of these statistics dropped like an atom bomb on a peacefully sleeping herd. They provoked outrage, alarm and astonishment and shocked the whole world.'[24]

In the England of the fifties the total legal prohibition against any homosexual activity between men, both in public and in private and regardless of their age, continued to remain in place. This prohibition was based on a law from 1885, known as Labouchere's Amendment, which replaced the previously applicable death penalty for sodomy. From this point on, homosexual activities of every kind were punished through prison terms lasting several years and to be served in a labour camp. It is also not surprising that Kinsey's core statement on the theme of homosexuality – that 37 % of the male population had at least one homosexual experience following puberty – unleashed corresponding fear and insecurity, as the results implied that homosexuality was present in every social class of the United Kingdom and was not the deviant behaviour of a small minority.[25] In his study *Sex, Death and Punishment: Attitudes to Sex and Sexuality in Britain Since the Renaissance*, Richard Davenport-Hines draws a chain of connections tying this situation to other elements of collective fears and points to possible links between the loss of political power and the fear of losing control over sexuality: 'Other events in 1951 added to the insecurities created by Kinsey. Britain lost its political control over Iran and Egypt, leading to a crisis of imperial self-confidence comparable with that of the 1890s when the degenerationist theories of Lombroso and Nordau had caused such anti-homosexual excitement in Britain. In the ensuing decade, as the British Empire disintegrated in Malaysia, Africa, and Cyprus, fears about military loss of control were over and over again identified with sexual lack of control: the disintegration of heterosexuality, it was reiterated, had been a feature of the disintegration of the Roman Empire, as it would be for the British Empire.'[26]

Police surveillance of 'suspects' and extremely harsh and indiscreet methods – such as questioning suspects at their workplaces or mass interrogations in cases where the occasion presented itself – were everyday practices and repeatedly led to mass arrests and show trials intended to strengthen and reinforce the general homophobic attitude. Thus in 1954–55 in the County of

Somerset, there was a series of mass interrogations and arrests of this kind, which would go down in history as the Somerset Pogroms: '[...] when an eighteen-year-old public school boy propositioned a fellow passenger on the train from Exeter to Taunton. The other man proved to be a railway police-man who initiated an investigation which resulted in 17 men being prose-cuted. [...] another 13 men were prosecuted at Taunton in 1955. [...] There was an identical pattern on each occasion. The police go round from house to house, bringing ruin in their train, always attacking the youngest men first, extracting information with lengthy questioning and specious promises of light sentences as they proceed from clue to clue, i.e. from home to home, often up to twenty.'[27]

In the Montagu-Wildeblood affair, a sensational 1954 trial against the aristocrat Lord Montagu of Beaulieu and two other co-defendants, the inves-tigators' extremely dubious practices led a part of public opinion to turn in favour of those convicted. Under the pressure of widespread popular protests and criticism in the media, the government found itself forced to reconsider the legislation and the practice of conviction. In *At Your Own Risk* Jarman remarks 'I was dimly aware that this national scandal related to me, though I had no words to describe it'.[28] But more than a decade was to pass before actual changes to the legislation were undertaken. However, as a direct consequence of the protests and in the wake of extremely heated discussions on the top-ic of homosexuality, the so-called Wolfenden Committee was formed by the Home Secretary before the end of 1954. It was placed under the direction of Sir John Wolfenden and was to occupy itself with potential reform measures. After three years of consultations, the fifteen members of the committee pub-lished the Wolfenden Report in 1957: this report arrived at the – when seen superficially and compared to the status quo of the time – liberal conclusion that consensual homosexual acts occurring in private and between men above the age of 21 should no longer be seen as crimes. However, the suggested age of consent was five years older than that for heterosexual encounters and the scope of the punishments for violations were to be substantially increased and intensified as compared to the existing situation.

The Report nonetheless led to countless negative reactions against these 'liberal' suggestions by parts of the Church, the medical profession and the media. The British Medical Association proved particularly dedicated in this context, presenting homosexuality as an infectious plague spread through in-cidental contact with foreigners. The homosexual became an 'enemy of the State' and 'attached to an alien ideology'. Heterosexuality, by contrast, was seen as 'the basis and strength of democracy'. As an antidote, the British Med-ical Association recommended 'religious conversion as a "cure" for homosex-uality, and included two appendices on the value of evangelism'.[29] As 'psy-chopaths', incorrigible homosexuals were to be isolated in psychiatric penal colonies. In keeping with these 'recommendations', homosexuality continued to manifest itself in the public consciousness in terms of an 'illness', a 'general issue of public health, comparable to that of tuberculosis'.

While dailies such as *The Times*, the *Manchester Guardian* or *The Observer* greeted the Report with some reservations, it was primarily the tabloids that provided support for this negative attitude of the public through the continued dissemination of irrational fears by sustainedly warning against the 'dangers of this infectious disease', which – if the suggestions of the Report were to be carried out – could even lead to the demise of the British Empire: 'The *Daily Telegraph* feared that homosexuality, if legalized, might spread like an infection. The *Sunday Times*, though not entirely hostile, warned that the "basic national moral standard" was being "undermined by libertarian cults and the steady sapping of welfare Socialism". The *Evening Standard* judged Wolfenden's proposals on homosexuality to be "bad, retrograde and utterly to be condemned". The *Daily Mail* judged that Wolfenden's "proposals to legalize degradation in our midst" would result in the fall of the Empire; the *Sunday Graphic* found that the Report extended a smiling benediction to the Sins of Sodom.'[30]

On account of these negative reactions and the mood of the general public, the results and recommendations of the Wolfenden Committee rapidly disappeared once more from the parliamentary calendar, and ten more years were to pass before the existing law in England and Wales would be replaced by the Sexual Offences Act of 1967 (see p. 88).

Images of Childhood in THE LAST OF ENGLAND: 'There's no place like the HOME movie'

One possibility of escape from this reality of the violent everyday life at school and outside of school was presented by the moving pictures of the 8 mm films of Jarman's father and grandfather, who were both enthusiastic amateur film-makers. Searching for a place called 'home', these home movies called up memories of the bygone years of his early childhood, and – for brief moments – they became safe havens within precisely that past. 'I think why I like THE WIZARD OF OZ so much is that at the end we return HOME, after hazardous adventures. There's no place like the HOME-movie.'[31] The black-and-white film material of his grandfather is from the late twenties and the thirties; his father began to film in colour in 1939, but he also retained his status of a private amateur film-maker during his service in the Second World War.[32] In his autobiographical writings, Jarman recalls home-movie nights: 'The "home movie" nights of my childhood were the most exciting. To watch Grandma Mimosa cutting up the Sunday chicken in 1929 seemed no less than a miracle [...]. Half-way, in 1939, when my father took over the filming, everything broke out into the most brilliant colour [...].'[33]

Numerous scenes or also sequences from his parents' and grandparents' stock of 8 mm films were incorporated as fragments into Jarman's film THE LAST OF ENGLAND, which he completed in 1987; in this way, he offers very personal glimpses of his own (family) history. The following descriptions of scenes are intended to provide a complete overview of the motifs and sources of this material. This is then discussed in terms of its contextual relationship with the film material surrounding it. All information provided, including the time indications, is based on the version of the film released by Second Sight (VFC 50992, 2NDVD 3055). The photographs of military stations are from Lossiemouth (during the war) and Abingdon (1948). However, a location cannot always be assigned with certainty to a given image. In a few of the descriptions of scenes, commentaries related to the given scene have been added from Jarman's texts. All comments and citations related to the listing have been gathered together under note 34.

Home-Movie Scenes in THE LAST OF ENGLAND

Scene 1 (begins: 7'15"/duration: 5", 1 shot)
Motif: Family, RAF station (Abingdon, 1948?): Jarman's mother in front of their housing area; she plucks a rose and fixes it to her clothes
Sound: Noise of film projector and voice-over of the opening line of Allen Ginsberg's 'Howl' (recited by Nigel Terry): 'I saw the best minds of my generation destroyed by madness, starving hysterical naked' (see pp. 44ff.)
Source: 8 mm film, colour, by his father
Jarman: 'I gave the desolation continuity in the film by relating it to the camouflaged married quarters at RAF Abingdon with their garden fences topped with barbed wire, and RAF Lossiemouth with its H-blocks.'

Scene 2 (begins: 8'46"/duration: 1", 1 shot)
Motif: Family, RAF station: Jarman's sister Gaye as a child; she runs across a meadow towards the camera (part of Scene 7)
Sound: Noise of film projector, gulls, bees
Source: 8 mm film, colour, by his father

Scene 3 (begins: 8'57"/duration: 5", 1 shot)
Motif: Family, Jarman playing with his sister in the garden
Sound: Music: 'The Last of England' (Simon Turner, CD, track 4)
Source: 8 mm film, colour, by his father

Scene 4 (begins: 18'12"/duration: 35", 7 shots)
Motif: Family, 'Sunday Lunch', Jarman's mother as a child at a family meal (1929)
Sound: 'Persistence of Memory' (Simon Turner, CD, track 6), noise of aircraft engines
Source: 8 mm film, b/w, by his grandfather
Jarman: 'The earliest footage dates from the end of the '20s. My grandfather, Harry,

who died before I was born filmed the family holidays in Bexhill. [...]
the Sunday Lunch, which is in THE LAST OF ENGLAND [...]'

Scene 5 (begins: 21'26"/duration: 26", 4 shots)

Motif: Family, Jarman's mother as a child
Sound: Background noise, sound of traffic
Source: 8 mm film, b/w, by his grandfather
Jarman: 'In my grandfather's home movie she blinked in the sunlight and smiled into the camera; a title appeared on the screen which introduced you to "ever-smiling Betty"'

Scene 6 (begins: 23'09"/duration: 10", 2 shots)

Motif: Family, RAF station: military buildings, Jarman's mother and sister in the garden in front of their housing area
Sound: 'Fina' (Simon Turner, CD, track 5)
Source: 8 mm film, colour, by his father

Scene 7 (begins: 23'20"/duration: 6", 2 shots)

Motif: Family, RAF station at Lossiemouth: Jarman's sister runs across a meadow and towards the camera with a tennis ball in her hand (see also Scene 2)
Sound: 'Fina' (Simon Turner, CD, track 5)
Source: 8 mm film, colour, by his father

Scene 8 (begins: 23'44"/duration: 14", 2 shots)

Motif: Family, RAF station: picnic in the meadow, Jarman with his mother; children playing in the water
Sound: 'Fina' (Simon Turner, CD, track 5)
Source: 8 mm film, colour, by his father

Scene 9 (begins: 24'12"/duration: 11")

Motif: Family, RAF station: Derek playing between the buildings of the station
Sound: 'Fina' (Simon Turner, CD, track 5)
Source: 8 mm film, colour, by his father

Scene 10 (begins: 24'31"/duration: 4", 1 shot)

Motif: Family, RAF station: picnic in the meadow, Jarman with his mother
Sound: 'Fina' (Simon Turner, CD, track 5)
Source: 8 mm film, colour, by his father

Scene 11 (begins: 24'48"/duration: 4", 1 shot)

Motif: Family. Jarman with his mother between the buildings of an RAF station
Sound: Igniting flare (see previous scene)
Source: 8 mm film, colour, by his father

Scene 12 (begins: 25'09"/duration: 33", 5 shots)

Motif: Family. RAF station at Abingdon (1948): Jarman, his sister and his mother playing ball in the garden of the RAF station; walls secured with barbed wire in the background
Sound: aircraft engines
Source: 8 mm film, colour, by his father
Jarman: '[...] my sister Gaye, and myself playing with a ball on the lawns of RAF Abingdon where my father was Station Commander – I'm six years old, it's the summer of 1948.'

Scene 13 (begins: 66'22"/duration: *c.*2'17" in total, 139 shots)

Motif: Travelling, Pakistan 1953/54: street life, military guard, marching soldiers, marching women in uniform, parade of tanks, cavalry, warplanes on an airfield *in between:* British terrace housing (b/w), military reception on an air field, market/bazaar, Jarman's mother in a garden at a military reception, his mother in the mountains in Pakistan, military reception, cavalry, marching soldiers *repeatedly in between* (filmed by Derek Jarman):
colour: Prince Albert Memorial
b/w: masked terrorists, fire, burning houses, rock-strewn fields, ruin-filled landscapes

Sound: Marching music: 'Pomp and Circumstance', op. 39, no. 1 in D minor (1901), 'Land of Hope and Glory', Edward Elgar (Sir Alexander Gibson/Scottish National Orchestra); car sirens, enthusiastic shouts from the crowd, air-raid sirens

Source: 8 mm film, colour, by his father

Jarman: 'I use the Albert Memorial, the great masterwork of the 19th century, in the sequence of Land of Hope and Glory with the family footage taken by my father when he was seconded to the Pakistan airforce.'

Scene 14 (begins: 70'15"/duration: 15", 4 shots)

Motif: Travelling, Jarman's parents at a mountain lake
Sound: Sounds of nature
Source: 8 mm film, colour, by his father

Scene 15 (begins: 70'37"/duration: 1', 10 shots)

Motif: Military, RAF station at Lossiemouth; winter, snow, transporting bombs, warplanes, warplanes being prepared for take-off, flight over the station, aerial footage of the base: H-shaped blocks, father collects mother, drive in a car
Sound: Noise of aircraft engines
Source: 8 mm film, colour, by his father
Jarman: 'He [Jarman's father] shot the footage of the Wellington bombers at Lossiemouth in the film.'

Scene 16 (begins: 71'39"/duration: 15", 1 shot)

Motif: Family, RAF station at Wittan: mother lifts Jarman out of a pram
Sound: Explosion of airborne bombs
Source: 8 mm film, colour, by his father
Jarman: '[...] I make my film debut in my mother's arms in the garden of a house they rented at RAF Wittan: I have used this at the end of THE LAST OF ENGLAND.'

THE LAST OF ENGLAND was created in 1986–87, during the transition from Margaret Thatcher's second to her third term in office – a period in which the repressive elements of her law-and-order politics and their consequences for societal structures in general and for the areas of culture and welfare in particular were being felt more and more clearly. The patriotic jubilation over the victory in the Falklands War (1982) had soon dissipated and was able to drown out neither the extensive race riots of the early eighties nor the extreme rise in unemployment: in Thatcher's first term, from 1979 to 1983, it had risen around 141 %.[35] This disenchantment was followed by the deployment of cruise missiles in December of 1983 and the extended coal-miners' strikes of 1984 and 1985, which would lead to a further polarisation of the political climate in the UK. It would nonetheless be an excessively one-dimensional perspective to look at the THE LAST OF ENGLAND exclusively as a reflection upon a politics that Jarman experienced in terms of a political 'state of war' and the accompanying state of society during the Thatcher era. Instead, the film is an autobiographical converging point, where multiple personal events come together before the background of the consequences of this political setting: Jarman's father died in November of 1986, and Jarman learned in December of the same year that he was HIV-positive. The political state of war was joined by a private one.

The kaleidoscopic montage of scenes in extremely rapid succession in THE LAST OF ENGLAND (filmed on Super 8, transferred to video, edited and copied on to 35 mm film) causes new, previously undiscovered images to emerge with every viewing of the film and these are conveyed almost exclusively at emotional and associative levels. They appear not just in the form of a personal taking stock but also as the visual realisation of a personal affective state and an exploration and return to Jarman's own past – an inward state projected outwards. Although life and work always formed an indivisible unity for Jarman, there is no other film in which he so consistently and exclusively collages elements from his own personal past, his personal history, with scenarios representing a contemporary emotional state, in order to form an autobiographical work. 'With THE LAST OF ENGLAND I've made a journey back of a different sort. THE TEMPEST and CARAVAGGIO allowed me to form a perspective, to stand back. Now I'm going back to my roots, to lay bare the contradictions.'[36] Here, in a manner related to the home-movie evenings of his childhood, the images of the home-movie fragments of his parents and grandparents symbolically become an opportunity for withdrawing, for an inner emigration, offering a view of a bygone, seemingly peaceful period in which there was still hope.

The film's title also points to the theme of emigration – in this case, an actual emigration – by citing the painting of the same name by Ford Madox Brown. The work depicts the departure for Australia of the sculptor Thomas Woolner, a member of the Pre-Raphaelite group of artists founded in London in 1848 (see fig. 2). For Jarman a chain of associations links this painting with his own ancestors' immigration to New Zealand: 'Suddenly one day I remembered the painting of the emigrants leaving the white cliffs behind for a life in the new world. My great-grandparents had done that. Left their farm in Middle Combe, Uplowman, Devon, to go to New Zealand. I have an extraordinary picture of them taken in the 1850s. I decided on THE LAST OF ENGLAND.'[37]

Among the total of sixteen scenes taken from the home-movie material that Jarman integrated into his film, two scenes were shot by his grandfather and fourteen scenes by his father. The scenes recorded by his grandfather consist exclusively of scenes of filmed family life of a kind that is 'classic' for 8 mm films; those of his father, on the other hand, can be categorised into three different groups of motifs:

- family (11 scenes)
- travels (2 scenes)
- military (1 scene)

Only Jarman, his mother and his sister are to be seen in the family scenes; his father is present exclusively in a travel scene and a military scene (Scenes 14 and 15). By operating the camera he has – in classic home-movie tradition – nearly eliminated himself from the visual history of the private moving picture and thus stands in the lineage of almost all filming fathers of recent generations: they themselves remain invisible – it is only their gaze upon the world that is revealed to us. The chronological sequence and montage of the individual scenes within the context of the complete material of the film is also worth noting: while scenes 1 to 5 have been inserted in a scattered sequence during the first 21 minutes of the film, scenes 6 to 12 and 14 to 16 follow almost directly upon one another, with only a few intervening shots, thus associatively conjuring up a thematic framework as they are viewed.

Scene 13 ('Land of Hope and Glory') occupies a special position: here Jarman has merged his own material with footage that his father shot while he was stationed in Pakistan to create a veritable flood of images featuring extremely rapidly cut sequences of shots (sometimes under a second per shot). In the course of a total duration of 137 seconds, this scene contains 139 shots! Here Jarman's material represents a thematic extension of the already familiar images; however, they are combined with the newly incorporated theme of the Albert Memorial.

With the exception of two civilian scenes about street life and a market in Pakistan, his father's material almost exclusively documents events related to military demonstrations of power, such as military parades, marching military guards, convoys of tanks and military receptions. The documentary character of these home-movie images and the military Scene 15 is, in addition to the motifs, primarily conveyed through the use of the camera. In contrast to the family scenes, Jarman's father does not attempt to personally participate in the events by means of the camera; instead, he observes what is going on from a corresponding distance. In these scenes the camera is not a mobile instrument following the objects being filmed; instead, with the exception of a few pans, it statically films what is happening from a single standpoint.

The entire montaged scene from 'Land of Hope and Glory' appears to form the point of intersection between the thematic axes of the film: here, on

Fig. 2: Ford Madox Brown, *The Last of England*, 1855

the journey to his personal origins, links between private and political as well as colonial history emerge – the ruin-filled landscape of the present and the imperial Albert Memorial are at war. The triumphal tones of Edward Elgar's march set the tone. 'The Albert memorial, is the summing up, the cross supported by the angels. Prince Albert as paterfamilias in the middle, sitting on art, architecture, music, and the sciences. Spread out at the four corners are the four continents of the earth, of the Empire. It's the most important "official" work of the 19th century; it attempts to bring everything together and centralise it under the British Monarchy. The attempt failed.'[38]

Jarman interweaves contemporary images of state power with demonstrations of power from the past, and in doing so he exposes subtle and repeatedly recurring parallels in the structuring of power. Jarman's father himself is – once again invisibly – present in the sequence of his own images: 'Who was my father fighting for? Was he fighting a just war? Or any old war? Was it possible to fight for the good cause?'[39]

In contrast to the documentary character of the images of military and travel scenes, the family scenes filmed by Jarman's father show pictures of a personal life-world. They belong to that category of images of private events that we know from various and innumerable home-movie family histories – including our own. At first glance the private aspect of these scenes seems ordinary and incidental; however, while the recordings may suggest chance observations of everyday situations, every one of them is an event staged for the camera. The camera itself rarely remains still, stationary, focused on a defined framing of its subject. Instead it is almost always flexible, in motion, following the events and movements in the image. The protagonists act – to the extent that they are not unsettled by the presence of the camera – for the camera and often towards it. Their direct gazes into the camera can often be observed, and this is simultaneously also an attempt to involve the filming member of the family in what is happening.

In Jarman's case the motifs conjure up apparently romantic images of the idyllic, of innocence and of timelessness: Jarman's mother plucking a rose and fixing it to her clothes, carefree children running through a meadow (Jarman and his sister), a picnic on a lawn, cheerful ball games between brick buildings, etc. However, even in the thin outward surface of these images there are clear hints of an environment that, through the presence of particular elements, leads to an inversion of this idyll and innocence: we see the green lawn of a military station secured by means of barbed wire, and the brick buildings are barracks that multiply monotonously in the background. The attempt at a conciliatory gaze back into the past is only partially successful. Thus, while that yearning for 'home', for a more humane environment felt to have been lost – for a 'lost landscape' (see also p. 181), as the American film scholar Chris Lippard, editor of the scholarly anthology *By Angels Driven: The Films of Derek Jarman*, referred to in a talk with Derek Jarman –[40] certainly becomes perceptible, clear cracks can be seen in the window of retreat through which Jarman gazes.

After all, the images of those old and grainy 8 mm films in their characteristically garish colours or saturated and monochrome tones of brown must be seen within the framework of the images surrounding them, even if they represent an independent category in terms of aesthetics and content. This framework is characterised by violence and decay, and we find ourselves back once more in Jarman's vision of the present – a corrupt system without hope. An inner dialogue at the beginning of the film formulates a few of the questions that emerge out of these images:

- What do you see in those heavy waters? I ask.
- Nothing but a bureaucrat from the ministry poisoning the buttercups with a new defoliant.
- What's that I hear?
- The sound of Gershwin on his ghetto blaster.
- What else?
- The atom splitting,
- And the whispering?
- Half-truths spilling from the minister's case Wriggling in the sunlight.
- What are they saying?
- All's well, no comment. Some of them are silent. Ah here's the guard.
- What's the password?
- EVASION
- What else do you see?
- Lies flowing through the national grid, and bribery.
- All's normal then.
- Yes.
- Where's Hope?
- The little white lies have carried her off beyond the cabbage patch.
- They've murdered her?
- Yes.
- And Tomorrow?
- Tomorrow's been cancelled owing to lack of interest. [...][41]

These are scenarios of a diseased world whose inhabitants have become the victims of a violent power penetrating every realm. In a series of extremely rapidly cut shots, combinations of images emerge which reassemble themselves anew with every viewing. A selective perception of individual details of images becomes almost impossible during a conventional, continuous viewing of the film – only certain suggested thematic threads are recognisable. Two young men wander aimlessly across fields covered with rubble and rocks, landscapes of a destroyed nature. In contrast to THE ANGELIC CONVERSATION (see pp. 169 ff.), the two will never find each other in THE LAST OF ENGLAND. Before the background of a red-coloured sky, emigrants await their departure, and that figure who – like a magician – seeks to light up the darkness with a Bengal flare finds the same uncertainty before him as the group of people in a boat who move away from the viewer and into this same darkness at the end of the film. Jarman sketches the image of a devastated post-industrial cityscape consisting of ruinous structures, concrete bunkers and buildings going up in flames – reflecting equally devastated human existences.

Representative Terror

Terrorist units represent the dominant power in THE LAST OF ENGLAND. Here the masked figures of terror appear not as enemies of the state but as a state of enmity whose actions are hostile and display a scorn for humanity; they appear as a system felt to be inhuman. Jarman also makes use of this metaphor in his later film THE GARDEN, where he presents terrorists armed with cameras as representatives of the media, particularly the tabloid and sensationalist press, which permeate every area of life. In this context the British tabloid *The Sun* was one of his favourite sources of inspiration and is an integral part of numerous works. In one scene in THE LAST OF ENGLAND, an infant in a pram is covered with a front page from *The Sun* which features a headline on the Falklands War: 'God be with you' (see fig. 3). He repeatedly points to the potential of the power of the media, which actively shapes public consciousness in a consistently regressive form and persistently rejects or censures positive and emancipatory tendencies – as always, profitable reporting is still expected to stand under a negative aspect. 'I cannot remember ever seeing an article in the British press which didn't see my sexuality in a negative light', is Jarman's summary of the situation in his autobiography *At Your Own Risk – A Saint's Testament*, where he juxtaposes thematically related texts from gay media with more than forty homophobic headlines from current tabloids.[42]

> 'Poll verdict on gay vicars: kick 'em out',
> 'Aids: Boy George is tested for killer plague',
> 'I'd shoot my son if he had aids, says vicar',
> 'Top lawyer exposed in rent boy scandal', etc.

Finally, great numbers of these front pages from *The Sun* and other daily papers provide the basis for many of the large-format paintings of the *Queer Series* (1992).[43] Thus, for example, the entire background of the painting *Letter to the Minister* consists of multiple photocopies of a front page of *The Sun* with the headline: 'VILE BOOK IN SCHOOL – Pupils see pictures of

Fig. 3: 'The royal baby' in the film THE LAST OF ENGLAND, Derek Jarman, 1987

gay lovers' (see fig. 4). Here Jarman breaks with the fragmentary intention of traditional collage and mounts complete reproductions of the front pages in a documentary sense. This repeatedly replicated message from the media is painted over multiple times with broad brushstrokes of thickly applied oil paint and rendered partially unrecognisable – it is made to disappear. Jarman then used a grattage technique in the oil paint to inscribe a text that – in an appeal to the Minister for the Arts! – seeks to use the accumulation of the names of numerous homosexual artists from recent centuries to reduce to absurdity both the strategies of denial in education and in scholarship and the press's attempts to manufacture scandal:

> 'Copies sent to the arts minister.
> Dear William Shakespeare
> I am 14 years old and I'm
> queer like you. I'm learning
> art. I want to be a queer artist
> like Leonardo or Michelangelo.
> But I like Francis Bacon best.
> I read Allen Ginsber [*sic*], Rimbaud.
> I love Tchaikovsky. If I make films
> I will make them like Eisenstein Murnau
> Pasolini Visconti. Love from Derek.'

(Regarding this painting, see also Roger Wollen's more detailed remarks in 'Facets of Derek Jarman', in *Derek Jarman: A Portrait*.)[44]

Over thirty years lie between the 'recommendations' of the British Medical Association, the hostile reactions in the press regarding the activities of the Wolfenden Committee and the present homophobic headlines of the British tabloids. Things nonetheless seem to have come full circle, as these ultimately resemble those outrageous statements of the fifties, with their expressions of scorn for fellow human beings. It is only the choice of topics that has changed, the perspective that has shifted somewhat, the attitude has not: the emergence of HIV and Aids ('the killer plague') in the early eighties changed homosexuals from manifestations of what was in itself an illness into carriers of an illness – and sometimes into both. The lack of social recognition, not to mention equality, and the corresponding lack of ways of life with which Jarman could identify form a common thread running throughout his biography. Clearly referring to the total prohibition of homosexual acts that existed until 1967 and to the subsequent introduction of 21 as an unequal age of consent, he stated in retrospect: 'For the first twenty-five years of my life I lived as a criminal, and the next twenty-five were spent as a second-class citizen, deprived of equality and human rights. [...] I have lived for fifty years as an unequal in this country, enveloped by hate; to ignore it I insulated myself, subtly changed my

Fig. 4: Derek Jarman, *Letter to the Minister*, 1992

life. No man is an island, but each man created his own island to cope with the prejudice and censure. The time for politeness had to end.'[45]

The Strategy of the Autobiographical and the Strategy of Naming – Painting as Self-Defence

Within this flood of prejudice and acts of censorship, Jarman gradually developed individual islands of personal strategies. Through his constant experience of the absence of positively connoted identities and models with which to identify himself, his own person became the thematic focus of his statements, his autobiographical confrontation became the central element of his works. Life and work became joined into an indivisible unity whose 'point of departure [became] always the feeling and thinking of his own person, his personal and often autobiographical confrontation with his surroundings'.[46] With this 'strategy of the autobiographical', as I refer to it, he sought to counter the constant experience of the absence of an identity-building environment, past and history. Jarman counters disinterested (artistic) statements – carried out from a distanced and secure standpoint and attempting to avoid personal responsibility to a greater or lesser degree – with his 'I', with 'working in the first person'. In his essay 'Post-larmoyante Kunst', Les Levine undertook an attempt to move closer to a concept of the artwork that is very close to precisely this self-concept of Jarman. He does so by defining an artistic manifestation as a personally intended, but nonetheless simultaneously also – in the broadest sense – political manifestation: 'An artwork is a metaphor for how one sees the world and how one finds his or her place in it and is able to act there. But more than anything else, an artwork permits one to be what one sees, to participate in the vision brought forth; it empowers us to have thoughts or to realise activities.'[47]

The strategy of the autobiographical becomes legible in Jarman's writings, which begin in 1984 with *Dancing Ledge*. The strategy had already become visible significantly earlier in his home movies – which recount personal (hi)stories – and later also very concretely in his feature films, such as THE LAST OF ENGLAND, THE GARDEN or BLUE, and in numerous paintings, collages, combine paintings and assemblages. Here it is particularly after 1986, the year in which Jarman learned that he was infected with HIV, that autobiographical elements take on a clearly pre-eminent role: this is most apparent in the late *Black & Gold Paintings*, the *Queer Series* and in his final works (see also pp. 67 f.).

'When I was young the absence of the past was a terror. [...] There wasn't much gay autobiography, some tentative beginnings in the gay press but no-one had written an autobiography in which they described a sex act – except

Tom Driberg – certainly no-one in my generation. That seemed to be a good reason to fill in the blank and to start putting in the "I" rather than the "they"; and having made the decision about the "I" to show how things related to me so that I wasn't talking of others – *they* were doing this and *they* were doing that. It was very important to find the "I": *I* feel this, this happened to *me*, I did this. I wanted to read that. My obsession with biography is to find these "I's". The subtext of my films have been the books, putting myself back into the picture. There's a huge self-censorship because we're terrified of betraying ourselves. We don't want people to know.'[48]

Jarman counters this 'self-censorship' – as he refers to the often discernible tendency to deny homosexual identities and intensities in the field of (auto) biographical works – with the concrete thematisation and naming of sexuality in his own works. This is not a speculative element but a way to tear away the veil of silence, of denial and of ignorance. Jarman removes them from their preformed peripheries and taboo zones and inserts them into the centre of the confrontation. Bit by bit, clear contours were to emerge from the insecurities and diffuse grey areas surrounding them. With this strategy, which I refer to as the 'strategy of naming', he not only undermines those moral principles defined as norms and cemented in the mind of the public through the media and the culture industry – he also ruptures the discreet silence of (art) historical discourses that reproduce the centuries-old denial of homosexual qualities in looking at their subject matter: 'It's important for us to talk about sex, to define ourselves in a world which has never talked about us or even let us talk about ourselves. If people can't understand that, they are very foolish. When you start to talk, it confirms you are living. If you are living under psychological terror what deals do you make with your oppressors?'[49]

Jarman presents them, for example, with their own highest and holiest cultural heritage through a perspective that had previously been carefully excluded. This technique can be seen clearly in works such as *Letter to the Minister*, the previously mentioned painting from the *Queer Series* in which Jarman once again toys with Shakespeare's possibly homosexual orientation (see also pp. 173 f.) and, in the role of a fourteen-year-old schoolboy, begins adoringly praising a whole collection of gay writers, painters and film directors. These are well-known figures whose life and work – subjected to a dogged exclusion of their sexual identity – were also taught about in the schools, which is precisely the reason why he wants to name them as his role models. They are, in fact, precisely those figures who are referred to in Kate Chedgzoy's *Shakespeare's Queer Children* as the 'international homosexual "great tradition" which includes Caravaggio, Marlowe and Britten as well as Shakespeare'.[50] Jarman repeatedly unearths new, previously silenced levels and taboo areas through his deliberate ignoring of established conventions and his free and – in a positive sense – uninhibited treatment of historical or classical material (e.g. THE TEMPEST, WAR REQUIEM or EDWARD II), myths (e.g. SEBASTIANE) or personal portraits (e.g. CARAVAGGIO and WITTGENSTEIN). His works are never about historically 'correct' reconstructions within the framework of existing (art) historical discourses or presentational conventions but instead about a critical questioning of historically developed constructions and attempts to transport their significance into the present. The material becomes a means to an end; its desexualised historical transmission is unmasked.

Among the different strategies for confronting the reality of life surrounding him, painting would become the primary form he pursued. In contrast to his later, deliberately employed, proactive strategies of the autobiographical and of naming, painting – during Jarman's childhood and his years at various boarding schools – represented above all the possibility of withdrawing into the free space of an environment created by himself: 'I knew I wanted to paint very early on – painting was my secret garden. My art was an escape out of Heterosoc.'[51] He saw it as a form of self-defence against the attacks directed against him from the outside; painting became his 'secret garden' within the normative 'Heterosoc' – the term he uses retrospectively in *At Your Own Risk* to refer to the surrounding heterosexual society in its attempts to mould him.

Painting was to become his most important and direct medium of expression, his 'lifeline'. While he would later become known to a broader public above all through the medium of film, he nonetheless never saw himself as both a film-maker and also a painter, but instead always as primarily a painter: 'I've never not been a painter. Painting takes into consideration the films in a way. I don't see gaps between things. It's all a continuum, so that ideas that are floating around can be expressed in various ways, either in film or in paint, or written [...].'[52] An associative, fragmentary and collage-like visualisation always forms the basis of his pictorial expression in the different areas and forms of his work. In the process the boundaries of the individual disciplines dividing painting, film, text, text and image or text in film disintegrate. The focus is on his desire to visually realise a message; the appropriate medium was selected during the search for the form of realisation corresponding to the given case.

[3]

Go West! Influences from Painting and Literature

Beat Power

AFTER COMPLETING BOARDING SCHOOL, Jarman's greatest wish was to attend an art school, specifically the Slade School of Fine Art at University College London. However, because his father was more concerned with an – in his eyes – solid university education for his son, Jarman made a deal with him: if he were to be accepted into both a general university course and by the Slade School of Fine Art, then he would first complete his university course and only afterwards begin his education at the art school. In 1960 he was accepted at King's College London: in the years that followed he studied History, Art History and English and graduated in 1963. For the first two years, still living with his parents in Northwood, he commuted every day from the London suburb to the university. The social climate of the early fifties clearly left its mark on him, and several of Jarman's diary entries reveal that he experienced this period as a student in a very withdrawn manner: 'At Kings I was not much nearer solving my problems. There was no gay society in those days, and I had no idea of the existence or whereabouts of pubs or clubs – even had I known, I was much too shy or inhibited to make a first move. So at Kings I bought any books that had a gay subject-matter.'[53] Jarman began reading the works of Walt Whitman, Oscar Wilde, Jean Cocteau and Jean Genet. Through his teacher – the writer, editor and critic Eric Mottram – he became familiar with the works of Allen Ginsberg, William S. Burroughs and Jack

Kerouac, the most important literary protagonists of the Beat Generation. Since 1960 Mottram had held the first professorship specifically devoted to American Studies at the University of London and was intensely committed to increasing awareness of and disseminating American contemporary literature in England. His main focus was on the Black Mountain College writers around Charles Olson, the so-called San Francisco Renaissance (authors like Lawrence Ferlinghetti or Gary Snyder) and the Beat Poets.

In the beginning the Beat Poets consisted only of a small group of friends in New York and San Francisco. The previously mentioned authors Ginsberg, Burroughs and Kerouac are consistently associated with its inner circle: they met in the mid-forties in the context of New York's Columbia University. Kerouac had created the term 'Beat Generation' in a 1948 discussion with the writer John Clellon Holmes, who presented it to the general public and turned it into a catchphrase with his article 'This Is the Beat Generation', published four years later in the *New York Times*. The movement of the Beat Generation would emerge only later – a movement that would interact with and contribute to fields far beyond literature, in a crossover extending to the areas of music, the visual arts and (experimental) film. At the same time it would also become the post-war generation's first protest movement, which also demanded changes to our ways of life.

'The origins of the word "beat" are obscure, but the meaning is only too clear to most Americans. More than mere weariness, it implies the feeling of having been used, of being raw. It involves a sort of nakedness of mind, and, ultimately, of soul; a feeling of being reduced to the bedrock of consciousness. In short, it means being undramatically pushed up against the wall of oneself. A man is beat whenever he goes for broke and wagers the sum of his resources on a single number; and the young generation has done that continually from early youth. [...]

'Their brothers, husbands, fathers or boy friends turned up dead one day at the other end of a telegram. At the four trembling corners of the world, or in the home town invaded by factories or lonely servicemen, they had intimate experience with the nadir and the zenith of human conduct, and little time for much that came between. The peace they inherited was only as secure as the next headline. It was a cold peace. Their own lust for freedom, and the ability to live at a pace that kills (to which the war had adjusted them), led to black markets, bebop, narcotics, sexual promiscuity, hucksterism, and Jean-Paul Sartre. The beatness set in later.

'It is a postwar generation, and, in a world which seems to mark its cycles by its wars, it is already being compared to that other postwar generation, which dubbed itself "lost". The Roaring Twenties, and the generation that made them roar, are going through a sentimental revival, and the comparison is valuable. [...] But the wild boys of today are not lost.'[54]

With their term, Kerouac and Holmes draw an analogy to Ernest Hemingway's 'Lost Generation', another post-war generation – of the First World War. The semantic associations and connotations of 'beat' are numerous and varied: 'to be beaten' in the sense of 'being hit' is mentioned, but also in the sense of 'defeat', 'resignation', 'disappointment' – always in close connection with the attitude towards life among parts of that young post-war generation who had grown up during the war years of the Second World War and did not want to or were not able to make themselves seamlessly conform to the social norms created in connection with the image of an economic boom in the post-war period. As nuanced as the actually intended semantic associations of 'beat' were, the ideas and aims of the authors of the Beat Generation emerged in a form that was no less multifaceted. The focus was, on the one hand, on an attempt at a spiritual and intellectual emancipation from homogenised thought structures and behavioural norms: including the demand for living out a liberated and thus liberating experience of sexuality. On the other hand – with anti-establishment political rhetoric, experimentation with drugs and visionary societal utopias – the outward battle was to be taken up against conservative forces and structures and their prescriptions and prohibitions: 'The Beat Generation's message of liberation of the individual struck a chord with many young Americans at the end of the 1950s, and consequently served as a model for whole generations of rebellion around the world – from the beatniks and hippies of the 1960s to the punks and alternative "slacker" and "grunge" subcultures of the '80s and '90s.'[55]

When Jarman was a student at King's College in the early sixties, the Beat Generation in America had already become a part of a broader youth and counterculture.[56] These ideas were on their way to Europe and were also transferred to the UK – not least thanks to the dedicated efforts of Mottram, who presented the Beat Poets to the public. In the UK they would lastingly and substantially influence the youth culture that was then in the process of developing. For the first time, viable critical approaches and ideological utopias and alternatives to the societal status quo of post-war Britain seemed to open up, because the works of the movement's proponents were able to fill precisely the emotional and conceptual vacuum of that generation which had grown up during the war years and directly afterwards. Finally, in June of 1965, Ginsberg stayed in London in connection with the International Poetry Incarnation and held a public reading at Royal Albert Hall, together with Lawrence Ferlinghetti, Gregory Corso and other Beat Poets. This reading is simultaneously also seen as the moment when London's underground and psychedelic scene was born. Emerging out of legendary clubs like the Marquee or the UFO Club, groups like Pink Floyd or The Soft Machine (named after Burroughs's book of the same name) became known to a wide audience.

Allen Ginsberg

The fact that the 'Beats' would pioneer or provide the spiritual and intellectual background for extremely diverse youth and countercultures in the second half of the twentieth century is to be attributed above all to Ginsberg's many-sided commitments. The scope of his activities stretches from the hippy and anti-war movements of the sixties to punk rock (he performed together with The Clash) and all the way to Generation X. Ginsberg became a key figure in the international protest movement and almost never passed over an occasion for political protest: he was expelled from both Czechoslovakia and Cuba (where he had criticised the persecution of homosexuals) and played a substantial part in the anti-Vietnam-War movement. The fact that the 1969 Stonewall Riots in New York took place without him did not prevent him from pledging his support immediately afterwards. Together with Burroughs, Ginsberg was one of the first public figures of the post-war period to not only live an openly gay life but also to make homosexuality a political question.

Formally, breaking open literary forms and unquestioningly adopted traditions and styles stood at the heart of the works of Ginsberg and the Beat authors. They favoured and cultivated spontaneous compositions and free language as well as open verse forms and rhythms, as opposed to metrics and measures. Particularly in connection with Ginsberg's work, the free narrative style of Walt Whitman's poems has been seen as a prototype and precursor; this is also true of Whitman's concept of 'candour', an open and free language in which the boundaries between public and private are to be blurred. Ginsberg first became known to a broader public through the 1955 performance of his poem 'Howl'. The text celebrates revolt and the desperate search for freedom and uninhibitedness; it deals with and explicitly refers to themes including gay sex and drugs in what was at that time a manner unprecedentedly free of taboos. While it may not be shocking from today's perspective, 'Howl' nonetheless unleashed a scandal in the late fifties. Because of its anti-Establishment visions and because its text was classified as pornographic, the poem's publication in the year after its public reading was followed by confiscations, prohibitions against its sale and subsequently a trial that went on for years – in the course of which a series of scholars and writers finally succeeded in convincing the court that the work was to be seen not as obscene but as art.

Ginsberg's 'Howl' would advance to become the central work of the Beat Generation. Years later, Jarman – who had first occupied himself with the text at King's College – integrated the opening line of 'Howl' into his film THE LAST OF ENGLAND (for the sequence of scenes, see note 5):

> 'I saw the best minds of my generation destroyed by madness,
> starving hysterical naked [...]'.[57]

Where Ginsberg's line introduces his autobiographically tinted visions of liberation from a degenerate American society that had exhausted itself, Jarman has removed its semantic content from the post-war environment in which it was written and placed it in a new and altered temporal context. The sentence is cited in one of the film's key scenes, introducing viewers to Scene 1 of the integrated home-movie fragments (see pp. 26 ff.), with the preliminary declaration: 'We heard prophetic voices [...]'. It thus commences the series of montaged private Super 8 material by Jarman's father and grandfather.

Instead of continuing on with the next line of 'Howl', which contains the first direct reference to drugs ('[...] dragging themselves through the negro streets at dawn looking for an angry fix [...]'), Jarman anticipates this aspect through a visual allusion: directly before Scene 1 of the home-movie fragments, a sequence shows the image of a junkie in the rubble of British buildings reduced to ruins. He is fixing a tourniquet to his left arm in order to shoot up. This is followed by the home-movie scene with Jarman's mother in front of the RAF housing area in the forties. The shot that follows immediately after this shows Jarman in a panoramic shot during the shooting of THE LAST OF ENGLAND. With a Super 8 camera in his hand, he now films himself in the post-industrial, ruin-filled landscape of the eighties, underlaid with the commentary:

'Not with a bang but a whimper
and gathered everything you threw out of your dreamhouses [...]'.

Both in 'Howl' and in THE LAST OF ENGLAND, the members of a new 'Lost Generation' appear in the form of a result, as 'products' of the social landscape surrounding them: no-future figures aimlessly wandering about in a broken world that they have become cut off from and which turns too fast for them. And in Jarman's films we repeatedly find the metaphor of a globe racing round in circles: for the first time in JUBILEE (1978), where a rotating globe is abruptly stopped and the inscription 'NEGATIVE WORLD STATUS – NO REASON FOR EXISTANCE [sic] – OBSOLETE' becomes visible over the Soviet Union ('negative world status – no reason for existance') and India ('obsolete'). In THE GARDEN it is the scene described on pp. 18 f. of Chapter 2, in which a schoolboy sets an old globe spinning in ever faster rotations before a gathering of scholars. THE LAST OF ENGLAND also contains two sequences with a globe metaphor of this kind. The first is accompanied by the words: 'What proof do you need? The world is coiling up like an autumn leaf. A storm is coming to blow it into the final winter. Can't you feel the days are getting shorter?' The second sequence comes later and is preceded by the following words: 'In the silence of an English suburb power and secrecy dwell in the same house, while far away in the big city the A to Z clamped a grid on despair.' The racing sphere of the earth is already covered by flames.

In THE LAST OF ENGLAND the first line of Ginsberg's 'Howl' marks the first interface between the images of the present and the private Super 8 images of the past. It can serve as a kind of key for deciphering this multilayered theme in Jarman's film (as discussed in Chapter 2) – revealing the individual levels. It thus becomes possible to read 'I saw the best minds of my generation destroyed by madness, starving hysterical naked' in multiple ways. On the one hand, through its linking with the home-movie fragment, the sentence points directly back to those post-war years with which Ginsberg carries out a reckoning in 'Howl'. At the same time, the images of personal and urban destruction inserted before and after this fragment open up levels of meaning that lead into the present. One of these levels relates to Jarman's sense of an absence of perspectives as well as of social and cultural loss in the United Kingdom of the early eighties under Thatcher's government; another relates to his personal experience of losing numerous friends through Aids. Jarman himself lost a large number of good friends and acquaintances even during the initial years of the epidemic (which was still untreatable at that time, with the immune deficiency leading to death in most cases), and he invokes the not entirely unproblematic comparison between those who died from the effects of Aids and victims of war multiple times in his texts. He draws an initial, personal balance in *Modern Nature* (1991): 'So many friends dead or dying – since autumn: Terry, Robert, David, Ken, Paul, Howard. All the brightest and the best trampled to death – surely even the Great War brought no more loss into one life in just twelve months, and all this as we made love not war.'[58] One year later he recalls this once more in *At Your Own Risk*: 'Ten years into the epidemic, HIV has killed more young men in the States than in the Vietnam war. At the moment – New Year 1992 – there have been a quarter of a million admitted deaths – many more are unrecognised, or deliberately misattributed.'[59] However, the different results of different destructive events that take on the form of a state of war or of a war-like state resonate at various associative levels within the film. Their victims – 'the best minds of my generation' – are presented in THE LAST OF ENGLAND.

A Finger in the Fishes Mouth

The influence of the Beat Poets' works on Jarman had already become recognisable significantly earlier in a different area, namely, that of literature. His first book, *A Finger in the Fishes Mouth*, was published in 1972.[60] It is a collection of thirty-two poems that were all written in the mid-sixties. Many of them were written during his first, three-month stay in America in the summer of 1964 and several others during stays abroad in Italy and Greece. The book's title corresponds to the photograph reproduced on the cover: Wilhelm von Gloeden's 1895 photo *Boy with a Flying Fish*.

In Jarman's texts we can clearly recognise formal techniques and aims of the Beat Poets, such as open verse and free rhythms, spontaneous composition and the discarding – and thus questioning – of familiar semantic contexts. In many cases his poems convey the impression that they are texts without beginning and end, that they are reflective excerpts of an experienced and also lived reality. One characteristic feature that directly conveys this impression of the fragmentary, of the excerpt-like, is the lack of punctuation in most of the poems. Only the poems numbers 15, 18, 20, 25 and 28 are provided with sporadic punctuation. In this context 'Words written without any stopping' (no. 28) is surely the most concrete example of a spontaneous poem. Here Jarman explicitly takes up the associative technique of the Beat Poets and Ginsberg's demand for a free and natural idiom. With no concern – or only a very marginal concern – for the conventions of spelling and grammar, he finally sets an abrupt end to this recording of his free flow of thoughts and words with the written-out words of the punctuation mark: 'full stop'.

At the level of content, he often contrasts romanticising images with terms from the realms of contemporary mass culture and technology ('billboard', 'superhighway', 'emergency exit', etc.) and inserts them into new and semantically seemingly irreconcilable contexts, thus producing the impression of a critical statement – though only indirectly. This critique is not articulated in concrete terms, and it is not politically direct in a narrower sense. It can only be read between the lines and is conveyed through situational, subjective descriptions that make it possible to recognise states of disillusionment, resignation or hopelessness.

(19) CALGARY JULY 64
the mountains ring the edge of the world
and the city watches
the river flows from the mountains of
the edge of the world
through wild rose woods
and circles the city
punctuating its superhighways with bridges

(27) MOON
[...]
moon skates between
elms telegraph poles and
chimney pots

in the mansions of the moon
the man with a loony
mask tearing the paper
at the edge of the field
tearing the world at the
edge of the superhighway
moonstruck

His two texts 'Moon' (no. 27) and 'Calgary July 64' (no. 19) are good examples of contrasts of this kind. In both of them clichéd images of nature, which can simultaneously also symbolise purity and beauty ('moon', 'river', 'mountains', 'wild rose woods'), are ruptured by means of 'the edge of the world', 'superhighways' or 'telegraph poles'. Here nature and civilisation have become mutually threatening opposites. In these poems, for the first time, we are able to sense Jarman's idealising yearning for a bygone period (in some cases, one not even experienced by him) that has been buried under the events of the present and that he feels to be irrevocably lost. This yearning later emerges both in some of his paintings, for example, in several of the *Black & Gold Paintings*, and also in his films in a substantially clearer form. In a podium discussion with Simon Field, Jarman explained his desire to preserve and conserve in more detail:

'I am a very traditional filmmaker, a conservative with a small c.

'[...] I said, I never made a film, if I didn't think it was sort of conservative. I never actually thought of my films as being radical. They are in a long tradition, like I don't see Pasolini [as a radical]. I see Pasolini as a conservative. It's possible to see Pasolini as an extreme conservative who attempted to preserve parts of Italian life. You can see him as a revolutionary if you like. I saw the same thing in Caravaggio, I thought of him as a conservative artist.

'The true conservation of things [...]! I like to bring back to people driving through the countryside all the meadows. Look there is a meadow there. You can go for ten miles! I remember when the whole of the countryside was full of flowers. It's all been destroyed for commercial interests ...'.[61]

Unlike the previous examples, images bringing about a yearning for a bygone period are entirely absent from Jarman's 'Manhattan' (no. 23). The poem can be seen as an example of the influence of those coinages based on Ginsberg's style and involving social criticism and an expressionist tendency. Here the influence of Ginsberg's critical attitude towards society becomes tangible not only from a formal perspective but also – and primarily – in the critical and criticising standpoint occupied by Jarman. A feeling of the loss of a mythicised image resonates in the resigned observation 'Now I have seen screaming manhattan' and in the lines that follow. The scenario that is evoked seems inhuman, blindingly fast and highly technological. The images of the 'stainless steel corsets', 'subways' and 'elevators' are no longer countered by any images of hope. People find themselves – like piles of rubbish – along the kerbs of the Lower East Side: 'I have walked through lives littering the lower east side'. These are the only people that Jarman mentions here.[62]

A little over a hundred years before, Walt Whitman had also recorded impressions of Manhattan in his 'Calamus Poems' numbers 18 and 19.[63] If we compare Jarman's text with that of Whitman, it is precisely the obvious difference between them that illustrates the above-mentioned idealising yearning for lost aspects of a bygone period. Both reflect subjective impressions of the New York borough of Manhattan: Whitman's in the mid-nineteenth century and Jarman's in 1964, during his first stay in America. The hopelessly apocalyptic image conjured up by Jarman is no less disillusioning than the image of Whitman appears to be romanticising and idealising. Whitman's poems symbolically represent precisely that yearning for a lost past that Jarman thematises by way of contrast in other texts, but whose place remains empty here. The exclamation 'City of my walks and joys!' that Whitman places at the beginning of his poem is followed by a depiction of urban life formulated in positive and richly detailed images. However, the endless rows of buildings, the ships in the harbour and the gleaming displays of the shops are not what primarily impresses Whitman either: it is the people, specifically, the desirous gazes of approaching men, which he perceives with pleasure and which inspire him to strike up an ode to this city. And while Whitman begins to dream in another passage – 'I dreamed in a dream, I saw a city invincible to the attacks of the whole of the rest of the earth, I dreamed that was the new City of Friends' – Jarman's city finally fades away 'like a kodak dream'.[64]

Walt Whitman: CALAMUS POEM 18
City of my walks and joys!
City whom that I have lived and sung there will one
    day make you illustrious,
Not the pageants of you – not your shifting tableaux,
    your spectacles, repay me,
Not the interminable rows of your houses – nor the
    ships at the wharves,
Nor the processions in the streets, nor the bright
    windows, with goods in them,
Nor to converse with learned persons, or bear my
    share in the soiree or feast;
Nor those – but, as I pass, O Manhattan! your frequent
    and swift flash of eyes offering me love,
Offering me the response of my own – these repay me,
    Lovers, continual lovers, only repay me.

Derek Jarman: (23) MANHATTAN
Now I have seen
screaming manhattan
thrusting to burst bounds
crush the sky
and wade into cool waters
I have seen
serpent taxis
jewly gemming
winding through stainless steel corsets
narcissistically reflecting
and scratching the sky
I have walked through
lives littering the lower east side
dominoes with death
and the rat crumbling
furnaces of july dwellings
dreaming of time sapped Europe
now I have ridden subways at 100 mph
elevators 40 storeys a minute
glittered in the electric wastes of
park avenue
rode the staten island ferry
and watched this city
recede like a kodak dream

The attempt to break up unquestioningly accepted traditions and styles as well as Jarman's spontaneous composition and improvisation became integral elements of his manner of working in both painting and film. They also make it possible to recognise direct or indirect parallels to the Beats. Thus, during his intense occupation with the medium of Super 8, he began to develop his 'cinema of small gestures' (see pp. 157 ff.), which is characterised by open filmic verse forms (i.e. double and multiple exposures) and autonomous rhythms (i.e. recordings in slow motion). Improvisational and collage techniques are just as inherent to his works as are elements of the fragmentary, the rejection of familiar semantic contexts for the sake of an associative reception and politically formulated statements that also reveal themselves through a subtle playing with irony or provocation.

Beat Generation approaches calling society into question, as well as the critical cultural and political ideas of the sixties would subtly shape very diverse areas of his style of working and living and his political principles. His resolutely anti-Establishment attitude, his pacifistic outlook and his demand for an openly and freely lived-out sexuality can be mentioned here – as well as his aversion to every form of authority, to established power structures and to mechanisms of repression. However, his commitment is always an individual one. Without the emergence of any superstructure defined in terms of political ideology – which also seemed suspicious to him on account of its typically authoritarian and absolute nature – he sought paths of his own and began to write, paint and film against his enemies. Similarly to that already mythical political motto of the sixties protest movement – 'the private is political' – he developed his own personally motivated 'politics in the first person', as he later referred to it in *At Your Own Risk*.[65]

This 'politics in the first person' is directly connected with the strategy of the autobiographical discussed in Chapter 2, and it is not to be understood in a static-dogmatic sense based on definitive guiding principles. Instead, in the decades that followed, he subjected his critical attitude, his development of strategies and his forms of working to a constant assessment, renewal and adaptation to the realities surrounding him. Thus, for example, in the early seventies he attended the doctrinaire, radically political gatherings of the Gay Liberation Front (GLF) more or less sporadically and in the role of an outside observer who looked with scepticism upon their theoretical and revolutionary demands.[66] 'I still feel that there is no sexual liberation unless it's personal. Struggle to find out who you are. It's no good joining a group and making speeches about what you want to be, life is to be lived first and proselytised after', is what he says on the topic in *At Your Own Risk*.[67] Twenty years later, in the early nineties, he became active in the context of the newly created, no less radical but concretely political 'queer politics' of ACT UP and OutRage! and took a public stand against the censorship regulations of Clauses 25 and 28, against discrimination towards people with HIV and for making the homosexual age of consent the same as that for the rest of the population.

Above all else there was his aspiration to always look at his work as an extension of his life, never detached from his direct and personal experiences: 'When you are making a film which doesn't have a script, it becomes an extension of your life.'[68] It was not only in his first home movies that the process of filming was to retain a private and improvisational character. Since his earliest films Jarman had collaborated with a stable circle of friends that continually expanded in the course of time, and he did not look at himself in terms of the traditional programmatic role of the director in his later feature films either. It was only in this way that he was able to develop most of his films improvisationally, together with those taking part in them. He often – as was also the case in films such as JUBILEE, THE LAST OF ENGLAND, EDWARD II or THE GARDEN – worked without a script that had been completed in advance. '... The element that I felt I could throw a party, in my filming, it was very important. Everybody used to come along and I would try to give them another good day, you know. It was happy work. That was my aim really and that's probably all I actually ever wanted out of the whole thing. It's quite simple [...]'

'THE GARDEN was a sort of a home movie really, because I was actually filming the garden [...]. And then James, my producer, said let's try and make

a feature film out of all this and there was a house, it was desperately inco-
herent pieces of Super 8, and then we got a gang of people down for a couple
weeks and attempted to make some sort of order by building roughly around
the Gospel story.'[69]

The working process, which he repeatedly referred to as 'a party with
friends', was absolutely the primary focus for him and the result was secondary. The expansion of the concept of the private and the unity of art and life
become particularly clear in his two films THE GARDEN and BLUE, both of
which are thematically and associatively already deeply permeated with his
own illness, but this is also true of his last large-format paintings of the *Evil
Queen Series*. Severely impaired by the numerous illnesses stemming from his
HIV infection and almost entirely blind, he created these last paintings in
simultaneous working processes, together with his assistants Karl Lydon and
Piers Clemett. Jarman articulated his mental images and gave instructions
regarding the choice of colours and the manner of applying the paint and
was thus able to complete a few of these paintings 'with a little help from my
friends', as he expressed it himself.[70]

Slade School of Fine Art

During his years at King's College, Jarman had already occupied himself
intensively with both painting and the design of theatrical sets for the school's
theatre, and he repeatedly spent his free time at the studios of The Slade. In
1961 he took part in the competition of the University of London Union Art
Exhibition with his figurative painting *We Wait and Wait*. He won the shared
prize in the amateur division, and in this connection he met David Hockney
for the first time; the latter had won in the professional division, and the two
would get to know each other better a few years later. In 1963 Jarman was
finally able to begin studying painting and stage design at the Slade School of
Fine Art, and this was simultaneously the beginning of a period of years which
he experienced as increasingly liberating and liberated in various regards. He
moved from his parents' house in Northwood to London that year and experienced the art school in terms of 'a fortress against another reality, a defence
against an everyday existence that was awry'.[71] Until the total legal prohibition
against homosexual acts was repealed in 1967, the social compulsion to conform still remained omnipresent, although it was no longer as concretely tangible as in the fifties: 'The repression was difficult to confront – like finding
your way down a foggy street. In the sixties, we were to be open but still illegal.
This did not make it easy to form relationships and led to fumbling, furtive
sex. There was little or no celebration until the end of the decade, although
things were getting better.'[72]

Nonetheless, familiar feelings of isolation and exclusion also appeared during the initial period at art school, 'where it was difficult to be openly gay'.[73] And this was the case in spite of the fact that, from a historical perspective, Jarman could know that he was in excellent company: since its founding in 1871 the Slade School of Fine Art had, after all, provided the education of numerous artists who either remarkably intensively – though thematically still encoded and transferred to meta-levels – turned to the (nude) male body as a motif in their works or took up themes that were even explicitly homoerotic in themselves or openly conveyed homosexual content. Henry Scott Tuke (1858–1929), Duncan Grant (1885–1978), Alvaro Guevara (1894–1951), Rex Whistler (1905–1944), Robert Medley (1905–1994) and Mario Dubsky (1939–1985) are only a few of the best-known painters to be mentioned along these lines as graduates of The Slade.[74]

During the first year of his artistic education Jarman attended the course for Stage Design, and he was soon forced to note subtle external pressures to also assimilate himself in the realm of art and style. In previous years he had enthusiastically admired the works of the Impressionists and Neo-Impressionists, studied the biographies of Monet, Gaugin and van Gogh and personally preferred to paint landscapes and still lifes. However, at art school – on account of contemporary influences and tendencies – it gradually came to seem impossible to him to carry out more works in this form. Not without an undertone of resignation, he states:

'I was painting landscapes, close to the red earth of north Somerset, the flowers, butterflies in the meadows. My influences? William Scott's pots and pans, Paul Nash and the megaliths. It was impossible to paint these landscapes at The Slade in 1964; everyone was falling over themselves for pop-art, we were focussed on Manhattan. The "new" art was an urban art, the art of the glass-topped coffee table with the flower arrangement on it, the comic, the poster: one measured oneself against that.'[75]

The romantic motifs of his early paintings, which he had created in seclusion from his surroundings and 'in self-defence', were to temporarily become a thing of the past. It was not until ten years later that he would take them up again in a modified form and by way of a different medium, namely, in several of his early Super 8 films. He did so, for example, in the grainy landscape images in JOURNEY TO AVEBURY (1972), which are further developed and superimposed with other images in IN THE SHADOW OF THE SUN (1972/80), or in the shots of the decrepit boathouse and the surrounding landscape of Essex filmed using the 'single-frame' technique (see pp. 125 ff.) in GERALD'S FILM (1976).

In England, as in most other Western European countries, primarily two essential tendencies could be noted in the field of visual art during the first two decades after the Second World War. On the one hand there was the attempt to establish a link to what has been called 'Classical Modernism' and to the avant-garde concepts of the first decades of the century; on the other hand there was an orientation directly and very concretely based on the art currently being produced in the US. This art had been influenced and broadened in a not insubstantial way through the immigration of numerous protagonists of that same European avant-garde before or during the Second World War, including André Breton, Marcel Duchamp, Max Ernst, Fernand Léger, Piet Mondrian, +, Hans Richter and many others. Techniques of the fragmentary and associative, theoretical models like the fundamental principle of simultaneity – characterised by the negation of chronologically narrated history and linear time – and above all the fundamental demand for the unity of art and life that had been vehemently championed by the protagonists of Futurism and later also in the areas of Dadaism and Surrealism were all taken up once more in the Fluxus movement and the happenings of the late fifties and the sixties. 'If you want to send a message use a telegram!' was a well-known aphorism of the post-war period, and it expressed the negative attitude towards closed narrative discourse and the communication of unambiguous messages. The strict negation of narrative elements was to call into question seemingly universally valid images of reality and the claims to truth derived from them. Representations were transferred from the absolute realm of closed narrative discourses into ambiguity – but without becoming 'speechless' in any sense.

If these developments in the visual arts are compared with those in the performing arts, they seem to indicate efforts in opposite directions; however, both are based on a critical approach to or questioning of the substance of reality, which can be traced all the way back to initial efforts at the beginning of the twentieth century. We can say that the entry of the written, painted and later collaged word into painting was aimed at an 'emancipatory', progressive function or effect similar to that of language's exit from areas of the theatre – as is the case in the happening, performance art, dance and movement theatre and mime. When it is used there, language appears in a similarly fragmentary or collaged form. In the realm of the performing arts the medium of language had now been fundamentally called into question and more or less radical demands were presented that language be minimised in or banned from the theatrical event (e.g. by Edward Gordon Craig, Jacques Copeau and Etienne Decroux). This was intended to liberate theatre from the dominant naturalistic norms of the nineteenth century. By contrast, words and text were introduced into visual art at approximately the same time in a diametrically opposed development. Here the entry of writing into painting had similar causes and consequences on a different level: in this context the conclusive suspension of the 'appearance' of naturalistic depiction and the overcoming of the Impressionist style in the painted picture also imply a questioning of the truth contained in images, the unambiguousness of the word and language and the associated sense for 'reality'.

The first visualised texts by Stéphane Mallarmé or Guillaume Apollinaire, which were created around the turn of the century, are to be mentioned as precursors in this realm: their authors undertook an attempt to represent language in the form of an image. The first pictorial-linguistic articulations in painting were undertaken almost simultaneously by Georges Braque and Pablo Picasso, who applied words, parts of words and letters to the canvas – in part with the help of stencils. These already appear 'as a necessary element of the image, not as an annotation foreign to it, as an added commentary or as an inscribed title'.[76] By directly gluing (textual) materials in a painting – with 'glued pictures', that is, the so-called *papiers-collés* – Picasso and Braque subsequently laid the foundation for the technique of collage. By means of collage, protagonists of Dadaism (e.g. John Heartfield or Kurt Schwitters) and Surrealism finally further advanced the integration of text by mounting textual and pictorial materials – generally taken from newspapers – together on to the surface of the image in new and altered semantic contexts. In doing so both the associative semantic or interpretive value of a message and the pure composition of forms could be the primary focus in the new compositions thus created. The boundaries between different fields of art were increasingly in a state of dissolution, and stylistic devices or techniques were utilised more and more in an intermedial fashion because, as noted by Toni Stooss: 'With Cubism, Futurism and Dadaism as well as and above all with the work of Duchamp, the foundations were established for literature and visual art's natural convergence and for the boundaries once established between visual representation and verbal statement becoming increasingly blurred.'[77]

The American Dream

This multi-layered dissolution of boundaries becomes manifest in every area of Jarman's work: techniques of collage, associative elements of the fragmentary and thus also inherently open narrative forms become elementary means of communication in his paintings, films and texts. In the latter area it is not only the poems and literary texts but also his autobiographical writings *Dancing Ledge*, *The Last of England*, *Modern Nature*, *At Your Own Risk* and *Chroma* (actually a meditation on the subjective meanings of colours) that display numerous characteristics of the non-chronological, the associative and the fragmentary as well as the breaks and discontinuities inherent to them. In these writings he also repeatedly points to concrete influences of that period: the attempts to further develop the avant-garde concepts of modernism, the uninterrupted or rediscovered relevancy of the ideas of the Bauhaus as well as the works of Mies van der Rohe and Le Corbusier and also the general reorientation based on post-war American art. 'At school I'd left the Post-Impressionists behind, had dabbled like a child in a sweatshop in Cubism, Suprematism, Surrealism, Dada (which, I noted, wasn't an "...ism") and finally in Tachism and Action painting.'[78] His description of the current situation in the field of painting as he found it at art school is not without an ironic undertone. And in numerous other passages he repeatedly articulates his enthusiasm for America and the contemporary art there, specifically that 'new [...] urban art' mentioned above. This enthusiasm was shared by a number of British artists of that period, such as David Hockney or Mario Dubsky: 'Growing up in the 1950s we dreamed the American dream. England was grey and sober. [...] Over the Atlantic lay the land of cockaigne; they had fridges and cars, TV and supermarkets. All bigger and better than ours. [...] How we yearned for America! And longed to go west. In 1960 every young English artist had an eye across the Atlantic.'[79] Jarman recalls the 'New Generation Show' multiple times: this exhibition was held in London's Whitechapel Gallery in 1962 and introduced numerous protagonists of the contemporary American art of that period to Britain. However, this was not the first major event to occupy itself with this topic in a wider sense: as early as 1955 (!) a symposium on 'pop culture' had already been held in London and an exhibition entitled 'This Is Tomorrow' was held the next year. Looking back, Jarman acknowledged gaining impulses from this period above all through David Hockney, Robert Rauschenberg and Andy Warhol, but also Kenneth Anger and Maya Deren – in terms of both his painting and later also his works on Super 8 film.[80]

In this context not only the dissolution of these boundaries but also Jarman's personal demand for a unity of art and life could, in one form or another, be convincingly traced back to the happenings of the sixties and from there to similarly formulated demands of the Surrealists and Dadaists and then all the way back to the protagonists of Futurism. However, no attempt is to be made here to examine, trace or – above all – to classify Jarman's works with regard to the categories of art historical development or the spheres of influence of individual 'schools'. A classification understood in this form and the associated attempt at fixing his position would lead only to limitations, not to a closer understanding of Jarman's works – and Jarman himself never associated himself with belonging to one of these categories or schools. Instead, in a manner similar to the area of the 'Beat authors', individual areas of influence and points of contact will be revealed in an exemplary manner. Accordingly, in what follows, individual aspects from works by Robert Rauschenberg, David Hockney and Yves Klein will be set in relationship to Jarman, for whom they were significant for very different reasons.

Parallels to Rauschenberg

Rauschenberg's early works were created during a period defined primarily by works of Abstract Expressionism, whose most important protagonists included Jackson Pollock, Willem de Kooning, Ad Reinhardt and Mark Rothko, among others. Here the conceptual category 'Abstract Expressionism' is not meant to delineate a specific stylistic tendency or technique that can consistently be identified in the different works. Instead it is to be understood in terms of a common denominator under which the different works can be subsumed. The concept is an attempt to summarise the shared intentions of a group of artists. In their works these are characterised above all by a negative attitude towards unambiguously narrative elements, geometrical abstraction and Socialist Realism. Similarly to the aspirations of the Beat Poets in the area of literature, the focus here is once again on individuality, spontaneous improvisation and the demand for a free artistic expression, and these are to find their most direct realisation in the processual form of 'Action painting': 'In the elaboration upon Surrealist ideas about automatism, the painted canvas of the processual Action painting is the manifestation of the real identity of art and life in the act of painting, because the artwork realises the absolute liberation from all norms of aesthetic thought as a dramatic document of the self, as a spontaneous outpouring of the inner movement revealing itself.'[81] Here the direct link between art and life and the liberation from internalised norms and patterns is to be realised in the spontaneous act of painting. Or at least this is to be attempted, because, of course, a new aesthetic norm – that of the 'Action painting' created by Harold Rosenberg in 1952 – came into being conceptually in the same moment.[82]

During the same period a contrary tendency led to a radical rejection of personal expression and to the production of 'anonymous' works that undertake the attempt to be free of any individual references to the given artist, to his or her personal 'hand'. The reductivist colour-field painting belongs to this tendency, as do the monochrome series of Yves Klein or Robert Rauschenberg. Rauschenberg used a paint roller to create his monochrome works of the early fifties, such as the *White Paintings* (1951) or the uniformly black *Untitled* (matte black triptych, 1951), which consist of panels in unvarying white or black multiplied into series. And although Rauschenberg saw white as an independent colour and not as an absence, the *White Paintings*, for example, suggest a 'neutral' emptiness and an absence lined up in repetition because of their entirely unvarying application of the paint and their serial execution.[83] Thus these *White Paintings* provided the decisive impulse leading John Cage to compose his famous piece *4'33"*, which consists of precisely that amount of time – namely, from the opening of the keylid to its closing – of absolute silence and draws full attention to the chance and always differing sounds of its surroundings. However, Rauschenberg turned away from this form of extreme reduction only shortly after creating these series of paintings. This reorientation becomes readily recognisable through the incorporation of add-itional materials – such as newspapers, gold, copper, ink and enamel paints, which are to be found in his subsequent series of black paintings *Untitled* (glossy black painting; *c*.1951) and *Untitled* (black painting on paper, 1952) – as well as through his use of gold leaf in paintings including *Untitled* (Gold Painting; *c*.1953). The materials present in these works communicate a life of their own, a surface structure and a history – in the sense of transience – and they establish interrelationships among themselves.

At this point Rauschenberg began to experiment with different techniques and stylistic devices and to integrate numerous elements and materials into his early works. These facets are also found years later in Jarman's work in a manner that is formally sometimes astonishingly similar, though they have been modified and are in altered, new contexts (see fig. 5 to 16). These consist primarily of:

The colours black and gold as well as the application of elements like bitumen/tar, gold leaf and gold dust:

Rauschenberg: in his so-called Black Paintings (various untitled works, 1951–53) and Gold Paintings (various untitled works, 1953), which usually display a heavily textured surface

Jarman: in the *Black & Gold Paintings*, e.g. in *United* (1983) or *Heart's Ease* (1984), *Fine Balance* (1986) or also tar (bitumen) in *Untitled* (keys, 1989)

Text – autonomous characters, words and sentences inscribed into the painted surface of the work:

Rauschenberg: e.g. in *22 The Lily White* (*c*.1950): textures and writing inscribed in the white paint with a pencil

Jarman: in some of the early and late *Black & Gold Paintings*, e.g. *Dead Souls Whisper* (1982), *God Bless American Express* (1987) or *The Mistake* (1987); in many of his large-format paintings from the *Queer Series* and *Evil Queen Series*, e.g. *Blood* (1992) or *Scream* (1993)

Objets trouvés: The use of everyday found objects, such as newspapers, labels, (post) cards, various textile or metal goods, etc.:

Rauschenberg: in his collages, combines and assemblages
Jarman: in some of his *Black & Gold Paintings*, in the assemblages and garden sculptures in Dungeness

Collages:

Rauschenberg: works that contain paper and newspaper fragments, whole newspaper pages, cards, printed reproductions, numbers and characters, among other things; *Should Love Come First?* (*c*. 1951) was one of his first collages, and he overpainted it in black in 1953 (*Untitled*, small black painting, 1953); followed in 1952 by various other *Untitled* (Hotel Bilbao, Frog and Turtle, Palm of Hand, Face in Bottle, etc.; *c.*1952)

Jarman: integration of newspapers in the *Queer Series*

Newspapers – integrated in two different forms:

(1) newspaper pages are fixed to the support as a ground and painted over: not collages in the true sense, because the newspapers disappear behind the paint applied over them, become invisible and appear in the work only in the form of its undulating surface

Rauschenberg: some of his Black Paintings, Gold Paintings and Red Paintings, e.g. *Untitled* (glossy black four-panel painting, *c.*1951), *Untitled* (Gold Painting, *c.*1953) or *Red Import* (*c.*1954)

Jarman: in some paintings from the *Queer Series* and *Evil Queen Series* the newspaper photocopies fixed to the support are completely concealed by the layers of paint covering them, e.g. in *Queer* (1992) or *Infection* (1993)

(2) newspaper pages are integrated into the work as partially or entirely recognisable collage elements

Rauschenberg: in some of the Black Paintings, Gold Paintings and Red Paintings, e.g. *Untitled* (matte black painting with Asheville Citizen; *c.*1952), *Elaine's Party* (1954), *Untitled* (Gold Painting, *c.*1953) or *Untitled* (Red Painting, 1954)

Jarman: in numerous works from the *Queer Series*, e.g. *Blood* (1992), *Letter to the Minister* (1992), etc.

Combines:

elaboration upon the 'ready-made' technique, which was essentially introduced and developed by Marcel Duchamp and in which found and often industrially produced utilitarian objects are provided with titles and declared to be artworks

Rauschenberg: integrates objects into the 'easel painting', e.g. *Bed* (1955), *Allegory* (1959/60) and *First Landing Jump* (1961)

Jarman: in numerous *Black & Gold Paintings*, e.g. *God Bless American Express* (1987), *Madonna* (1988), *TB or not TB that is the Question* (1990), etc.

Assemblages – a further development of the collaging combines:

the flat easel painting is extended by forming diverse materials into three-dimensional images and sculptures

Rauschenberg: sculptures made out of utilitarian objects, e.g. *Untitled* (washboard assemblage; *c.*1952) and metal-and-stone sculptures (e.g. various *Untitled*, Elemental Sculptures; *c.*1953)

Jarman: e.g. *K.Y.* (1988), *A Plant* (1989) or *Untitled* (pearl and stone, 1987) and sculptures in the garden at Dungeness

Action painting:

Rauschenberg: in the series *Night Blooming* (*Untitled*; *c.*1951), in which asphalt has been used in addition to oil paint, Rauschenberg comes closest to Harold Rosenberg's claims for an 'Action painting' in which the painter's actions and reactions during the process of painting generate the form given to the work

Jarman: the large-format paintings of the *Queer Series* and *Evil Queen Series*: Jarman – or, in the late paintings, his assistants – apply parts of the paint and text with their hands

After Rauschenberg's early rejection of his own attempts at total reduction, his works nonetheless remain closely connected with the aspirations of 'Abstract Expressionism'. The materials and elements placed in connection with one another do not reveal any semantic levels of direct messages or statements. Instead, the works open up several interpretive possibilities to the viewer, who is thus made into an active 'reader' who subjectively completes the work, a 'co-creator', as Armin Zweite has referred to it in this context: 'They are, as has repeatedly been emphasised, open works of art, and in this context it can be mentioned that Umberto Eco's formative book *Opera aperta* was published in Milan in 1962. The "open work" is to be understood as a field of interpretive possibilities or, alternatively, as a configuration of indeterminacies that stimulate the viewer to engage in a series of variable interpretations and thus make him a kind of co-creator of the work.'[84]

However, regarding these points, it is also important to record the fundamental differences relative to comparable works by Jarman. Where Rauschenberg attempts – as he puts it – to make 'the gap between art and life' his sphere of action, Jarman closes this gap: both areas overlap and become a single shared field of action. While experimentation with materials, abstraction and avoiding messages or narrative elements are Rauschenberg's primary focus, many of Jarman's works utilising comparable techniques and materials contain subjective content that often conveys messages with a social or political intention. In Jarman's case the 'configuration of indeterminacies' is reduced and limited by the intention to communicate. The materials and elements placed in connection with one another are meant to produce statements, to 'narrate' something in the broadest sense of the word.

In the case of Rauschenberg's works, viewers are forced to become active through the absence of any direct message. They have to first position the individual elements within a (semantic) context, and within this framework they can form any meanings they want. With Jarman, on the other hand, they are forced to react: the intended statements in Jarman's works demand reactions. However, viewers are not assigned the role of a passive recipient here either, instead – through their reaction – they find their own personal position for subjectively 'reading' and completing the messages and statements. In Jarman's case the formal abstraction is no longer carried out for its own sake, instead, it has become a means to a communicative end. It opens up an associative field giving viewers the freedom to subjectively assess and adapt statements, to develop their own feelings and thoughts and – in connection with the given content – to project them on to this field. Abstraction serves the subjective reception of the message inherent to the given work. In this sense the works' viewers become 'co-creators' here as well, because they are able to associatively elaborate upon them for themselves.

tar and bitumen

Fig. 5:
Robert Rauschenberg,
Untitled (Night Blooming),
*c.*1951

Fig. 6:
Derek Jarman, *Untitled* (keys),
1989

Fig. 7:
Robert Rauschenberg,
Untitled (Gold Painting),
*c.*1953

Fig. 8:
Derek Jarman,
Fine Balance,
1986

newspaper collage and inscriptions

Fig. 9:
Robert Rauschenberg,
Untitled,
1954

Fig. 10:
Derek Jarman, *Blood*,
1992

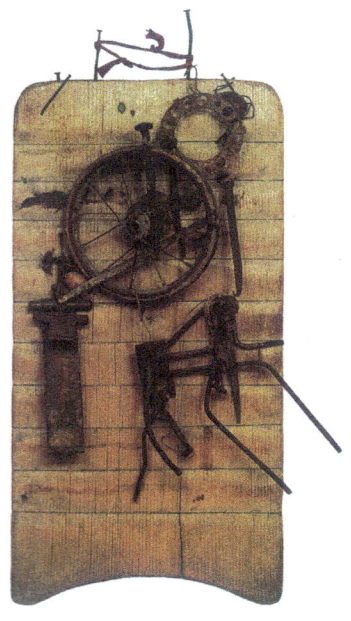

Fig. 11:
Robert Rauschenberg, *Untitled*
(washboard assemblage),
*c.*1952

Fig. 12:
Derek Jarman, *A Plant*,
1989

combines

Fig. 13:
Robert Rauschenberg, *Bed*,
1955

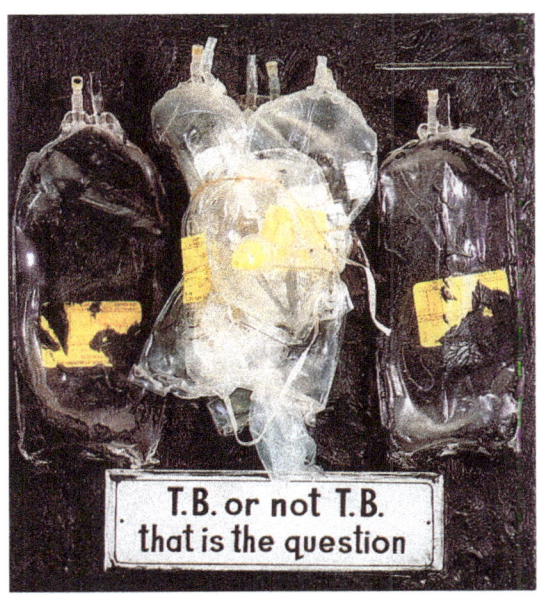

Fig. 14:
Derek Jarman, *TB or not TB
that is the question*,
1990

Fig. 15:
Robert Rauschenberg, *Untitled*
(Elemental Sculpture),
*c.*1953

Fig. 16:
Derek Jarman,
Garden sculpture at Dungeness

The formal parallels in the use of individual elements and techniques presented here in connection with Rauschenberg can be concretely identified from Jarman's early *Black & Gold Paintings*, begun in 1982, onwards. These works were created during a period defined by deep and widespread insecurity and uncertainties within the gay (sub)culture caused by the appearance of the first cases of Aids, which simultaneously multiplied at an extremely rapid rate. This – at that point in time – new 'mysterious illness', which seemed to threaten only homosexual men, was indicatively still referred to under the medical label GRID ('gay-related immune deficiency') in the early eighties. In these early works by Jarman we find exclusively these two elements of black and gold: 'The black paint is like the universe. Black is the colour that binds the universe: it is all infinity: the void that binds everything.'[85] Gold emerges out of this void in the form of shadow-like suggestions of the depicted subject. It seems to enter into a – so to speak – alchemical link with the endless black out of which dream images, fears or yearnings grow. The sketchily indicated naked bodies of young men emerge, engraved into the thin layer of black paint applied to the gold leaf. Vague and apparently static or frozen, they find themselves within an unbounded space, e.g. in *Dead Souls Whisper* (1982), *All we see is sleep, all we see awake is death* (1983) or *Heart's Ease* (1984). In some other compositions featuring a substantially more emphatic effect, the vague word 'Love' emerges out of the dark background, e.g. in *United* (1983) or *Thames at Night* (1984).

From 1986 onwards, however, the *Black & Gold Paintings* are expanded through key elements: the black layers of paint or tar are now added in a thick coat, objects are integrated, the paintings emerge out of their two-dimensionality to become sculptural and three-dimensional combines and the messages to be conveyed become more direct (e.g. *The Mistake*, 1987). Jarman learned of his HIV infection in that year and was able to buy Prospect Cottage, an old fishers' house he discovered on the beach of Dungeness while shooting THE LAST OF ENGLAND. Many of his subsequent paintings would be created there. Gold and black continue to remain constant elements in these works. They are joined by new, periodically appearing elements, such as broken mirrors, shards of mirrors (*Silence* and *Fine Balance*, both 1986) and various found objects. These very literally 'found' objects often consist of driftwood and other things washed up on the beach – rotted-out, rusty or algae-covered objects fixed to the canvas to create brittle, three-dimensional combines. Like these combines, Jarman's assemblages made of weathered wood, stones or shells – including *Untitled* (pearl and stone, 1987) and *Untitled* (shell, stone and wood, 1988) – and the gradually assembled garden sculptures at Dungeness convey a sense of the transformation of matter and material, of decay and transience. They are landscapes of decay, which always seem to express a certain yearning desire to hold on to that which is transient, but which also repeatedly display ironic ruptures. Words or sentences have been inscribed into some of the paintings. The writing scratched into the paint becomes an inscription. In the late eighties the references to Aids become more and more concrete in the combines and assemblages. They seem to reflect the states of decay brought about through illnesses, the progressive destruction and simultaneously the powerlessness of one's own body. The objects mounted on the canvas or constructed into assemblages, including condoms (e.g. *Praise God and Pass the Ammunition*, 1987, or *Untitled*, comb, 1989), squeezed-out tubes of lubricant (*K.Y.*, 1988), candles (*Caravaggio*, 1986) or crucifixes (*Short Circuit, Exit*, 1988, or *Sands of Time*, 1988) enable associative reflections on illness, blood, death, suffering, poisoned bodies and hypocritical morals. Not hopeless or loudly reproachful but quiet and reserved, looking back upon a time from which there is nothing left to salvage – the mirrors are broken.

The large-format paintings of the *Queer Series* and *Evil Queen Series* appear very different: these works combine the techniques of collage and grattage as well as inscribed writing, and they were created in the early nineties, closely based on the technique of Action painting. In this context, associations with the works of Jackson Pollock are nearly unavoidable. He had been the first to 'apply' paint to large-format canvasses by means of gestural actions and with his hands or in the form of drip painting and to avoid all of the conventions of a central motif. Particularly in several paintings from Jarman's *Evil Queen Series*, we rediscover elements of drip painting, for example, in *Drop Dead* or *Dipsy Do (Sinister)*, both of 1993.

At this point in time Jarman had already battled with countless severe infections and illnesses brought about by HIV, and in these series he gives voice to his feelings – particularly his hopelessness, sadness and anger – through the expressive, forceful and wild application of paint. His anger derived above all from the tabloid press and its inhuman headlines on the topics of Aids and homosexuality but also from the ignorance and homophobic mental attitude of the society around him. These paintings are no longer reserved, instead, they are active, passionate and confrontational. The garish colours have been applied, for example, in the form of painting by brush or by hand over the multiplied copies of tabloid front pages laid out on the canvas. Jarman subsequently reworks the paint with his hands: in the process he forms lines, individual words and sentences. The messages that appear no longer leave any room for a detached consideration, instead, they confrontationally cry out for action, for example, in *Time* and *Love, Sex, Death* (both 1992) or *Ataxia (Aids is Fun)* (1993) and many others.

'In this context it is important to note that, from the very beginning, the influx of written language, of typographical elements, into the image also implied the influx of the "everyday".'[86] Toni Stooss's statement, formulated as a generalisation in the art historical context of the example of Braque, can be concretely exemplified using Jarman's work: alongside the various 'everyday objects' in the combines and assemblages it is, namely, primarily his own inscriptions and borrowed typographical materials (the newspapers) and finally the combination of both that incorporate the everyday and, here, in particular, everyday experiences – which Jarman increasingly formulates into concrete messages. Whether figuratively, like the black paintings and combines and assemblages, or abstractly, like the *Queer Series* and *Evil Queen Series*, many of these works convey concrete content and it is possible to note in generalising terms that the later the works were created, the more virulent the messages become, which enter more and more clearly and vehemently into the foreground. This development and this change in the statements of those works created from the early eighties onwards are also to be seen in connection with HIV and Aids – initially indirectly and later directly.

Painting It Out: David Hockney

In the summer of 1964 Jarman embarked upon his first journey to America, from July until the end of September. After a stay in New York he travelled on to Canada to visit his friend Ron, whom he had met in London. Many of the poems later published in *A Finger in the Fishes Mouth* were written at this time. As Jarman repeatedly emphasises in his autobiographical writings,[87] his first journey to America and the impressions and encounters associated with it provided a decisive impulse for his consciously realised coming out and his wish for a more liberated and self-determined life. Having returned to London after his first, three-month stay in America, Jarman encountered David Hockney at a Picasso exhibition in the Tate Gallery: 'In the autumn of 1964, Ossie Clarke and I visited the Picasso Show at the Tate and collided with David straight off the plane from L.A. He invited us back to his freezing flat for tea and we climbed into his bed to keep warm as he unpacked his suitcase full of bright fluorescent socks and underwear and the first *Physique Pictorials* I had ever seen.'[88]

Jarman subsequently got to know Hockney better and became a part of his closer circle of friends around Ossie Clarke and Patrick Procktor – whose role he would play years later in Stephen Frear's film PRICK UP YOUR EARS (UK, 1987) – and in this way he met numerous young contemporary artists from the London and international scenes. The period of isolation, seclusion and loneliness seemed to be at an end. In the second half of the sixties an increasingly freer life became possible, one that could be shaped counter to a public sphere that continued to remain repressive: 'Through David and his friend Patrick Procktor I met all the young painters; this changed my life. There were shows and parties and nights on the town; we all fell in and out of each other's beds. It was enriching. Sex was bonding, pedagogic, a way of learning.'[89]

As a painter in the United Kingdom of the sixties, Hockney was not only among the first to break a societal taboo still seen as absolute at that time, by publicly affirming his homosexuality – in addition he had also begun to directly, unambiguously and straightforwardly thematise homosexuality in his works. The primary focus in Hockney's work is not on styles and techniques of working but on his life and lifestyle, which are repeatedly present in his work, occupy the centre of attention and also appeared to Jarman as something of not insignificant importance. Hockney's statements, which were extraordinarily courageous at that time, provided a model for a whole generation. In this context this model is to be attributed an essential and integrative function in the achievement of both a personal and a general, societal self-concept – not only for Hockney himself but also for those artists and friends that he gathered around him. Jarman repeatedly points to the liberating power and the influence that Hockney's open lifestyle and his works exercised far beyond the boundaries of the realm of art, extending all the way to the emergence of the Gay Liberation Movement in the late sixties: 'He completely altered a whole generation's view of homosexuality, with a few strokes of an etching needle. He was the first artist to be so open about his private life, and he had a huge influence because of that. Gay liberation grew out of gestures like this later on in the decade. Both David and Patrick lived this open lifestyle, but David was a much more public figure, much more in the limelight. [...] The path they forged is commonplace now – all young people live in its aftermath and what is quite ordinary was a revolution. There hasn't been a revolution in our lifestyles of that nature since. The 70's and 80's are just re-interpreting that period.'[90] In an essay on Hockney, Jarman describes how, for example, a superficiality like Hockney's dyed-blond hair – which seems so unexceptionable and commonplace from today's perspective – broke the strict conventions of masculine appearance in the sixties: 'When David dyed his hair blonde, he lit up more than his bathroom mirror. It seems such a small gesture now but then it broke every convention of the ghastly fifties. The grey suits and black shoes, stiff collars and ties, the tight furled umbrellas of the middle classes barely ruffled by the wind of change, a fucked up closet culture where queers were bashed in the tabloids.'[91]

Hockney's works are autobiographical, their themes are directly connected with him, his sexuality and the environment of his private life. As reserved or cryptic as some of the very early works may appear from today's perspective, even many of them already thematise homosexuality as their subject in a direct and immediate form that was new, 'shocking' and 'scandalous' for that period. In the early sixties, while a student at London's Royal College of Art, he created an initial series of so-called 'coming out' paintings, including a portrait of Walt Whitman, to whom references can also repeatedly be found in other works. The well-known painting *We Two Boys Together Clinging* was created in 1961: two embracing men can be recognised in it and the phrase of its title, the first line from Whitman's 'Calamus Poem No. 26', has been inscribed into it. Hockney's painting *Adhesiveness* (1960) also makes reference to a term used by Whitman, with which he tries to give a name to close friendships between men.[92]

In another student project created in 1961 at the Royal College of Art, Hockney also occupied himself with Ford Madox Brown's painting *The Last of England*. He inserts an entirely personal narrative into his 'copy' of the painting – which he has renamed into the questioning *The Last of England?* – by putting himself in the place of Brown and his heart-throb Cliff Richard in the place of Brown's wife (see fig. 17). In his biography of Hockney, Peter Webb explains the background behind this work:

'At the Royal College, students were set the project of copying a famous painting and Hockney chose Brown's *The Last of England*. He rejected the pathos of the original as well as its sharp focus. Instead, he depicted himself (labelled 4.8 in his alphabetical code which equalled D.H.) with his arm round his fantasy lover, Cliff Richard (D.B. for Doll Boy). However, he kept Brown's circular format and added the title made into a question: "The Last of England? Transcribed by David Hockney 1961". [...]

'Hockney has borrowed the schoolboy code of one of his favourite poets, the homosexual Walt Whitman, in which 1=A, 2=B and so on. Thus 3.18=C.R., which identifies the figure as the singer Cliff Richard. Hockney was at this time infatuated with Cliff Richard and had decorated his studio cubicle with photographs of the singer whose current hit record was entitled "Living Doll". The song was about a girl, but David changed the sexual roles and made Cliff his "Doll Boy" [also the title of a painting of 1960], the object of his love and at the same time his chosen symbol of sexual repression.'[93]

Private themes become more and more dominant motifs in his work: Hockney's friends, his long-time partner Peter Schlesinger, his family, the boys around the pools of America's West Coast, his travels, his 'daily life' can be seen in many of his paintings. In Jarman's words: 'He chased the shadows from his work, the shadows that hide our lives.'[94] Hockney now deliberately ignored traditional taboos and thematised corporality and gay sexuality in his works in a way that gradually became more and more immediate and direct. In the mid-sixties he created the series of the so-called Cavafy etchings as illustrations of poems by the Greek writer Constantine P. Cavafy. This series visualises Hockney's personal and extremely intimate impressions in a naturalism that was directly provocative at the time: in its aesthetic disinterest it no longer seeks to beautify, conceal or euphemise anything. The studies of nudes and the recorded scenarios resist almost any idealisation in a classical sense. Like snapshots they seem to approach towards realistically accurate images and to suggest an everyday and commonplace quality. Jarman presents them as diametrically opposed to the idealised figures of Jean Cocteau: 'When I saw David Hockney's Cavafy etchings of very ordinary young men in bed together, they were something quite new; if you look at Cocteau's boys, they were idealised; these were very honest. David was honest to the point of naïvety.'[95] In the first half of the sixties Hockney became one of the first to unreservedly and radically turn his back on romanticising motifs used to serve as alibis. He tore away the veil of masks and ambiguously interpretable suggestiveness by rejecting the available store of stereotypical, mythological or antique motifs and drawing the content of his works out of his personal, lived present.

Even in the late sixties and in both photography and the other visual arts, openly thematising and depicting male sexuality, nude male bodies and corporality – not to mention homosexual connotations, content and themes – were almost exclusively relegated to the level of metaphor and could be expressed almost exclusively by this indirect means. The idealisation of the perfect, strong and active male body was still omnipresent at that time, both in photography and the other visual arts.

The content of these representations could never be permitted to draw too close to the reality of the present, let alone permit direct associations with the individual realities of their viewers' lives. Stretching back for decades and centuries themes had been based on classical motifs and their ideals, and mythological subjects or themes from Roman or Greek antiquity were repeatedly utilised to provide pretexts to permit the depiction of the nude, active or battling male body. Concerned to achieve a more or less correct classical contrapposto attitude, poses were staged, surrounded with fake Doric columns or other stereotypical antique props. The thematic sequences of romantic bathing youths, of sailors in Cocteau's and others' prior works and of fighting, wrestling, swimming, hunting and heroically posing men can be continued almost indefinitely.

Physique Pictorial

The photographs and drawings published in the fifties and sixties in the American magazine *Physique Pictorial* provide, so to speak, a reproduction of this entire palette of motifs and themes of athletic manliness. Here – unlike other comparable 'athletics magazines' published at that time, which continued to utilise topics regarding physical health and conditioning as pretexts – the aestheticisation of the male body was the exclusive focus of interest for the first time. This interest was extraordinary at that time, because: 'There was an unspoken agreement that men never took their clothes off just to be admired for their looks. What *Physique Pictorial* did was to strip away all that

Fig. 17: David Hockney, *The Last of England?*, 1961

obfuscation. [...] No serious attempt was made to gloss over the fact that those attractive young men were naked to be looked at and enjoyed. Men, naked for the pleasure of others? That, in the fifties, was dangerously radical.'[96] This repertoire of images attempted to reproduce every one of the above-mentioned thematic sequences of athletic manliness in the published photographs and drawings of *Physique Pictorial*. Among them, two repeatedly recurring groups of themes are to be emphasised: the shower scenes shot in countless variations and the theme of wrestling. For years the former inspired Hockney to create numerous works, and the latter – the motif of men wrestling with each other – is later to be found once more in passages from several films by Jarman.

Hockney, who came across *Physique Pictorial Magazine* for the first time in America, was fascinated by the unmistakable significance possessed by the subject of the shower – both in the series of photographic motifs in the magazine and in real life on the West Coast. What is special about the shower scenes (see fig. 19) is that they are the first (and the only) thematic sequence among the photographic material of *Physique Pictorial* that seems to entirely liberate the models from their heroic and rehearsed poses (see fig. 18). The photographs suggest the snapshot aesthetic of a scene catching its subjects unawares and they show the models in 'natural', unrehearsed poses for the first time. Here only the selected location of the shower remains as a means to legitimate the photos. This is what permits the nudity, corporality and physical contact – which at that time still necessitated extensive 'explanatory' captions as a consequence: 'Double Bath: After every posing session the fellows like to shower and get rid of the oil and dirt they have picked up in rough and tumble wrestling and posing. We have only a small hot water tank, so if two fellows have posed they usually have to share the shower afterwards so that there will be enough hot water for both. Too, they are able to help each other to remove the oil, etc.'[97]

Alongside his famous swimming pool motifs, showers became a favourite and repeatedly recurring subject in Hockney's works. In this context he often utilised the photographs of showering men from *Physique Pictorial* to provide inspiration and source material (see fig. 20), for example, in *American Boys Showering* (1964), *Domestic Scene, Los Angeles* and *Two Men in a Shower* (both 1963) or *Boy About to Take a Shower* (1964).[98] In a 1994 interview with Paul Melia he remarked regarding this: 'A shower is much more interesting for the artist because you see the body. [...] Remember, I'm drawing from life and not wanting to draw from life [laughter] in the sense that drawing from life at the art school was one thing but here it has to be another. [...] Because a person's actually doing something in a naked form. There's a clear reason, bathing. It's an old subject yet it's a totally different way from the nude bather by Renoir ...'.[99] For Hockney it is only the location of the activity that remains as a 'pretext'. It forms the framework of the narrative that Hockney individually elab-

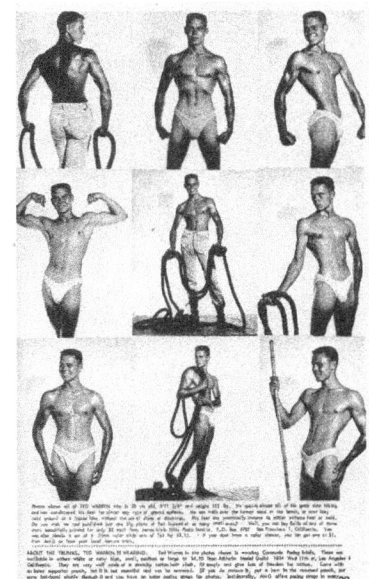

Fig. 18:
Heroic and rehearsed poses:
Ted Warren, in: *Phyisque Pictorial*,
January 1960

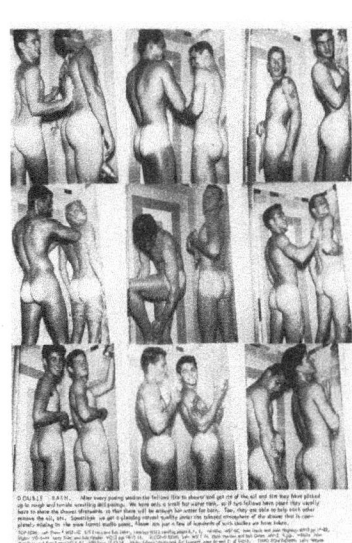

Fig. 19:
Snapshot aesthetic:
Double Bath, in: *Phyisque Pictorial*,
January 1961

Fig. 20: David Hockney, *American Boys Showering*, 1963

orates upon in his paintings by either replacing individual models from his photographic source material with his own friends (for example, in *Two Men in a Shower*) or creating entirely new, independent scenarios filled exclusively with people from his own personal surroundings ('I'm drawing from life'). In this way the already individualised poses of the models become personalised and personal; images with explicitly sexual connotations are rid of the aura of the extraordinary. Hockney thus created his own individual and open form of expression that both negates any idealisation of the depicted people and causes their actions to appear typical and everyday.

The Motif of Wrestling in Jarman's Films

The motif of men wrestling with one another, which we will find again years later in individual sequences from several of Jarman's films, is omnipresent in the photographs of *Physique Pictorial*. Countless images there present the most fanciful contortions of men's bodies wrapped tightly around one another 'in struggle' – always making an effort to emphasise the 'athletic element'. However, the theme was by no means an invention of this period, instead, it can be traced back in the field of photography to Eadweard Muybridge and his well-known motion study of the two wrestlers in *The Complete Human and Animal Locomotion* of 1887. In the field of fine art the motif can point to a substantially longer history of representation and in the twentieth century alone it was taken up in numerous works by artists such as Duncan Grant (*Two Wrestlers*, c.1920–24), Keith Vaughan (*Wrestler*, 1948) or Robert Medley (*Slave and Wrestlers*, 1953), to mention just a few examples. For a long time the theme of wrestling, with its representation of a socially legitimated struggle, was the only one to permit direct male-male proximity and physical contact, because 'the image of two men wrestling successfully evokes a sexuality that can only safely be expressed in physical struggle'.[100] Prohibitions and censorship could be circumvented in this way: the wrestling men were struggling but nonetheless united, the images became readable – in this way or that.

For decades Francis Bacon occupied himself with this motif and possible ways to dissipate the stereotypes inherent to it. In works like *Two Figures* (1953) or in the central painting of the triptych *Studies from the Human Body* (1970), which also explicitly make use of the Muybridge's above-mentioned photographs as source material, the distance that is normally preserved between the depicted figures is almost entirely dissolved for the first time: the boundaries at points of contact are blurred, become invisible, and the body is robbed of any athleticism. The theme of the struggle now figures only vaguely, because here, alongside that component of violence inherent to the gesture of the struggle, that of sexuality emphatically and unambiguously makes its way into the foreground for the first time: '[...] it is sight, touch, tension, orgasm, together'.[101]

In elaborating upon the motif of wrestling, artists like Hockney were primarily pursuing efforts directed towards an emancipatory dissipation of the stereotypes and clichés inherent to it by establishing subjective and personal approaches in their depictions. In the case of Jarman, however, the motif becomes an entirely self-sufficient, thematic element. In any case the images of wrestling men in Jarman's work stand for themselves: they have emancipated themselves and lead a life of their own. They no longer point to something else – they have become something else. The taboo against the depiction of male-male sexuality and the obligatory requirement of legitimisation implied by it have fallen. Accordingly there has also been a shift in the function and status of the motif as we find it in very different thematic contexts in sequences from his films SEBASTIANE, THE ANGELIC CONVERSATION and EDWARD II. Jarman is not concerned – as is Hockney, for example – with a personal 'appropriation' of, elaboration upon and removal of the taboo on this specific motif. Instead it is the overriding narrative framework and the themes themselves that he resolutely attempts to expose and reveal through his strategy of naming. The common denominator in all of this is always the thematising of society's repression of sexuality.

In order to do so Jarman makes use of 'classic' themes like the legend of St Sebastian, the love poems of Shakespeare in THE ANGELIC CONVERSATION or Christopher Marlowe's royal drama surrounding EDWARD II, and he unmistakably places the either suppressed or cryptically communicated theme of homosexuality at the centre of his explorations. Within these treatments the images of men wrestling with one another no longer seem ambiguously interpretable in the previously mentioned sense. Instead they are deliberately deployed quotations that stand for themselves and produce and convey independent statements within the overall context, the 'plot'.

The most direct associations with the antique poses of the images from *Physique Pictorial* are surely evoked in the scenes of struggle in SEBASTIANE, where the protagonists literally wrestle for physical, bodily closeness.[102] Initially approaching one another by way of seemingly playful struggles – a classical wrestling match in the sand or tussling in the water – each of these activities are followed by unambiguous, deliberate physical contact, embraces and sexual encounters clearly distinguished from those of the struggle. In contrast to the depictions in *Physique Pictorial*, the arrangements of the scenes in SEBASTIANE are no longer shifted to the level of metaphor. Instead, by elaborating upon and clearly formulating underlying intentions, they are led out of the realm of hints and ambiguities. The 'forbidden desire' that had previously been covertly expressed within classical wrestling scenes is explicitly stated here in independent images. In SEBASTIANE Jarman dismantles the figural shell of this saint: a representation that, over centuries, both became the ideal artistic subject for the depiction of the male body within and under the scrutiny of the Catholic Church and – to the same degree – advanced to become an icon of repressed homosexual desire. At the same time, however, Jarman also dismantles the figural shell of countless Spartan or Roman warriors and gladiators frozen into images: he achieves this by freeing them from their poses – distanced in their struggle – and acknowledging their desire and passion.

The eight-minute sequence of the two men wrestling with each other in THE ANGELIC CONVERSATION (see pp. 183 f.) occupies a central position. The 'struggle' – which is preceded by a lengthy search, an aimless wandering about, by the two young men – begins directly after the final lines of a Shakespeare sonnet recited by Judi Dench:

'So, till the judgement that yourself arise,
You live in this, and dwell in lovers' eyes.'[103]

Here it is less the gestures of violence and struggle that Jarman reveals through the movements reproduced in slow motion than the otherwise invisible details of physical contact that lie concealed behind them and appear gentle and sensitive in their slowed state. Wrestling with one another becomes an initial, very close encounter, and in their slowed sequence the motions are invested with an intimate and tender expression. Because almost the entire film has been shot in slow motion, two short scenes inserted in real time stand in all the sharper contrast to the meditatively timeless effect of the sequences of images of struggle surrounding them: lasting only four seconds, an inserted repetition of a movement breaks in among the other images with a brutality and intensity that is just as immense as that of the scene of an embrace ending their struggle.

In EDWARD II, on the other hand, the motif is to be seen not in the form of a central scene but as a brief fade-in directly after the signing of the edict on the banishment of Edward's lover, Gaveston.[104] Like a vision, a group of nude young men testing their strength appear out of the darkness before the eyes of Edward's son, the young Prince Edward. They move within a dark space lit only by the cone of light emitted by a pocket torch – clenched together and step by step, they move forward and back according to their relative strength. Here the primary focus is not on the direct thematising of corporality or revealing the physical contact inherent to it. Instead, in EDWARD II, the motif appears as the open formulation of an ambiguously interpretable metaphor for inward states and it can be read in the context of different struggles being fought out at the level of the film's content. Here, in spite of the apparent directness and quotation-like unambiguousness of the image, viewers nonetheless remain able to associatively interpret and elaborate upon the theme within the recounted narrative, which seeks to force King Edward to also sign the edict and causes Gaveston to tear it up.

Yves Klein – Blue

Blue. Deep, luminous blue – nothing else. No more images, only this single, powerful colour makes its way out from the screen and floods over the viewers of Jarman's last film, BLUE. It is the French painter Yves Klein's ultramarine in which our gaze loses itself: that colour which, for Klein, was situated beyond all of the dimensions inherent to the other colours. It is a blue that seems to convey both a deep, almost unbounded distance and an expression – through its luminous presence – of immediate and inescapable proximity: we wish to grasp out at it, but nonetheless find only a void.

BLUE invites us to engage in an associative meditation: sounds, noises, voices and music can be heard, simultaneously distant and near. 'The present is filled by echoes of past …', writes Jarman in his last book, *Chroma*, an associative discourse on colours.[105] And for seventy-four minutes it is precisely this resonance, this echo of memories of experienced situations and events that fills the acoustic part of this film, the present. BLUE is a collage of thoughts and memories that Jarman recites with the help of his diaries: conversations with friends in a street cafe or reflections on his long, uncertain and torturous dying with Aids – repelled by all the empty phrases of positive thinking, he once stated: 'I don't *live* with Aids, I *die* with Aids!' In BLUE – alongside all of his experiences in the consulting rooms of the hospitals, the well-meant advice of his doctor or the endless, sometimes life-threatening (and in the context, seemingly absurd) side effects of a single medication – transience, dying and death nonetheless begin to take on concrete form, their contours becoming more and clear: 'Love is life that lasts forever.'[106]

In the final two years of his life, Jarman was almost completely blind, and in this film he has found his path to a quintessential expression: an expression of the visual and simultaneously associative, that which he had sought as a painter in many of his films. 'It definitely has roots in painting, like Yves Klein and whatever, and it is very much a painter's film. On the other hand it *is* a film, which is quite interesting, because technically speaking it shouldn't be. It should be some experiment, you know. It isn't an experiment. It's not an experimental film of any sort whatsoever. And for some reason or other it was obviously the best solution for the subject that there should be no images on it. I can't imagine it with images.'[107] In BLUE, through this rigorous reduction to a single monochrome blue, which simultaneously appears in the form of a single picture, no new images of horror, decay and suffering are played out for the eye accustomed to them – no staged and canned reality show. Instead, numerous immediate and unpredictable images repeatedly emerge anew: directly in the many different and unpredictable minds of those watching.

In a brief period of only around seven years, during the fifties and sixties, the French painter Yves Klein, also known as 'Yves le Monochrome', created over a thousand works, and he had already been of very special interest to Jarman since his years at art school: in addition to the monochromes – the absolute reduction to a single colour, which left behind absolutely no traces of the figurative on the canvas – it was above all his characteristic, all-pervading blue that fascinated Jarman. Klein vehemently rejected every subjective artistic gesture of expression based on communication and catharsis and strove to open up the widest possible space of experiential freedom to the viewers of his works. In order to achieve this, in order to avoid the expression of any sort of personal gesture in his works, Klein went so far as to replace his brush with a roller: in applying the paint he was thus able to avoid providing any indication of his hand and the associated distinctive brushstroke of a given artist. And in this way he created those monochromes that are very personally and unmistakably associated with him ...

Klein's theoretical pursuit of an absolute and primal freedom, which was to be subjected neither to narrative content nor to any dogmatic symbolic systems of an art historical nature, is to be understood in its close connection with the world of social experience in the post-war Europe of the mid-twentieth century – a world that was closely tied to the philosophies of Phenomenology and Existentialism in France. Klein had radically forbidden to himself any sort of personal expression in his art and he was, as noted by Sidra Stich in her monograph: 'not the only one who turned away from the self as the subject of art. The "Death of the author" was the theme of the post-war avant-garde. Even before Roland Barthes formulated this phenomenon in 1968, it could already be observed in the plays of Samuel Beckett and Eugène Ionesco, the novels of Alain Robbe-Grillet and the films of Jean-Luc Godard and François Truffaut as well as the music of John Cage and Pierre Schäffer.'[108]

Pierre Restany argues that Klein's works are related to a complex merging of ideas based on the writings of Gaston Bachelard, Eugène Delacroix, Max Heindel and C.G. Jung.[109] Klein's affinity for ideas and approaches from the fields of alchemy, philosophy and psychoanalysis is clearly recognisable in his numerous gold and fire paintings. However, it is also present in his actions involving materials and space, for example, the ritual transfers of immateriality or the presentation of a *Zone de sensibilité picturale immatérielle*: in the former action he scattered gold leaf in the Seine and in the latter he established empty zones within an exhibition, which were intended to illustrate the ultimately immaterial, non-quantifiable value of art. In the early sixties, in the works known as *Anthropometries of the Blue Epoch*, Klein was able to realise his idea of 'painting with a living brush' in performance-like actions: bodies coated with blue pigment suspended in emulsion left behind their imprints in the form of fragmentary traces of the body on paper or silk cloth. A series of over 150 blue body images was created: the dematerialisation that took place in the process reveals an interesting analogy to Rauschenberg's monoprints and to Jarman's BLUE (see fig. 21 and 22). While in Klein's case the bodies of the models were the 'living brush' that left behind traces by means of paint, Rauschenberg had produced blue impressions of the body in large-format blueprints ten years before that time. These were modulated not through the application of paint but by means of light: 'Through the blurry transparency of the technical medium, the effect of a dematerialised silhouette is intensified into an illusionistic weightlessness.'[110] Jarman had already viewed the camera as a brush during his work with Super 8 (see pp. 122 ff.) – in BLUE he then finally realised a comparable dematerialisation. Here colour is projected on to the white screen by means of light and via the medium of film, producing a similarly illusionistic weightlessness: through its projection by means of light, the unvarying blue appears to be constantly changing, seeming to live with the words, to breathe. The materiality of the body has disintegrated – it has (already) vanished.

Klein's occupation with the element of fire led him to the extreme limits within the transmutation of colours. For Klein the trilogy of the colours blue, pink and gold is to be found in their logical synthesis in the flame of a fire – beyond fire lies the immaterial.[111] These would become the universally defining colours of his monochromes, with blue occupying a central role (see fig. 24–26). Like the endless blue of the sky, which is reflected in the blue of the sea and has its imaginary intersection in the immateriality of the horizon, this blue – as the colour of the distant, of yearning and endlessness – is to lead to an altered sensibility while it is viewed, to the greatest possible freedom of individual perception.

Klein long experimented in search of a blue pigment corresponding to his notions, one that – in the intensity of its saturation – would also retain its luminosity after being applied to its support and that, when viewed, would achieve that visual immateriality that he desired and which he succinctly describes with reference to his paintings for the opera house and theatre in Gelsenkirchen, Germany: 'I find that, here, it is possible to speak of an alchemy of painting, born in the tension of every instant of the material (painting material). It is the suggestion of bathing in a space that is vaster than the infinite. The blue is the invisible becoming visible.'[112] He finally found the answer for this blue, which unites both endless vastness and direct proximity, in an intensely luminous ultramarine. For him it was the 'most perfect expression of blue', a colour that he subsequently had patented as his own invention under the name IKB, the abbreviation for International Klein Blue.

Fig. 21:
Robert Rauschenberg, *Balance*,
*c.*1951

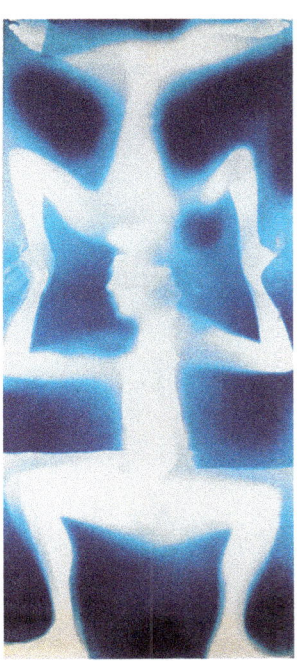

Fig. 22:
Yves Klein, *Anthropometrie,
Untitled* (ANT 63),
1961

Fig. 23:
James Turrell, *Wide Out,*
1998

Fig. 24:
Yves Klein, *IKB 3,*
1960

Fig. 25:
Yves Klein, *MG 18*,
1961

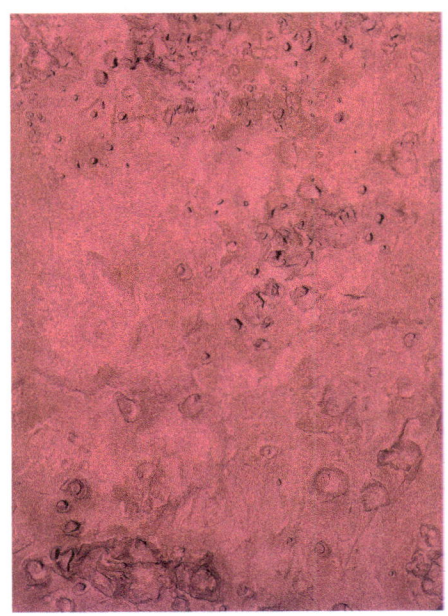

Fig. 26:
Yves Klein, *La Lune I* (RP 22),
1961

In the course of a relatively long and intense viewing of a blue mono-chrome by Klein, familiar limits of perception, the conscious distinction be-tween the subject and object of viewing, really do seem to disintegrate. No fixed point in space can be distinguished anymore, the viewer's gaze sinks into the depth of a chromatic sensation that simultaneously seems to expressively spread out across the perceived space.

In BLUE Jarman uses the ultramarine-coloured film material to place pre-cisely this colour of Klein not on the canvas but on the screen, the surface on which the film is projected. At that point in time it seemed to him to be the sole remaining possible and adequate way to realise in cinematic form his account of himself and of his living and dying with Aids. Nearly blind, his perception of his own surroundings, his own 'reality', has been fundamentally altered. However, in addition to conveying precisely this altered perception, Jarman was primarily seeking to avoid causing preformed images to appear in the minds of his viewers. Instead, the meditative immersion in the deep-blue projected light enables viewers to embark upon an associative journey into their own selves, based on the perceived words, noises and sounds, and in doing so to find themselves in an inner dialogue with what they perceive. The distinction between the subject and object of viewing seems to have actually been suspended.

Where, in Jarman's case, the blue in which we are immersed is the colour of the film projected on to a screen, the American light artist James Turrell expands this experience into a genuinely spatial one in his light spaces. In his installation *Twilight Arch* (1991, Museum für Moderne Kunst, Frankfurt am Main), the 'viewer' enters into a large, rectangular, darkened room filled with a diffuse, bluish light that seems to materialise in a large, rectangular and luminously blue field, a 'picture' on the opposite wall. Our eyes slowly adjust to the darkness and, as we approach step by step, our perception changes: the picture becomes lighter, the blue slowly turns into a milkily luminous fog of light. Having arrived directly in front of it, the picture dissolves the instant that we attempt to touch it: we grasp into the void. The bright rectangle is a space that is without perceptible boundaries and which is lit by unseen UV light sources: a light-picture. This perception is of a similar intensity to that of viewing the projected blue light in the film BLUE. The distinction be-tween subject and object also appears to be suspended in *Twilight Arch*, where the feeling emerges that we no longer see anything, but nonetheless perceive something – something that is intangible in its form: light. 'What we see is a light space of "immeasurable" depth. At the same time, however, all depth seems to have collected on the "surface" of the light-picture and to flare up there. The spatial light is characterised by both an immaterial transparency and a directly substantial tangibility. The light phenomenon before our eyes is one of transparent intransparency.'[113]

In his installation *Wide Out* (1998), created on the occasion of the exhibition *the other horizon* at the Museum für angewandte Kunst in Vienna, Turrell finally really did suspend that distinction between subject and object: *Wide Out* expands *Twilight Arch* into something that can be experienced spatially (see fig. 23). Viewers initially find themselves before a large, luminously blue 'picture' with a deep and intense luminosity. People moving within the image are seen as black, silhouette-like shadows whose contours become blurred. A few steps lead up to a pedestal and to the lower edge of the 'frame'. We climb into the picture and find ourselves within the pictorial space: a long room with a white floor and white walls extends approximately 15 metres – it is immersed in a luminous, fluorescent blue light. The white and the white air appear milky, radiant. At the far edge, a further frame becomes visible: a luminously milky blue and apparently endless space opens up behind it – similar to the 'pictorial space' in *Twilight Arch*. It becomes possible to experience the colour, the coloured light in three dimensions: it surrounds our bodies, which are immersed in colour. Depending upon the viewer's position and the length and intensity of viewing, the blue changes: it becomes lighter or darker, shifts towards a reddish violet or greyish black. The experience of the body bathed in light is just as subjective as it is ever-changing, and in his light spaces Turrell seems to have transposed what Klein describes as the 'suggestion of bathing in a space that is wider than the infinite' into a genuinely perceptible form. This blue has become the 'invisible becoming visible'.

Empty Spaces

In 1967 Jarman completed his studies at the Slade School of Fine Art. He showed his work in exhibitions at London and Liverpool galleries and was also invited to both the Open 100 in Edinburgh and the fifth Biennale des Jeunes Artistes at the Musée d'art moderne in Paris, where he was able to exhibit his model for a set design for Sergei Prokofiev's ballet *The Prodigal Son*. His painting *Cool Waters* (1966/67) was awarded the Peter Stuyvesant Foundation Prize at the *Young Contemporaries* exhibition in the Tate Gallery. Simultaneously, during his last two years at The Slade he had already occupied himself less with painting than with the design of stage sets. As he describes in *Dancing Ledge*, he felt how the group work involved in theatrical projects removed him from the isolation whose presence he repeatedly became aware of when painting. In contrast to that extremely individualised field of work, he furthermore sensed greater freedoms and possibilities in the aesthetic designing of stage sets: 'I like working on shared projects. It breaks down the isolation of working as a painter. There is much greater aesthetic freedom. The theatre is not subject to the same strict rules we surround ourselves with as individual producers: I can employ imagery I would not dare or wish to use in my painting. So I'm definitely working as a theatre designer, not as a painter imposing an individual vision.'[114] In those years – in addition to his work for Prokofiev's *Prodigal Son* (1967) – he thus also created models for works including Ben Jonson's *Volpone* (1966), Jean-Paul Sartre's *Huis Clos* (1967) and Igor Stravinsky's ballet *Orpheus* (1966), integrating photographs from *Physique Pictorial* magazines into the scenery for the gate to the underworld in a collage-like form. Through Sir Frederick Ashton, principal choreographer of the Royal Ballet, Jarman finally received his first major commission: designing the set and costumes for the ballet *Jazz Calender* by R.R. Bennett, which premiered at the Royal Opera House in January of 1968. By the end of the year, John Gielgud had already invited him to design the stage set for Mozart's *Don Giovanni* at the English National Opera. Through his coincidental acquaintance with Janet Deuter, a friend of Ken Russel, the latter also became aware of Jarman's work: during the years that followed he hired Jarman to serve as production designer for his two films THE DEVILS (1970) and SAVAGE MESSIAH (1971).

The year that Jarman concluded his studies at The Slade was the same year that decisive legislative reform was implemented which revoked the total prohibition of all homosexual acts enforced up to that time. It was not until July of 1967, ten years after the publication of the Wolfenden Report, that the so-called Sexual Offences Act became law. According to this act – and in keeping with the recommendations of the Report – sexual acts taking place in private and between two men aged 21 or older were no longer punishable offences in England and Wales (however, the prohibition remained applicable in Scotland and Northern Ireland until 1980 and 1982, respectively).[115] The revocation of this prohibition of 'buggery' – which bore penalties of up to twenty years in prison – and the limited attempt at a decriminalisation implied by it nevertheless led to only a partial improvement of living conditions within society. The Sexual Offences Act was not passed on the basis of a changing and more tolerant attitude, instead, it was pursued as a strategy to shift the very broadly defined category of 'sexual acts' exclusively into the private sphere and to limit this sphere and the number of those involved as much as possible, in order to be able to subject them to the highest degree of scrutiny and control. Male homosexuality was not to be legalised and granted the same status as heterosexual desire, instead, it was merely to be permitted under precisely defined circumstances. The consequences of this 'liberalisation' were a significantly more rigorous prosecution of 'offences' in a public that was now precisely defined, a jump in the number of filed charges and convictions and a renewed flourishing of the above-mentioned, pseudo-medicinal attempts at therapies and cures. Jeffrey Weeks, sociologist and gender theorist, succinctly describes this situation in the course of his theoretical reflections in 'Capitalism and the Organisation of Sex': 'Thus the crucial factor about Wolfenden and the 1967 sexual law reform was the role of the distinction between the public sphere and the private. Homosexuality was defined as something which is acceptable because unavoidable, in private, between consenting adults, but something which is not acceptable in public. [...] Homosexuality, in other words, has not been accepted in society at large; rather, the target for its control has switched.'[116]

Without a doubt, the introduction of the Sexual Offences Act fostered a withdrawal into the private sphere, within which a space of legal freedom had now opened up for the individual. At the same time, however, the first hesitant attempts were being undertaken to open things up in the direction of the public sphere and visibility. In the late sixties many people within the youth (sub)cultures and the general protest movement – particularly those living in a university environment – no longer wished to allow themselves to be intimidated by this kind of state measures of regulation and control. Even before Woodstock (1969) the music of the time had already become a substantial vehicle for general political protest, and the expression of dance further developed and corresponded to this. However, when two men danced together in public, they additionally became a political statement per se: 'We always said in the Sixties, before the Gay Liberation Front was founded, that the most sensible thing to do was to dance together. It was a political statement. We went into somewhere like our college and we danced together. It must have been like an OutRage! demo in Canterbury for the other students because they were all so shocked, but we were having a good time and I think that's important. Otherwise it all becomes mind and not body. The idea of a demo turning you on and being sexy is so good.'[117]

In various passages from his autobiographical writings, Jarman describes in depth his attitude towards a life defined by moral hypocrisy and talks about his attempts to break out of an all-pervasive 'normality' and about the late sixties, which he accordingly experienced in terms of an increasingly liberated but also politicised period: 'We spent the rest of the decade celebrating wider horizons, throwing out the furniture, sitting on the floor, in brighter and brighter clothes. The music grew wilder, the Beatles were displaced by The Who and The Stones, they in turn by The Doors [...]'and 'the last four years of the 60's were one long dance'.[118]

However, Jarman's works of these years convey nothing of this newly developed attitude towards life. There are neither indications of his relationship to the shifting social and societal environment nor concrete references to his sexuality and the strategies of living out and impressions of the experiences that it involved. The thematisation and artistic transposition of personal, private areas seems to be entirely omitted or, as Tony Rayns puts it: 'While his former fellow student David Hockney exuberantly celebrated the festival of the sixties with his "male art", in Jarman's paintings there was not a single level touching on Jarman's homosexuality.'[119] The theme of the landscape still continued to remain at the centre of his interest. However, in contrast to his very early naturalistic motifs in the traditional landscape paintings and still lifes that he created before he began at the Slade School of Fine Art, the landscapes in the works of the late sixties appear in a form that is strongly abstract and is balanced out in linear paths and strict geometries. Impressed by Duchamp, de Chirico, Morris Louis and Richard Smith, but also by the protagonists of Cubism, Jarman inscribed objects into some of the monochrome colour fields of his paintings in a quotation-like manner, in the form of a trompe-l'œil or also by mounting actual objects on the canvas. Nevertheless this semi-abstract, geometrical occupation with landscape and space did not remain limited to a two-dimensional depiction in the form of an easel painting. It is also evident in several of his works in set design, such as *Jazz Calendar*, but above all in John Gielgud's staging of *Don Giovanni*, whose protagonists make their way through a stage landscape defined by over-sized cubes, blocks and cylinders.

By contrast, Jarman's paintings show completely lifeless landscapes devoid of people and evincing a cool detachment and foreignness. When viewed, their experiments with colour, with contrasts of black and white and with surfaces, lines and geometries cause a mute emptiness and indefinable distance to arise, and they associatively bring about a feeling of loneliness, total disorientation or of being lost within the three-dimensional space they evoke: this finds its pendant in titles like *Deserted Landscape* (1967), *Landscape with a Blue Pool* (1967), *Cool Waters* (1966/67) or *The Shore* (1968). While Jarman's very early paintings remained naturalistic in a traditional sense and figuratively conceived – and, by contrast, his late works of the *Queer Series* and *Evil Queen Series* abstract and non-figurative, but often invested with precise and emphatic messages – the semi-abstract, figurative works of the late sixties close themselves to almost any kind of statement. 'Meanwhile my paintings unlike my theatre work, became emptier and emptier; their titles tell the story "Stony Ground", "Cool Waters". My final picture of the decade was called "Deserts". Then I picked up a Super 8 camera in 1970 and started to populate these dreary pictures with my friends – clothed, I should add; I was too shy to get their pants off on camera ...'.[120] Jarman's occupation with the medium of Super 8 film began in the years that followed and would enable him to leave behind the empty surfaces of his paintings and, in the moving pictures of his home movies, to fill them with very personal levels of content and autobiographical aspects. In his book *The Last of England*, he remarks that 'my first films filled in the empty spaces of my painting',[121] and these really do form the polar opposite of his lifeless landscape paintings devoid of people: here the cool detachment and foreignness of geometric forms is dissipated by the improvisational intimacy of spontaneously captured personal events and encounters.

[4]

Beware of Definitions: Demarcation of the Rhetoric of Film Theory

'BEWARE OF DEFINITIONS. NO GREAT painter can be reduced to a category. One can say such and such a painter is an Impressionist, others are Expressionists, and others are Cubists, but basically you're saying nothing at all; in saying that you're simply identifying a style that says nothing about the painting itself.'[122] In a discussion with Michel Archimbaud, Francis Bacon uses the example of the stylistic complexity and heterogeneity of individual representatives of Impressionism, such as Manet, Monet and Cézanne, but also van Gogh, to convincingly illustrate the limiting and reductive consequences of art historical attempts at categorisation, and he also questions their meaningfulness in general. As little as a style is able to make concrete statements about a concrete work – it says no more about its creator. Monet himself, whose 1873 painting *Impression, soleil levant* (Impression, Sunrise) suggested the name given to an entire group of artists, was originally very concerned to reserve the term Impressionism only for specific aspects of his own works, and years later he stated in a letter: 'I still very much regret having caused the naming of a group whose majority had nothing impressionist about it.'[123]

Jarman's understanding of himself as an artist was defined primarily by this understanding of painting, and he consistently and vehemently rejected all attempts to appropriate or classify himself. Interestingly, in the existing secondary literature on Jarman's work, it is rarely in relation to his artworks but, instead, almost exclusively in relation to his filmic work that repeated attempts have been made to come to grips with his work by means of categorisations in terms of the history and aesthetics of film. In numerous and certainly also in-depth analyses or essays this applies both to limitingly subsuming his films under a specific style as well as to what is – in my opinion – a misleading occupation with the narrative element in his films. Before going into more detail regarding his Super 8 films and his 'cinema of small gestures' in the next two chapters, in the following pages I use several theoretical reflections – selected for their exemplary nature – in order to discuss the difficulties or also contradictions involved in the attempts to fix the position of these aspects in this way. Regardless of the question concerning the general meaningfulness of such enterprises, Jarman's works cannot be unqualifiedly classified according to the categories of art terminology or film history. They can neither be placed in the tradition nor, alternatively, among the successors of the 'classic' avant-garde film nor do they possess direct points of contact with the various aesthetic categories subsumed under the overarching term of experimental film – such as the abstract film, the materialist film or the structural film. Their protagonists – film-makers like Hans Richter, Oskar Fischinger, Ernie Gehr, Ken Jacobs, Malcolm Le Grice and Michael Snow, among others – primarily sought to realise experimental projects in order to analyse and verify theoretical considerations regarding film, film material and the reception of films. This formal exploration and formalist realisation is at the centre of interest there: the component of content is of subordinate importance. In *Visionary Film* Peter A. Sitney describes his concept of the 'structural film' as follows: '[...] a cinema of structure in which the shape of the whole film is predetermined and simplified, and it is that shape which is the primal impression of the film. [...] The structural film insists on its shape, and what content it has is minimal and subsidiary to the outline.'[124] In Jarman's work, however, he was not concerned with the theoretical and practical examination of the medium of film in its material and immaterial qualities: his primary interest lay not in the analysis of the 'truth' of the film material, as was the case among the protagonists of the structural film or the materialist film, for example. Visual motif, theme and content were more important to him than the formal experiment.

In the liberation from the frozen forms and the 'emptiness' that he himself criticised in his paintings of the late sixties and early seventies, Jarman looked at filming primarily as a continuation of painting by other means. Above all it was the medium of the Super 8 film that revealed possibilities to him for freeing himself from the obligatory conformism of painting and to discover and develop his own new aesthetic of pictorial representation. Thus, while gazing through his Super 8 camera, he could – among other things – rediscover the romantic landscape motifs of his early paintings. As previously mentioned, these motifs present themselves to us, for example, in JOURNEY TO AVE-BURY, IN THE SHADOW OF THE SUN and GERALD'S FILM in the form of their slow-motion sequences. However, this continuation of 'landscape painting' by other (filmic) means is clearly present not only in his early Super 8 films but also in some of his feature films, such as THE LAST OF ENGLAND and THE GARDEN. And his late 35 mm films – with their tableau-like, theatrical staging (WAR REQUIEM, EDWARD II or WITTGENSTEIN) – also indicate the perspective of a painter and set designer. Jarman's final film, BLUE, ultimately seems to be nothing but the logical conclusion of the path to projecting colour on to the cinema screen in the form of a pure, monochrome blue for the duration of seventy minutes.[125] But even the choice of this stylistically extreme form is founded exclusively in the attempt to fittingly visualise the extreme condition of living with the full-frame reality of Aids, because it is 'a painter's film. [...] But it isn't an experiment, it's not an experimental film of any sort whatsoever. And for some reason or other it was actually the best solution for the subject that there should be no images on it. I can't imagine it with images on it. [...] I'm very lucky, I mean, most of the people who are very ill just sit there being very ill. I must be lucky, I can actually turn it into something. [...] I thought someone should put some of it on record. And this was one way of doing it. I haven't seen anyone put any of this on record – not very well, at least. And by removing people from it, making it much more abstract, one left it free-floating for people to make up their own minds. It's sometimes difficult to identify with x person, you know? And also the other great problem is making films about illness is a very, very dodgy area. They don't work very often. I mean, who wants to go and see that? It's not artwork. However, in this particular case it seems to work. What the reason is, I don't know.'[126] It was not formal parameters or, alternatively, experiments per se that were of primary interest to Jarman, instead, it was – in the broadest sense – the motif to be captured and – in a narrower sense – the theme, a message, the 'content'. His experiment's origins lie in the search for the adequate means to realise his intentions and it is actually not so much an experiment as an expedition. On this journey into the unknown or into a new terrain, the material was not the centre of interest but merely a means to an end. It was the vehicle for those intentions, messages and statements which originated in the personal.

Questionable Categorisations

Nonetheless – with regard to the attempts to stylistically classify his filmic work in general, as well as his feature films, home movies and Super 8 films in particular – a great number of those keywords of 'avant-garde film', 'experimental film', 'underground film' and 'underground cinema' have already been called upon in the secondary literature in order to incorporate his works in one form or another into canonical categories of film aesthetics and to assign them a corresponding place. However, in approaching Jarman's works, labels of this kind lead not to an expansion of our understanding but to a limiting of the corresponding work. With regard to its terminology and its statements, the work is subsequently in danger of no longer being perceived in its openness and complexity but, instead, of being reduced to the parameters of the category assigned to it.

Thus, for example, in his essay 'An Archaeology of Soul', Gray Watson does indeed grant both Jarman's artistic foundation as a painter and the multilayeredness of his different approaches to working. However, in connection with 'his experiments with Super 8 that led him to create a type of cinema that was uniquely his own', he situates Jarman in line with the tradition and development of the American post-war cinematic avant-garde: 'Jarman's films need to be seen first of all within a tradition of artistic avantgarde film-making, and in particular that tradition of American avant-garde film whose leading figure was Stan Brakhage, and which was superbly chronicled by P. Adams Sitney in his *Visionary Film*, a book that Jarman respected enormously.'[127] In the preface to his standard work *Visionary Film* Sitney himself nonetheless very clearly points out the makeshift nature and complexity of naming aesthetic categories like 'experimental film' or 'avant-garde': 'Both names, like all the subsequent ones, are inaccurate and limiting. [...] Very few filmmakers were ever satisfied with any of these labels. "Avant-garde" is itself unfortunate. On the one hand, it implies a privileged relationship to a norm which I do not wish to affirm, and on the other hand it has been used to describe thousands of films which fall outside the scope of this book [...]. In the course of writing, historical patterns emerged which I have allowed to control the structure of the book. I have had to invent a series of terms – the trance film, the mythopoeic film, the structural film, and the participatory film – in order to describe this historical morphology. It is almost too obvious to point out that the film-makers themselves did not think in these categories when they made their films.'[128] Neither before, during nor after filming did Jarman think in terms of these categories or feel that he belonged to a certain line of development in the sense of a 'school' – on the contrary: he repeatedly rejected the countless attempts to classify his work on film and described his feelings of isolation and of being a loner artistically. In a conversation with Simon Field, Jarman answered the latter's question as to whether he saw himself as a part of a community of film-makers: 'I feel very isolated, although there are other filmmakers which I like very much – Sally Potter or Terence Davies' films for example are remarkable for their control and the use of the camera.'[129]

Michael O'Pray, a film scholar profoundly familiar with Jarman's work, attempts in a certain sense to do justice to this situation by also pointing to Jarman's background as a painter and, in several passages of his meticulously researched history of the film-maker's work, *Derek Jarman – Dreams of England*, by associating his Super 8 films not with the formal experiments of the London Film-makers' Co-operative but with the personally influenced realm of the 'underground film', which was influenced by the Beat Poets and developed out of an open, 'alternative' lifestyle: 'Jarman's experimental super-8s of the 70s and after are loosely connected to the avant-garde and underground cinemas of the 60s. The work of Andy Warhol, Kenneth Anger and other films seen in the late 60s had their effect [...]. In fact, Jarman is not a film-maker immersed in film history at all. To understand his style one is better served by looking at his education as a painter and his early forays into set design.

'[...] Although there is an eclecticism here, Jarman's main reference point was to underground film, or what was to be called "avant-garde" cinema. Unlike the formal film-making going on at the LFMC [London Film-makers' Co-operative] in the early 70s, underground cinema was not primarily concerned with formal experimentation at the price of content. Following the lead of the Beat writers, underground films were about alternative lifestyles, with drugs and "eccentric" sexual behaviour as their main impetus, as in the work of Jack Smith, Ron Rice and to some extent Warhol and Anger.'[130]

By contrast the film scholar Chris Lippard sees above all the Super 8 films, but also Jarman's feature films from the 'cinema of small gestures' that he created in the eighties, as 'avant-garde work': 'In the early 1980s he produced some of his most interesting avant-garde work, culminating in the feature-length THE ANGELIC CONVERSATION, a beautiful and meditative envisioning of the male body in labour and passion, shot on Super 8 and transferred to 35mm.'[131] In her essay, the American film theorist Tracy Biga even goes a step further and subsumes more or less Jarman's entire filmic oeuvre under the term avant-garde – also incorporating his late feature films. The use of techniques such as overlapping changes in exposure, shooting with large-grained film material or the juxtaposition of different film stocks 'distort', in her opinion, 'the image', '[...] emphasising its surface and the external mediation of the filmmaking process. A sense of spectacle is also created by the frontal orientation of Jarman's compositions which often slide into tableaux, most notably in CARAVAGGIO and WAR REQUIEM. The refusal of master-shots, eyeline-matches and the creation of 3-dimensional, realistic space implicit in this frontality mark even Jarman's more narratively conventional films as avant-garde.'[132]

In its original sense the term 'avant-garde' derives from military language and refers to the vanguard that marches ahead of a body of troops or an army that is under way. In the early twentieth century the term found its way into theoretical concepts from the visual arts, music and literature and was also adopted in those areas of film whose artistic aspirations were concentrated primarily on the discovery of new, altered experiences of vision and reception. It was not least for this reason that these stood in opposition to the commercial production system then establishing itself: 'The avant-garde film removed itself from the contexts of societal influences and it isolated itself from the commercialisation process of industry and society, which was linked to a specifically encoded and historically analysable use of the filmic expressive material. [...] The subversion of these films is the negation of the semantic networks of the kind typically woven by the texts of narrative cinema.'[133] While it is true that Jarman's films remove themselves (to varying degrees) from the 'commercialisation process of industry and society', they do not isolate themselves from the 'contexts of societal influences' – on the contrary, they grow out of these.

However, in its film historical sense, the traditional concept of the 'avant-garde', the 'avant-garde film', is primarily associated with the works of European artists of the inter-war period – Luis Buñuel, René Clair, Marcel Duchamp, Viking Eggeling, Oskar Fischinger, Fernand Léger and Hans Richter, among others. Their work was continued in the America of the forties to the sixties, where it was expanded through works including those of Maya Deren, Gregory Markopoulos, Stan Brakhage and Kenneth Anger, among others. It was only in the sixties and seventies that categories and labels like 'experimental film', 'underground film' and 'independent film' developed. The films classified in these categories are related above all through their being created outside of typical contexts of production and commercialisation. However, an exact distinction is no longer possible: the terminological boundaries have rapidly become blurred. The formal experiments of the experimental film have become diverse, encompassing a great variety of areas in the filmmaking process, such as camera movement, camera technique, acting, editing or presentation. Thus it is certainly possibly to classify an 'experimental film' as an 'underground film' or 'independent film', however, both of these categories specifically point to the societal implication of particular films within particular systems or subsystems. The term 'underground film' was originally ideologically closely interwoven with the political student and protest movement in the US of the sixties, while 'independent film' refers more to the form of commercialisation and its economic basis. Through the founding of various cooperative associations, such as the New American Cinema Group, the New York Film-Makers' Cooperative or the London Film-makers' Cooperative, autonomous organisational forms and distribution systems were created which sought independent niches for presenting their own works outside of the large mainstream companies.

In Ken McMullen's very sensitive and personal filmic portrait THERE WE ARE JOHN ... (UK, 1994) – which was to become one of the last interviews prior to Jarman's death in February of 1994 – the British art critic John Cartwright expresses a warning in connection with Jarman's work as a film-maker: 'But you are in danger, I think in a way, of being categorised. People always like to categorise film-makers, and you might be put in the position of being regarded as the avant-garde or the alternative film-maker.' And Jarman's response – which makes reference to that 'avant-garde' term used in a manner that is equally inflationary and lacking in due consideration – is not without a certain ironic undertone: 'I've never felt it myself. I just thought I was making films. And perhaps that I was making films in a way that was sometimes not the most conventional way of doing them. I don't think of myself as avant-garde. I think the avant-garde died with Marcel Duchamp before the war. So I find that all very odd with that category. I never made those categories. I mean I'm here to make films and that's it. I've never thought of myself like this. It's odd. I just thought, you know, I'm making films.'[134] He had already stated this in an even more direct fashion – and additionally incorporating the realm of the 'underground film' – years earlier, in his book *The Last of England*: 'Try explaining to them that I don't make underground films, I have never made underground films. I hate all the labelling, the boundaries drawn by the "communicators", the middle men who sit between the audience and the experience.'[135]

In the secondary literature on Jarman's work – almost all of which has appeared after his death – it is nevertheless also possible to identify positions that do not assess his work according to the keywords of film aesthetics and history discussed above. Instead, these emphasise his individual approach and, in occupying themselves with his work, they take into account the primary demands he placed upon himself and his manner of working: understanding film-making as an extension of his own life and also placing the work's creation itself, the creative process, above the finished product. Thus, in his essay on the aesthetic dimensions of Jarman's films, Richard Porton uses concrete examples like WITTGENSTEIN and BLUE to point out that, while his entire oeuvre as a film-maker can easily be placed within this or that aesthetic niche, from 'avant-garde' to 'postmodern', that oeuvre – based on personal experiential contexts – actually resists all such classifications. For Porton the personal strategies of finding and developing forms, which can simultaneously also contain statements on political levels, seem essential to the individuality and aesthetic independence of the works: 'Jarman's films resist facile classification. His work could easily find a niche within any of the "five faces of modernity" cited by critic Matei Calinescu – modernism, the avant-garde, decadence, kitsch and postmodernism. Whether we view Jarman as a modernist, postmodernist or unregenerate Romantic, it is clear that he was never wedded to monolithic assumptions concerning visual style or narrative structure. Jarman's aesthetic strategies are not influenced by a predetermined agenda, but emerge pragmatically from specific contexts. [...]

'Whether bracingly flamboyant or rigorously austere, all Jarman's films are prismatic expressions of his own identity. WITTGENSTEIN and BLUE are the most ascetic products of Jarman's fictive self. These films sum up the career of a director who never made concessions to popular taste, but who refused to be relegated to the realm of hermetic "avant-gardism".' The fact that Jarman's work, particularly his early films, can stimulate associations with artists like Kenneth Anger, Stan Brakhage or Jean Cocteau – who represent styles that are just as radically individualistic – is interpreted not as contradicting but as supporting his thesis: '[...] his work often evokes memories of such disparate figures as Kenneth Anger, Stan Brakhage, Michael Powell, Jean Cocteau and Pier Paolo Pasolini. All these directors are united by their hostility to mainstream naturalism and their radical individualism – an individualism that does not foreclose the cultivation of collective, but non-dogmatic, radical hopes.'[136]

In Lawrence Driscoll's attempt to position the film-maker's work, '"The rose revived": Derek Jarman and the British Tradition', the author also presents misleadingly used keywords that repeatedly refer to Jarman's works as 'characteristically anti-Establishment, non-canonical and controversial', points out the misreading of his works as 'radical' or 'alternative' and also takes into account the (practical) political dimension on which these assessments may be based. His argumentation is entirely consistent with Jarman's conservative self-concept – as the film-maker presents himself, for example, in his talk with Simon Field (see p. 48) ('I am a very traditional filmmaker, a conservative with a small c.') and his wish to preserve the bygone or transitory ('The true conservation of things [...]'). Driscoll sees Jarman's works as belonging to that old British tradition stretching back long before the twentieth century: '[...] he returns to an older tradition, aligning himself with a strain of cultural criticism evident in medieval literature, as well as in Shakespeare, Blake, Ruskin and Larkin.' At the same time, however, he also points to a practical political connection with the present, because – in his opinion – the image of the controversial film-maker emerged for the following reason: 'because he has chosen to speak for a very old British tradition, placing his faith in cultural values that are primarily aesthetic and historical. Jarman is perceived as radical because he worked in an environment in which this particular British tradition has been eroded both by the Left and by the Right. Given the failure of British postwar social and economic policies, Jarman is confronted with a cultural terrain torn between the failures of the Left and the inhumane alternatives of the Right. [...] His œuvre is thus best seen as a direct intervention, attempting to revitalize British culture by providing sustenance to its desiccated roots, enabling Britain, to become once again "the rose revived".'[137]

Where the arguments of Porton and Driscoll reveal the unclassifiable nature of Jarman's work on film, the two critics Keates and Romney go a step further. Independently of one another, in their analyses of WAR REQUIEM and

EDWARD II (both of them films that may be included among those aforementioned late works featuring a theatrical and tableau-like staging), they open up a new independent 'genre' of the 'Jarman film', a new aesthetic category of the 'Jarmanesque'.[138] In his article 'The Art of War' Keates describes the 'landscape of the imagination' created by Jarman, which he staged within the ruins of an abandoned psychiatric hospital to shoot WAR REQUIEM, and Keates draws attention to his pictorial visual orientation and his intense connections with colour and spatial arrangement. Keates views this as an essential element of that independent aesthetic: 'This sense of the painter's eye constantly alert to colour and texture is related, as in all Jarman's work, to a self-conscious theatricality [...]. For all its qualities of spareness and restraint, WAR REQUIEM is emphatically Jarmanesque in its idiosyncrasies.' Jonathan Romney uses ED-WARD II to establish an independent category of the 'Jarman film': 'partly recognisable as Marlowe and wholly recognisable as Jarman. After the imagistic patchwork of THE GARDEN, Jarman returns to the enclosed theatrical format of CARAVAGGIO, staging Marlowe's narrative on a sparse but adaptable single set.' Along with the royal drama's theatrical staging in the film version, it is primarily the thematic elaboration, the individual interpretation and Jarman's subjective adaptation of Marlowe's original text that are decisive for Romney's characterising the film as a 'Jarman film', in the sense of a genre of its own: 'Rather than present a clear-cut story of gay martyrdom, Jarman overlays the play's complexities with his own thematic obsessions, producing a contradictory film which is readable less in terms of sexual politics than in terms of the code of the "Jarman film" as a genre in itself. [...] These quintessentially Jarmanesque images add up to a contradictory surfeit of meaning that the text cannot accommodate.' Establishing the definition of an independent 'genre' in this manner may seem exaggerated and one-dimensional at first glance. Upon close examination of Jarman's filmic crossover through various formats and materials from Super 8 to 35 mm, from film to video and on to digitally edited images in some of his later films, such as THE LAST OF ENGLAND or THE GARDEN, the term nevertheless proves justified: it is the product of an entirely uncompromising elaboration upon that line of argumentation which appropriately seeks to distance Jarman's filmic work from the established and semantically defined terminology of film studies and succinctly expresses his permanent search for a personal and adequate realisation of his 'thematic obsessions' in filmic images.

Obsolete Categories of the Narrative

As already suggested at the outset, the second aspect deals with the question of the extent to which Jarman's filmic works can be meaningfully categorised in traditional categories like the 'narrative' and 'non-narrative'. In the context of his work on a 'cinema of small gestures' and specifically in connection with IN THE SHADOW OF THE SUN (1972/74/80) (see pp. 161 ff.), Jarman has elucidated a principle that he considered valid with regard to the equivalence of image and word or, alternatively, images and language: 'This is the way the Super 8s are structured from writing: the buried word-signs emphasize the fact that they convey a language. There is the image and the word, and the image of the word. The "poetry of fire" [here he is specifically referring to those superimposed images of glowing flames in IN THE SHADOW OF THE SUN] relies on a treatment of word and object as equivalent: both are signs; both are luminous and opaque. The pleasure of Super 8s is the pleasure of seeing language put through the magic lantern.'[139] There exists the image, the word and the image of the word (of the signified). Building on this thought, Jarman inscribes the perceptible image of an object and the conceivable image of a word in an equation of signs. These exist in balance with one another and, for him, they are equivalent in their representation of the objective – a representation which can nevertheless be subjectively experienced and can thus also be read and interpreted on many levels. At the same time, in the concrete case of IN THE SHADOW OF THE SUN, he rejects that form of interpretive reception which seeks 'to understand' a story. His intention here is not an interpreting but an experiencing of images: '[...] There is no narrative in the film. The first viewers wracked their brains for a meaning instead of relaxing into the ambient tapestry of random images. The language is there and it is conveyed – and you don't know what you have to say until you've said it. You can dream of lands far distant.'[140] When viewed multiple times, a seemingly unending series of new combinations of images and previously undiscovered scenes – comparable to the images of a kaleidoscope – emerge before the eyes of viewers, permitting them to dream of precisely those 'lands far distant'. In terms of their structure, none of his other films display a comparably intense web of images that enables free associations to such a great degree. Even in similarly associatively composed films like THE ANGELIC CONVERSATION, THE LAST OF ENGLAND or THE GARDEN, a substantially larger role is played by the representational quality of the sequences of images and the concrete message, which is intended to stimulate an interpretation.

In the film WITTGENSTEIN, which was created years later, Jarman once again takes up the question of the representative meaning of word and image by having the philosopher Ludwig Wittgenstein (played by Karl Johnson) declare to the circle of his students: 'I used to believe that language gave us a picture of the world. But it can't give us a picture of how it does that. That would be like trying to see yourself seeing something. How language does that is beyond expression. That is the mystery. That was all wrong. Language isn't a picture at all. It's a tool; an instrument. There isn't just one picture of the world, there are lots of different language games. Different forms of life, different ways of doing things with words – they don't all hang together. All I mean is "The limits of my language are the limits of my world". We keep running up against the walls of our cage.'[141] Wittgenstein's occupation with the role of language as a vehicle of meaning is central in his writings and he views it primarily as an instrument of communication; here he emphasises the diversity of the various existing 'language games', which can generate images of reality that are equally diverse. One's own world of ideas ends at the boundaries of one's own language, however, the images of different languages are numerous and diverse.

In his essay 'Language Games and Aesthetic Attitudes: Style and Ideology in Jarman's Late Films', Richard Porton pursues an enlightening approach to Jarman's filmic work by way of precisely this theoretical notion of Wittgenstein. Via Wittgenstein's concept of understanding human activity as a series of 'language games', he attempts to assess the different, but interrelated stylistic aims that Jarman developed as a film-maker. It is above all Wittgenstein's postulate that linguistic activity and its individual construction of meaning is always to be seen in the context of a specific social context ('different forms of life') that seems to be of central interest in this respect: 'Wittgenstein's anti-metaphysical and anti-ontological bias teaches us that even the deeply submerged vicissitudes of the self are tied to a social nexus. One of the most celebrated sections of the *Philosophical Investigations* debunks the notion of a "private language", since language is invariably linked to social interaction and is never merely solipsistic. Jarman's allegiance to sexual libertarianism and gay militancy has little relationship to Wittgenstein's own quietistic – even masochistic – sexual ethos.' However, the parallels here lie in the aim to view even what is most personal within an overriding social context and to expose so-called 'private' experiences to the public: '[...] films as disparate as SEBASTIANE and BLUE are aesthetic experiments that share the provisional quality of the *Philosophical Investigations* and partake of the Wittgensteinian desire to infuse private experience with a public resonance. Wittgenstein was fond of comparing language to a "tool-box", and Jarman shares the belief that art's reception and assimilation by actual viewers, readers and listeners are of more interest than abstract notions of beauty. [...] If Jarman's œuvre is viewed in its entirety, family resemblances between disparate narrative and stylistic strategies become apparent. The baroque early work, and the stylistically antithetical late films are equally determined to undermine the ideological solidity of what Jarman terms "Heterosoc", and to herald the emergence of a new gay subculture.'[142]

Specifically with regard to the narrative strategies in Jarman's films, a polarisation into the two categories of 'narrative' and 'non-narrative' can be noted in the secondary literature, and this is typically preceded by efforts to use the classification of Jarman's films into one of these categories to draw a conclusion about their conventional or unconventional structuring and the 'readability' implied by this. In this context the basis for the standard of conventionality always seems to be the concept of a cohesive narrative discourse in general or, alternatively, the hermetically constructed plot sequences of 'traditional' narrative cinema in particular.

Thus, for example, Tracy Biga ('The Principle of Non-Narration in the Films of Derek Jarman') considers the identifying characteristics of 'narration' to be very closely tied to the concept of a cohesive plot based on a traditional model in which the events of the recounted story have a fixed place in their sequence within the fundamental structure of introduction, main action and conclusion.[143] According to Biga, when 'logical' narrative sequences of this kind are ignored, it results in 'disruptions of this arrangement', which are said to limit the significance of the conclusion – an element that she identifies in all of Jarman's written and filmic work: 'These disruptions operate on the levels of both form and content, details and the overall patterns of texts, and they continually frustrate the progression of narrative.' The concept of 'narrative' is so narrowly defined here that even elements of form or content that attempt to break up the construct of a narrative unity or linearity of plot are already declared to be symptomatic of the non-narrative. Setting out from a starting point of this kind, it is almost inevitable that elements of the non-narrative reveal themselves to Biga throughout Jarman's work and that – elevating them to the level of a principle – she both interprets them as the expression of his artistic style and seeks to construe them as a deliberately utilised political strategy, an act of political dissent rejecting patriarchal hierarchies (of knowledge): 'Jarman's principle of non-narration can be seen as an element of his artistic style, linked to a political strategy. In particular, Jarman's art expresses a continual refusal of patriarchal logic and, with this refusal, a sense of undifferentiation inconsistent with the gendered law of the father. [...] The arrival of the father announces the differentiation of gender and induces conscience; it poses the barrier of love, as well as establishing the basis of hierarchy. Just as Jarman interrogates hierarchy thematically in his books and films, he also does so formally, contributing both the sense of experimentation associated with his work, and a principle of non-narration.'

Gray Watson also seems to understand 'narration' primarily in terms of the model of a cohesive, linear narrative or plot structure when he attests to Jarman's 'difficulty in creating convincing narratives'. He believes that he has recognised the general cause of this in Jarman's inability to pursue linear trains of thought: 'Partly this reflected Jarman's difficulty in creating convincing narratives – narrative dialogue in particular – a problem which he sometimes solved by taking a readymade script, as with THE TEMPEST and EDWARD II. His difficulty with narrative reflected his lack of affinity for linear thinking in general, and his preference for more loosely associative and poetic patterns of thought. This was just as evident in his books as in his film.'[144] Aside from the speculative nature of this thesis, the author here (as in numerous other theoretical analyses) also contrasts an understanding of the concept of narrative with apparently opposite categories – such as 'non-narrative', 'associative', 'poetic', etc. – without clarifying the parameters of their definitions and asking whether this really has to be a case of mutually exclusive opposites at all.

By contrast, Roger Wollen and David Hawkes deal with the issue of narrativity in connection with Jarman's filmic work in a substantially more nuanced manner. Wollen draws a decisive distinction between Jarman's 'artist's films' on Super 8 and video and his feature films, comparing the latter to Jarman's paintings and establishing parallels between elements from the fine arts and architecture and his films: 'His output was not compartmentalized: he put over his ideas in every medium open to him. As a result the work has a consistency and coherence, not only at any one time, but across his life and output as a whole. Compare, for example, his feature films with his painting. Few of his films are narrative works in the tradition of the commercial cinema; they are much more concerned with a flow of imagery, a series of two-dimensional compositions on screen, very much like paintings and collages. Where there is narrative it is often temporally disjointed and sophisticated, combining several time phases, viewpoints and character sets.'[145] The idea, the message, comes before the choice of medium. Wollen points to the coherency across Jarman's entire artistic output and resists its being posthumously split up into individual aesthetic disciplines. The filmic images are also to be looked at from the perspective of fine art, as two-dimensional compositions on the 'canvas' of the silver screen. The concept of the 'narrative' is placed in a concrete relationship with the general understanding of narration by commercial film within traditional narrative cinema: Wollen sees Jarman's feature films as situated largely outside of this realm, without denying that they contain individually formulated elements of the narrative. This form of narrativity instead corresponds to the collage-like compositions of plot-related patterns and images.

In his essay '"The shadow of this time": The Renaissance Cinema of Derek Jarman', Hawkes concretely describes precisely this individual, open form of narrative. He develops a more nuanced concept that he distinguishes from the general understanding of the 'realistic', hermetically cohesive construct of narration by pointing to the origins of this understanding of the traditional and linear narrative discourse – leading us back to the narrative culture of sixteenth- and seventeenth-century theatre: 'In the early modern theatre we can discern the emergence of the mode of storytelling known as "narrative realism". During the 16th and 17th centuries, the convention that a story should be a transparent representation of a realistic, linear sequence of events gradually displaced older emblematic and allegorical aesthetic techniques. [...]

In literature, narrative realism culminates in the 19th century novel; in cinema, it reaches its apotheosis in the still-dominant classical Hollywood tradition.'[146] At the same time, Hawkes emphasises the close connection between the rigid narrative conventions within traditional narrative cinema and the one-dimensional constructs of models of behaviour and perception of sexuality and gender identity that are linked to it. For him, the fundamental aesthetic rules of narrative realism are by no means the only possible way to construct a storyline. Hawkes clearly distinguishes between the concept of a cohesive narrative and the diverse variety of ways to construct a story, and he uses Jarman's film versions of THE TEMPEST and EDWARD II to show how the film-maker both ignores the closed discourses of narrative realism and calls into question the related filmic conventions regarding sexuality and gender roles. Flashbacks and visible cuts as well as stylistic, temporal or 'historical' ruptures – for example, the fashionable designer suits in EDWARD II – are only a few of the means used to avoid the linearity or chronology of a staged reality and its implicit claim to truth for the story: 'In Jarman's films, the spectacle re-emerges from the underground to disrupt and complicate the assumptions of narrative realism, and, in doing so, it challenges the definitions of sexuality and gender roles which have defined classical cinema. In Jarman's work, the fetishized body is always male.'[147]

Open Narration in Jarman's Work

In speaking of Jarman's filmic work, four general areas reveal themselves and need to be distinguished: his 'home movies', the short Super 8 films, the 'cinema of small gestures' that he developed and his feature films. All of his home movies are Super 8 films featuring private motifs, spontaneously filmed in connection with private occasions and not originally shot with any intention of public presentation. The short Super 8 films, on the other hand, exclusively contain scenes explicitly staged for the camera. The Super 8 films from Jarman's 'cinema of small gestures' were also staged for the camera, but they sometimes also contain material from home movies, and they feature a longer running time of up to 60 minutes. The feature films include his 'feature-length' films for the cinema, whose film material consists of Super 8, 16 mm, 35 mm and/or video or, alternatively, a crossover incorporating these individual formats.

Regardless of which of these formal aspects applies in the given case, all of the films nonetheless share the fact that they fulfil neither the criteria of being 'narrative' in the sense of cohesive narrative discourses nor 'non-narrative' in the sense of abstract sequences of images or compositions of colour. They reject the traditional concept of 'narrative realism', with its linear plot structure and hermetically cohesive narrative logic, and – with greatly varying intensity – they take the form of open, fragmentary visions related to a specific occasion (home movies), motif (Super 8 films) or theme ('cinema of small gestures' and feature films). However, in doing so they never become lost in abstract presentations of colours and forms comparable to the works of Oskar Fischinger, Hans Richter or the meditative image patterns of Jordan Belson in the seventies. Jarman's images – including those involving multiple exposures, editing or superimposition among his Super 8 films – represent a more or less concrete objectivity: the representation never becomes entirely abstracted from its motif.

In Jarman's case the concept of narration is in no way to be limited to those models of conventional narrative forms that utilise language as a vehicle. Instead, narration is to be understood in a substantially broader manner: even those repeatedly superimposed images, for example, in IN THE SHADOW OF THE SUN – with which Jarman wished to cause his viewers to 'dream of lands far distant' – are neither 'abstract' nor 'non-narrative'. Because they are representations of objective motifs – which establish interrelationships and which viewers can thus situate within semantic contexts that are often very individual and always new – they also have something to share, to report: something to tell, in the widest sense of the word. Here it is the images themselves that do the telling. Their open narrative structure enables every viewer to associatively dream his or her own dream.

In all of Jarman's films – from the early home movies to his feature films and extending on to BLUE – narrative elements or, alternatively, concrete narrative structures are present in various forms, however, as recognised by Porton, they resist a 'facile classification' based on conventional standards. Here the concept of 'narrative' has to be understood in a sense extending far beyond that limiting notion of reality of traditional narrative cinema and its conventional, restrictive parameters. Jarman has developed nuanced structures of an 'open narration': these permit ambiguity and thus open up a space providing freedom to the viewer's own 'self'. In this context we may recall THE LAST OF ENGLAND as a concrete and simultaneously also extreme example, whose structures cannot be unambiguously identified even after numerous viewings: 'Jarman's films are open-ended and inspire interpretations that are subject to constant revision; he reflexively examines the sometimes frustrating and often edifying confusions that language games engender.'[148] The narrative is no longer linear and cohesive, instead, it is forked and many-layered. Its framework has become variable and permeable, and the degree of associativeness corresponds to the given intensity of the narrative. This open narrative form provides viewers with room for associations and the opportunity to use their own experiences, thoughts and feelings to expand and elaborate upon what is visually perceived, the 'story'. Here, entirely in the sense of that approach pursued in Chapter 3 (p. 60) regarding Jarman's work as a fine artist, the viewer once more becomes an active 'reader', a 'co-creator' of the given work or, as succinctly described in a different context by William C. Wees, in his study on the visual aesthetic of the avant-garde film: 'To take film in, instead of being taken in by it, viewers cannot remain passive receivers of images. They must become engaged with film in a continual creative process of visual renewal [...].'[149]

Familiar chronologies within an outlined or concretely identifiable narrative are either entirely absent or – particularly in the feature films – their linearity is repeatedly suspended by flashforwards, flashbacks (e.g. in EDWARD II) or other techniques of discontinuous narration. Furthermore the continuity of those feature films which make use of 'historical' themes in the wider sense is repeatedly and deliberately ruptured by unsettling optical or acoustic stage elements inserted from the present, such as calculators and typewriters in CARAVAGGIO or the previously mentioned designer suits and the documentary images of a demonstration by the gay-and-lesbian activist organisation OutRage! in EDWARD II. This also applies to the claim to truth implicit in continuity and always inscribed upon the so-called 'grand historical narratives'. Jarman is thus also working to counter a distanced historicity and its unfulfillable claims to universal validity and universal truth – and he is therefore very concretely working towards what Peter Sloterdijk describes as the 'breaking up of the ancient European concept of truth. Once again very imprecisely formulated, this means that the three dimensions of the classical space of truth are drifting apart in irreconcilable directions. There is a tendency for the true to lose its connection to the beautiful and the good, the beautiful is emancipating itself from goodness and truth with a grandiose and threatening determination and the good is becoming entirely something that is too "beautiful" to be true.'[150]

With the recognition that reality cannot be 'directly' grasped, that it is not an unambiguous and absolute phenomenon, the 'grand narratives' and their claims to universal truth have also been obsolete since the arrival of modernism, at the latest. A wide array of modern art-making techniques – such as abstraction, the principle of defamiliarisation, the rejection of 'realistic' mimesis and the questioning of formal rules and harmonious 'principles' – have called into question and invalidated the concept of realism's monopolistic status as a way of understanding reality and also destroyed the trinity of the true, the good and the beautiful. According to Frederic Jameson, 'the work of art' is 'no longer unified or organic, but now a virtual grab bag or lumber room of disjoined subsystems and random raw materials and impulses of all kinds. The former work of art, in other words, has now turned out to be a text, whose reading proceeds by differentiation rather than by unification. [...] This new mode of relationship through difference may sometimes be an achieved new and original way of thinking and perceiving.'[151] Thus, for a long time, differentiation processes of this kind and the phenomena of ambiguity and 'inexplicability' (in the sense of a single, unambiguous 'truth') have been immanent in various formations within different areas of artistic creativity. The forms of different, open or fragmentary types of narration have become just as diverse in the medium of film as in the areas of video, literature, theatre or fine art. New narrative structures have been developed and these imply an equally new form of 'reading'. To the same extent that the forms of 'narration' have metamorphosed, the concept of narrativity, of telling a story, has also expanded. Habits of vision and 'reading' have changed massively, associative forms of open narration have become legible and interpretable to an increasingly general audience and the filling of gaps and empty spaces with content of one's own has become a matter of course. This is particularly clear in the field of music videos, for example, which utilise not only the most modern technologies but also the storehouse of classic avant-garde film in their innovative language of expression. In an interview with the London painter, film-maker and video artist John Maybury, who was a friend of Jarman and collaborated with him on a number of projects, he specifically points out the influences of popular culture in the form of music videos and pop promotional clips on conventions of vision and comprehension: 'People who started watching videos in 1983 at the age of 12 probably understand much more today about montage as a means to place images in relation to one another than a film scholar who has occupied himself with Eisenstein for twenty years – these kids have been exposed to a merciless bombardment with images that place entirely new demands on them every three minutes.'[152]

A fundamental problem with those theoretical reflections on the narrative aspect in Jarman's films discussed at the outset here is their clinging to an antiquated concept of narration and to the understanding of the representation of reality and truth implied by it – an understanding that is not interested in taking into account an altered, 'new and original way of thinking and perceiving'. Instead, the discussions are repeatedly based on those demands for the cohesive development of narratives or, alternatively, plots made by classic narrative cinema in the tradition of Hollywood, the so-called NRI cinema, that is: narrative (story), representative (content and 'presentation'), industrial (form of production) cinema. Once cohesive, linear narrative discourses in general and the hermetically constructed plot sequences of narrative cinema in particular have been elevated to the measure of all things, there is no room left within the narrative for other, open forms. These appear in terms of disruptive factors and they become a mutually exclusive antipode instead of an integral element within an expanded concept of the narrative.

However, it is not only because of their open narrative form that Jarman's filmic works stand outside of this realm and are not products of the NRI cinema: they are neither narrative in the sense of a cohesive narrative discourse nor are they representative with regard to the symbolism of the beautiful, the true and the good, in the sense of the 'classical space of truth' – and they are in no way industrial in terms of the process of their creation and production. Their economic circumstances are worth mentioning in this context, because their contribution to the development of Jarman's individual filmic form was not insubstantial. These circumstances were defined throughout all of his work in film by a permanent lack of the financial means which would have been required for the complex production structures of a film in the sense of NRI cinema: 'Looking at my film-making from 1980 to 1987, I find I have received £550,000 from all sources, with this I've established a reputation as a film-maker world-wide. The current going rate for one low-budget feature is three times this – about £1.5 million.'[153] Thus Jarman shot his first feature film, SEBASTIANE, with a budget of only £30,000; EDWARD II, on the other hand, was his most expensive film at £850,000. The production costs of the other feature films vary between these two sums and the share of grant money for each was relatively small.[154] Jarman himself repeatedly points out how much the financial means at his disposal – coupled with the selection of the film format and the corresponding materials and resources – also influenced how he worked and thus, as a contributing factor, directly influenced the form of the films' realisation and their narrative technique: '[...] quite honestly, without the Super 8 camera I wouldn't have been working. It enabled me to work at a time in which it was quite difficult to get funding.'[155] Elsewhere he said: 'I'm the film-maker who has gone the furthest with the least. I made all my films for about £1 million, when the present cost for a low budget feature film is a million and a half. This puts me in a true perspective and this is in part why my films look the way they do. From the beginning I had to write my own scripts, partly at least because no one else could understand how to make a film for so little. [...] I can't handle the narrative approach because it is too expensive! I have really made a virtue of necessity in avoiding this.'[155A]

This, for Jarman unrealisable, 'narrative approach' can be illustrated in an exemplary manner using three paradigms of NRI cinema: the striving for a perfect cinematic illusion of reality, a production process that remains invisible to the viewer and the resulting impression that the film narrates itself. Films that can be classified as NRI cinema are distinguished by their efforts to generate a nearly perfect illusion of reality, an illusory space of reality. Along with high-quality production equipment, it is primarily a meticulously elaborated canon of filming and editing techniques that brings about an illusion of this kind. In order to approximate a perfect illusion of reality in this way, the cinematic production process has to remain invisible. In the moment of viewing, nothing may be permitted to remind viewers that they are witnesses to the artificial product that is a film – although they naturally know this. Thus through the purposive utilisation of the entire canon of traditional principles of editing, including soft cuts, dissolves, crosscutting, the shot/countershot technique and acoustic overlapping, among other things, an attempt is made to 'construct the filmic situation as such in a way that it is invisible for the viewer. Through this denial of the manner of its production, NRI cinema succeeds in concealing the staging of its events [...].'[156] This concealment of its staging then ultimately causes the self-narrating impression of the film's action to emerge. The situations of the plot seem to emerge out of themselves, to produce and to elaborate upon themselves. The successful cinematic experience is cathartic, and it is for this reason that the films of the NRI cinema are to be intelligible upon their first viewing and are primarily conceived for one-time consumption.

Subjective Mode of Expression

In Jarman's films, on the other hand, a subjective mode of expression always surfaces, with varying intensity. Entirely in the sense of his strategies of the autobiographical and of naming (see pp. 38 ff.), Jarman does not hide himself in the background of a staged filmic illusion but is instead always present in the filmic expression as its 'author': 'So I make films to create – like painting. The fact that I was brought up as a painter says everything. I believe that film should be just as personal. My first criterion for judging a film I watch, irrespective of whether I like it or not is: do I think the author had a deep need to make this film? Can you feel the commitment as you watch it? So what I attempt in my films, in my art, is to uncover things about myself and the world around me – things I might be only dimly aware of. [...] Normally film is second hand! The director or producer buys a script, but he is being no more than the equivalent of an illustrator to a book, rather than its creator. Even if a script is written by the filmmaker, financiers decide whether it should or should not be made. But can you imagine Francis Bacon having to write out what he might paint next year?'[157]

The images of his films, which are narrated in this way, can clearly be perceived in terms of subjective and individual expressions, statements or visions and – in some cases, depending on how open the form of narration is – they can only be optically and thematically deciphered after multiple viewings. At the same time, the scenic sequences of images do not deny the filmic production process. Thus, for example, Jarman does not subject the material from some of his early home movies to any further editing or montage at all: here the sequence of scenes in the projected film corresponds precisely to that of the recorded scenes. On the other hand, in films like THE LAST OF ENGLAND or THE GARDEN, precisely the rapidly cut sequences or dissolves and the superimposing of two or more images are essential to the impression of the open narrative's arranged series of images and scenarios: 'Superimposition automatically destroys the single, fixed point of view essential to perspectivist representations of space. Collage techniques and masking can produce disproportionate sizes and conflicting vanishing points within the same image. Rapid camera movement can flatten space and shatter the edges separating objects from each other and the space around them [...]. Rapid intercutting of simple images and movements also flattens the perceived space, as Léger seems to have been the first to discover while making BALLET MÉCANIQUE (1924).'[158]

In the generation of images and their arrangement in sequences, the constructed nature of the editing is not concealed in Jarman's films – even in his feature films with more developed narrative structures, 'visible' cuts deliberately suggest the informal lining up of individual shots or scenes, so that the film is rid of its self-referentiality. The story does not develop out of sequences of scenes that seem to produce themselves, instead, it is told in the form of scenic tableaux. But Jarman also attempts to make the process of filming transparent in itself by making direct reference to it: thus the first shots of THE GARDEN, montaged into the opening credits, show the crew shooting in the film studio, and their voices and conversations can be heard. In other films, such as THE LAST OF ENGLAND (see pp. 25 ff.), the author even goes so far as to inscribe himself into the sequence of images as the film-maker.

The film does not tell itself: it is Jarman who tells it. In doing so Jarman is working not on the construction of cohesive narratives within illusory spaces of reality but on the constant deconstruction of false traditional claims to and ideals of truth – both within the context of a theme and, corresponding to this, in its adequate filmic realisation. The deliberately inserted ruptures and the absence of familiar chronologies and predictable linearities in the 'story' render an immediate identification of viewers with the events difficult or impossible. Instead they are invited to inscribe their own reality into the film and to associatively complete it.

In itself, this form of subjective elaboration does not represent anything out of the ordinary: it repeatedly shatters the hermetic categories of narrative realism only because – in its original form – the medium of film, cinematography in itself, was developed primarily to make it possible to objectify reality and to present it as such. In order to appear convincing in this form, viewers cannot be granted any room for individual freedoms or interventions. It is 'the product of a society that was constantly concerned with the potential mastery of this reality and that, in the cinematograph, had created an instrument for itself to make this mastery possible in a genuinely "fantastic" manner: from then on reality could be transformed in such a way that, through this transformation, something like meaning could be conceived through reality! In film, reality means what it is supposed to mean.'[159] This means that even those NRI cinema films constructed according to the minutely defined body of rules sketched above are not 'read' and understood on the basis of a self-evident narrative logic. Instead, like all other forms of filmic expression, they are merely a construct that functions on account of certain conventions: in order to produce meaning, in order to be capable of being interpreted as 'reality', they likewise have to be understood by viewers in terms of their body of rules and their conventions.

The Beautiful Illusion: Representation of Space

A concrete representation of space within the image is inseparably bound up with the construction of reality in traditional narrative cinema. The projected arrangement generates a unity of space and time, and this is accompanied by 'a unity of movement that cannot be more than an illusion, because the film consists of individual still photos lined up in a specific order(ing) and these photos all display the same characteristics: they are centred constructions in linear perspective of real perceptual impulses'.[160] Here NRI cinema utilises that technique of depiction in central perspective which – since its invention during the Renaissance and since Leonardo da Vinci's discussions of it – has been considered the universal, exact reproduction of the reality perceived by the human eye. After all, without the suggestion of spatial and three-dimensional sequences of images to bring about the appearance of such seemingly real sequences of events, the staging of filmic narration within a perfectly simulated illusion of reality would not be possible.

Through the use of central perspective, a complex system of rules was grafted on to the depiction of space: in their mathematical-geometrical construction these pursue the goal of depicting three-dimensional objects on a two-dimensional surface in such a way that the image appears to the viewer in the same way as the depicted object itself. Similarly to the viewer of the cinematic image, the viewer of the graphic image is assigned a fixed position, a point of view, from which the deception of the sense of vision can be maintained and from which the collective ensemble of the apparently three-dimensional depiction appears correct. In the process, spatial vision has been subjected to rules that then metamorphosed into conventions of spatial perception. And these can cause depictions to appear three-dimensional solely on the basis of certain assumptions, because the images that we experience as three-dimensional in our own understanding are nothing of the kind. We first have to 'read' them as such.

Since the beginnings of Cubism in painting, but also in photography, the central-perspectival illusion has been subjected to a fundamental questioning or, alternatively, invalidation – in the traditional film of narrative cinema, however, it still continues to represent a central element in the construction of meaning. Because film consists not of a single image but of a sequence of images, the dimension of time is constituted alongside that of space and 'a network of relationships must be created, which permits viewers to gain control over this fragmentation (in space and time). Thus, while perspective ensures that viewers always remain situated at/as the centre, the specific rules (rules which they do not need in the world outside of the film and many of which must be learned) allow them to experience a temporal and spatial continuity during the entire film.'[161] In Jarman's films this continuity is also repeatedly ruptured or suspended entirely through the techniques already mentioned.

I would like to use three concrete examples – a reflection by the philosopher Paul Feyerabend, a photograph by Jan Dibbets and a painting by Derek Jarman – to conclude this discussion of the dubiousness of these terms and concepts. All three examples thematise the manipulation of the gaze and illustrate how much the perception of illusory space and, directly connected with this, how much our grasp of (reproduced) reality and 'truth' are influenced and defined by learned visual conventions and unspoken norms.

In his two works *Wissenschaft als Kunst* (Art as science) and *Against Method*, Feyerabend critically discusses the concept of reality and the claim to truth implied by it in the realms of both science and fine art, and he makes extensive reference to the phenomenon of perspectival illusion.[162] He uses a simple graphic illustration to demonstrate the great degree to which perception is based on conventions and the decoding of what is depicted, because 'depictions of three-dimensional objects on a sheet of paper are like maps or models, and a key is required in order to understand them.

'The archaic artist treats the surface on which he paints as a writer might treat a piece of papyrus; it *is* a real surface, it is supposed to be *seen* as a real surface [...] The simple drawing [below], for example, may represent three paths meeting at a point:

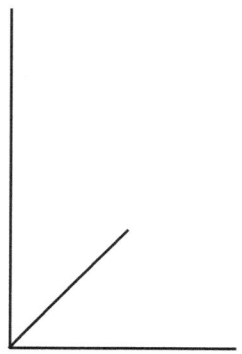

'The artist using perspective on the other hand, regards the surface and the marks he puts on it as *stimuli* that trigger the *illusion* of an arrangement of three-dimensional objects. The illusion occurs because the human mind is capable of producing illusory experiences when properly stimulated. The drawing is now seen either as the corner of a cube that extends towards the viewer, or as the corner of a cube that points away from him (and is seen from below), or else a plane floating above the surface of the paper carrying a two-dimensional drawing of three paths meeting.'

It is precisely this capacity of human consciousness, namely, the ability to produce illusory experiences from specific optical stimuli, that the Dutch photographer Jan Dibbets thematises and exposes in an astonishing manner in his series *Perspective Correction – My Studio II* (1969) (fig. 27 and 28).

Each of the reproductions shows a partial view of an emptied room, where the lines separating the walls and the floor seem to lead viewers' eyes into depth in a familiar manner. They convey spatiality and a sense of depth and, on the basis of several clues, such as the windows, the approximate size of the reproduced room can be – consciously or unconsciously – recognised. The camera has registered this depth, which is subsequently transferred from the two-dimensional surface of the film to that of the photograph. However, each photograph contains a disturbing detail: a square with intersecting lines inscribed inside produces the impression that it has been drawn on to the surface of the photograph after it was printed. However, the lines of this geometry are located not on the paper but in the photographically recorded space. Dibbets had fixed adhesive tape in the form of a trapezoid to the floor of the room or, alternatively, drawn a trapezoid on the wall of the studio – in each case, their receding sides counter the given perspectival diminution. For his photo Dibbets finally selected that vantage point from which perspective corrects the trapezoid into a square, whose edges now run parallel to those of the photograph. In this way the 'square' in the reproduction becomes a visible link, an interface, between the space of the studio and the two-dimensional reality of the photograph. Furthermore, the squares inscribed into the photographs also generate an additional, new spatial illusion: they convey a sense that the square projects from the wall into the room or, in the other case, that it stands upright on the floor in the middle of the room.

Finally, in his painting *Cool Waters* (1966–67), Jarman combines the illusory articulation of space with real objects that support and intensify the sense of simulated space through their genuine three-dimensionality (see fig. 29). Because of the horizontal bisection into a wide red and a narrow blue field, the planar, two-dimensional impression dominates at first glance. However, upon closer inspection, this is repeatedly disrupted by means of various elements: through the real objects mounted on the painting, through a suggestion of linear perspective and through a trompe-l'œil as well as two parallel horizontal lines. In this way multiple levels of simulated and real spatiality are created on the surface of the picture plane, and these both fictively lead into depth and really lead out from the surface.

If we were not conditioned to see in spatial, central-perspectival terms, we might identify the geometric figure at the lower left corner of the painting as the letter U, with a somewhat shortened right side – or we might simply identify it as three lines of different lengths placed on a plane and connected together. As it is, though, these diagonal lines lead our gaze into an imaginary depth, as in Feyerabend's cube example. The diagonal line subsequently appears to us as an edge joining a non-existent red floor to an equally non-existent side wall; the rear vertical line suggests a back wall. The drops of water added on the right side of the painting in trompe-l'œil technique correspond to this sense of depth: they seem to come out of a real water tap mounted on the surface of the painting (which is here consistent with the suggested back wall) and also to have formed small puddles on the surface of the floor. The towel rack mounted in the centre at the bottom optically suggests the front edge of a horizontal surface. When viewing the painting, however, our gaze is not steered in any clear direction; instead, it constantly shifts between the different levels of illusory depths and real protrusions. If our gaze finally wanders further up in the painting and fixes on the two parallel lines bounding its upper third, an entirely new level of perception is revealed: two pyramids and three smokestacks enter into view, located precisely on the boundary between the red and the blue fields. The red lower part of the painting, which had only just still been perceived as three-dimensional, now takes the form of the ground stretching horizontally back to the blue: the boundary line becomes a horizon and the blue becomes the sky.

In *Cool Waters* Jarman is already playing with that 'reality'-producing and linear-perspectival gaze, just as he later attempts to break through the code of spatial representation by means of various techniques in his films: here, as in the sequences of his films, the depiction is not linear and cohesive but forking and many-layered. New semantic levels and perspectives repeatedly reveal themselves in the image. Viewers' gazes are not directed to a position from which the individual elements coalesce into a seemingly unified whole, instead, viewers find room to associatively elaborate upon these elements and, accordingly, to formulate a subjective 'truth' (of their own). The content of this 'truth' can certainly base itself on that terminological demand expressed by Feyerabend in *Wissenschaft als Kunst*: for him, 'truth is what the style of thought says is the truth [...] The choice of a style, a reality, a form of truth, including criteria of reality and rationality, is the choice of the work of humanity. It is a *social act*, it depends upon the *historical situation*; it is occasionally a relatively conscious process – one considers different possibilities and then makes a selection – but it is much more often direct activity on the basis of strong in-

Fig. 27, 28: Jan Dibbets, *Perspective Correction – My Studio II*, 1969

tuitions. It is "objective" only in the sense dictated by the historical situation: objectivity is also a stylistic characteristic (compare, for example, Pointillism with Realism or Naturalism). One thus decides in favour of or against the sciences, just like one decides in favour of or against punk rock, but with the difference that the present social embedding of the sciences surrounds the former decision with much more chatter and also much more noise in general.'[163]

Fig. 29: Derek Jarman, *Cool Waters*, 1966–67

[5]

Home Movies
and Super 8 Short Films

STUDIO BANKSIDE –
Private Images of Inner Life and the Outside World

THE GAZE INWARD SHOWS images of interiors, everyday objects of personal value, beloved friends and a beloved place. These are private living and working spaces, the open and affectionate atmosphere of a studio, people, images, paintings or photographs that have a story of their own, that tell their own story.

The outward gaze shows the bridges of the Thames, ships, the unchanging flow of the water under the bridges and the anonymous stream of people and traffic. Abandoned sites of decay, tall old warehouses made of brick and low harbour buildings, remains of a Gothic church that has long since ceased to exist, views through shattered window panes, views into the uncertain – this is the Bankside district, captured one last time before its destruction.

These are the grainy, mostly static and tranquil images of STUDIO BANK-SIDE: Jarman's first, short Super 8 film would simultaneously become the beginning of an intensive occupation with the medium of film in general and with the Super 8 format in particular. Nonetheless, according to his own account, this first film was largely the result of a coincidence: Marc Balet, an architecture student from the US and later the art director of Andy Warhol's magazine *Interview*, had a Super 8 camera with him when he visited London in 1970. Jarman borrowed it and made this three-minute recording of his studio, located in a former warehouse in the old harbour district of Bankside. In the previous year Jarman had already moved into a studio in a vacant corset factory in Upper Ground. This was the first of that series of old factory and warehouse buildings situated in the middle of London, in the former harbour district on the right bank of the Thames, which would serve as the centre of his life and work during the next ten years. However, after only one year at Upper Ground, the factory was torn down and Jarman – together with several other artists, including Michael Ginsberg, Peter Logan and Jean Marc – moved into that warehouse in Bankside, where he occupied the top floor and was able to remain until it was destroyed in the autumn of 1972. His studio in Butler's Wharf, not far from Bankside, then became the third and also the longest station during the period he spent in the warehouses. Gradually, however, most of the old harbour buildings in this area were torn down or burned down – the latter occurring at Butler's Wharf in 1979. The redevelopment of the area along the Thames between the Waterloo Bridge and Tower Bridge in the years that followed was so thorough that the paths of its streets and its architectural substance seem entirely different and are now scarcely recognisable.

To be precise, STUDIO BANKSIDE consists of two parts which were recorded at different times and that differ not insubstantially both in terms of their film material and the structure of their sequences of images. Jarman combined both parts – underlaid with music by the British composer Edward Elgar – and he presented them to the public and commented upon them in this form during his retrospective at London's ICA in 1984.[164] The first three minutes of the film actually consist of those first recordings made in 1970. They were shot in colour and primarily show the above-mentioned life within the warehouse's studio spaces. Although the film was not edited after being shot and the projected sequence of the scenes thus corresponds to the sequence of their filming, this first part of STUDIO BANKSIDE displays both a rhythmically strictly structured progression as well as a simple, pre-planned and structured concept in terms of the choice of motifs. Jarman films individual photographs of the studio and in between, as though he were tracking down traces, he rerecords on film one of the motifs (objects) depicted in the photographs within the 'real space' of the studio. At the same time, the rhythm of the sequence of images is defined by repeatedly recurring, split-second cuts to a close-up of the filament of a light bulb and its warm, reddish-orange light. The images of the second part, the remaining three minutes of STUDIO BANKSIDE, were recorded only much later – namely, in 1972, two weeks before the warehouse's demolition. They were filmed using black-and-white film and as a series of brief shots; however, these do not possess the rhythm created by the intervening shots of the first part. Here Jarman has ventured the step from the inside to the outside and shows the surrounding area of Bankside – the old, defunct Docklands along the Thames, left to their destruction and demolition.

The calm and static images of STUDIO BANKSIDE communicate impressions of this newly won space of freedom and this creative environment – but simultaneously also the threat of losing the studio. 'In 1970, when Upper Ground was demolished, we moved to Bankside, which became the most beautiful living-space in London [...]. At Bankside there were film shows and poetry readings and parties. [...] Life in the warehouse brought fun and laughter into our lives with a thousand events. People camped out, swung or slept in the white hammock suspended across the room. Andrew kissed a thousand home-grown celebrities, and once Katy Hepburn came to tea.'[165] In that part of STUDIO BANKSIDE created in 1970 several different chronological layers become visible: by filming objects which were present in the space and had already been recorded – 'eternalised' – in photographs, Jarman momentarily transferred these out of the pose of the past and back into the present. For the duration of their filming, he fills them with new 'life' in order to then interweave them as filmed photographic images and filmed real objects within the film.

As in many of his other home movies, the images in STUDIO BANKSIDE show the passing and the past: they deal with the memory of ambiences, moments and encounters which are to be rid of their transience in their recording on film. In connection with the photographic portrait, Roland Barthes refers to this moment of reification, this objectification of a person or situation as 'that very subtle moment when [...] I am neither subject nor object but a subject who feels he is becoming an object: I then experience a micro-version of death (of parenthesis): I am truly becoming a spectre'.[166] This 'micro-version of death' in which the subject, trapped on film, freezes into an 'immortal' image, gives expression to that concrete wish to capture moments in time – to eternalise an event or to grant immortality to a loved one – which is inherent both to private (commemorative) photography and to traditional home movies (and later family videos). In a certain sense, Jarman himself saw the works created at this time as continuing the tradition of private home movies by his father and grandfather: 'These Super 8 films record the life of Bankside and Butler's Wharf. They are home movies, an extension of my father's and grandfather's work. The difference, of course, is that they don't record family life.'[167] Similarly to those home movies of his parents and grandparents, they document in the present moments from a time that is already in the past – in a certain sense representing 'historical footage', for example, of the no longer existent urban landscape in STUDIO BANKSIDE. Above all, however, they represent personal memories of private events and numerous friends who later died as a result of Aids.

Kodak Families

If we expand the concept of family by transferring it to Jarman's circle of friends, then the images of his home movies certainly record private 'family life', in this wider sense:

Recordings of
- friends (e.g. in STUDIO BANKSIDE and SLOANE SQUARE, 1975/76), private celebrations and birthday parties (e.g. ULLA'S FETE, 1975, and PICNIC AT RAE'S, 1975/76)
- excursions to the countryside (JOURNEY TO AVEBURY, 1972, and GERALD'S FILM, 1976)
- journeys (FIRE ISLAND, 1974; THE FOUNTAIN, 1978; THE PANTHEON, 1978, and PONTORMO AND PUNKS AT SANTA CROCE, 1982)

All of these films have in common that they were not originally shot with the intention of later being publicly presented, and some of them additionally reject consciously established scenic arrangements and staging: 'There was no intention ever with the early Super-8's to really show them to audiences. They were actually shown to the people who are in them.'[168] They are genuinely an extension of the traditional home movie, which primarily seeks to capture and document private events in its typically spontaneously realised recordings. In the early nineties, when the loss of close friends had taken on ever more dramatic proportions, Jarman himself sorrowfully and sadly formulated a newly emerged private dimension of these films during an interview: 'The only real thing I like about my films is that it is possible to see my dead and dying friends in all the nooks and crannies, and I like that. It's wonderful.'[169]

Originally 16 mm film was the only available 'amateur format', however, it remained the luxury plaything of a small privileged class on account of the high costs of the equipment and material. It was true that Kodak brought out a new double 8 mm format – a 16 mm film divided down the middle and run through the camera twice in opposite directions – and thus launched an attempt to offer a less expensive film format for leisure and amateur use. Nonetheless, the double 8 mm format was unable to establish itself as a film medium for everyday use. In the thirties, 8 mm film was placed on the market as an inexpensive and easy-to-use medium that was accessible to and affordable for the general public. Finally, in 1964/65, the Super 8 format was introduced. The new cameras, which were even easier to use, and Super 8 film cartridges displaced the 8 mm format that had been standard until that time and made Super 8 – alongside photography – the most popular and enjoyed medium for recording private events until into the eighties.

Not only did the development of home movies take place parallel to the international economic upswing, the so-called 'economic miracle' of the post-war years: it also documented this situation. It was, after all, first in this 'age of the home movie' that the opportunity was opened to everyone to capture private occasions of all kinds in the form of moving images on film. The film material and the technical equipment became cheaper and cheaper and the cameras easier and easier to operate. Still, from today's perspective – compared with the video systems that entered the market several years later – filming with 8 mm film was an activity that had to be carried out rationally and sparingly: the film cartridge's relatively short length of approximately three minutes defined the length of the recording and a restriction was also posed by its cost, which was several times higher than the price of a 240-minute VHS cassette. This economy of filming repeatedly becomes apparent in numerous home movies in the staged nature of individual scenes that seek to convey a sense of spontaneity, but only seem to have been casually recorded.

The images of private home movies suggest a sense of remembering what is now in the past, even when the motifs' creation and their contexts are unknown to the viewer. Entirely in the sense of Barthes's 'micro-version of death'. 8 mm images also conjure up sensations of the loss of a seemingly intact, secure world, whose scope was limited to the staged framing of the image. However, in the nostalgic melancholy of viewing, the question repeatedly forces its way into the foreground: 'Are home movies really about home? Or are those movies to home what canned laughter is to mirth? That is, home movies like canned laughter, are indexical signs which draw our attention to the illusive signifiers of shared good times and safe loving homes. Home movies are understood to be benign glimpses into a carefree time when both the children and parents were younger, their relationships unsullied by the complications of adult life. These ghosts of parents and siblings that drift out of projectors and shimmer across movie screens couldn't possibly ridicule, terrorize, beat and abandon. These are Kodak families, and Kodak families just smile, smile, smile.'[170]

The smile seems to be frozen in place, the joyfulness has vanished and nonetheless: although darker memories from behind the smiling family facades certainly can resurface and become present in the later consciousness of the viewer, it is only too easy for these fleeting spotlight snapshots to congeal into idealising images representing whole periods of our lives. Because the images of home movies repeatedly generate anew a few selective memories of happy moments and recall long-gone feelings of 'home' and carefree security, they play a role in contributing to concepts such as 'happy childhood' and 'carefree youth', which are always retrospective and produced in the memory.

Jarman, who grew up within precisely this tradition of the classic home movie and himself appeared in numerous recordings by his father, extended this tradition while modifying it. He began his personal search for a new, more open form of capturing private events on Super 8, attempting to rid the home movies of his parents of their one-dimensionality as idealised commemorative images and to permit a few of the darker landscapes of his childhood to reveal themselves. While the home-movie evenings of Jarman's childhood still signified a withdrawal into the secure environment of 'home', in works like THE LAST OF ENGLAND the home-movie fragments reveal parts of that environment from which he had wanted to escape at that time. Jarman has robbed the old images of their inherent innocence and snatched them out of their isolated and seemingly intact world by placing them in new and changed contexts (see pp. 29 ff.). He has not only inscribed the 'happy' childhood images into present-day, violent surroundings but also collaged them with his father's 'documentary' military footage and retroactively overlaid them with corresponding military and war sounds. Aircraft engines drone in the background during their carefree ball game in a garden secured with barbed wire and located at an RAF station. When he is lifted out of his pram by his mother, the explosions of dropping bombs can be heard, and the dark-red brick buildings of the military settlements form the omnipresent backdrop of his childhood idyll. A crack has appeared in the seemingly intact world in Kodak colour and the violence that otherwise lies more or less hidden in the background of the Super 8 images of his childhood is rendered discernible, tangible: the militarised environment of his childhood, the barracks of the post-war period, the authoritarian upbringing, his military father ...

'The Super-8s were always intended to be home movies. It's the best form of filmmaking. It would be great to have a TV channel of home movies, where you would see the sorts of things that people really do. My father's and grandfather's home movies are fabulous now; they're as good as any filmmaking from the 1920s, because they show bourgeois life then absolutely perfectly, in a way that René Clair might not have imagined. The great thing about Super-8 is that you can switch it on to automatic and get beyond all those technicalities.'[171] In the early seventies, when Jarman was trying to free himself from the outwardly imposed conventions of painting at that time, there were a number of reasons why he felt the Super 8 camera was the ideal means to do so. It was easy to use and did not require any complex technology of the kind that he always considered obstructive in his creative working process. Compared with 'professional' formats, the costs involved were very limited and the camera could be used spontaneously and flexibly. Thus the images of his first Super 8 films displaced the impersonal, geometrical surfaces of his paintings. His camera (a Nizo S 480) became his brush, light took the place of paint and the canvas was replaced by the Super 8 film material. Jarman began to rigorously continue his development of that aesthetic of the private gaze inherent to the Super 8 image by trying out unconventional shooting techniques, the deliberate use of staging and post-production processing: 'I got involved in Super 8 films, and I was able to do it all myself. You just put the film in the camera, press the button, and a film comes out. Eureka! They become part and parcel of recording my world along with my painting.'[172]

Not an Experiment but an Expedition

As has already been shown in the previous chapter, Jarman's Super 8 films can be divided up into three different groups in terms of their motifs and editing techniques:

- The private 'home movies':
  These are personal motifs filmed on private occasions; they were not staged for their shooting, but some of them have undergone editing. These include ULLA'S FETE (1975), GERALD'S FILM (1976) and JORDAN'S WEDDING (1981), among others.

- The Super 8 short films:
  These were staged for their shooting and edited. They include GARDEN OF LUXOR (1972) and THE ART OF MIRRORS (1973), among others.

- The 'cinema of small gestures':
  These represent a further development of the short Super 8 films and sometimes feature characteristic home-movie elements (see pp. 157 ff.). They include IN THE SHADOW OF THE SUN (1972–74/1980), IMAGINING OCTOBER (1984) and THE ANGELIC CONVERSATION (1985).

If we compare the images of Jarman's personal home movies with old, traditional home-movie footage, we can identify a clear change: the artificial poses of the protagonists have disappeared and the events and scenarios are no longer consciously staged for and towards the camera. Instead Jarman has recorded them without drawing attention to himself and in a largely casual manner. Here the moment of filming has shifted from the focal point of the events to their unremarkable margins. It is no longer the people captured on film who stage themselves for the camera but Jarman himself who introduces various forms of staging through his handling of the camera or his editing of the exposed film after shooting. However, in contrast to these private home movies, many of his short Super 8 films and the portrait-like films about artists with whom he was friends – such as those about Andrew Logan, Christopher Hobbs or Duggie Fields (ANDREW LOGAN KISSES THE GLITTERATI, 1972; TAROT, 1972; DUGGIE FIELDS, 1975/76) – exhibit clearly conceived structures or were staged explicitly for and towards the camera. Jarman was captivated by the creative potential that the medium of Super 8 film opened to him and later, with his 'cinema of small gestures', he finally undertook an attempt to establish Super 8 film as an equally valid medium alongside the 'commercial formats'. The 'cinema of small gestures' as well as the films IN THE SHADOW OF THE SUN and THE ANGELIC CONVERSATION will be discussed in detail in the next chapter.

As vehement as was Jarman's rejection of restrictive theoretical categories and concepts that attempted to place his works in questionable overarching aesthetic or film-historical contexts – the experiments that he carried out with this medium were no less rigorous and diverse. As has already been mentioned (see p. 93), this was not based on a wish to investigate formal filmic structures and phenomena, instead, these experiments were primarily a means to an end – a means to transform personal intentions into corresponding images. For this reason, I prefer to characterise his search for adequate possibilities for realising his intentions as an 'expedition' rather than as an 'experiment'. Always looking at things from the perspective of the painter, he tried out extremely diverse techniques of shooting as well as manipulating and editing Super 8 material and later also video, 35 mm film and digital images. Thus, at that time, he stood at a great distance from the then much-celebrated structural film, the active film scene and the circle surrounding the London Film-makers' Co-operative. However, Jarman stood at a distance not only from the formalist-dominated, experimental area of film but also from the abstractly theoretical ideological practice of the protest generation of that period. Instead he seems to have simply taken the then-popular slogan 'The private is political' literally, in the sense that he both captured everyday scenes without any grand theoretical superstructure and also unhesitatingly experimented without concerning himself with which tendencies were currently being celebrated. Years later, John Maybury provided a very succinct description of that form of experimentation which had increasingly come up against a dead end at that time – as well as the almost anarchical role in which the medium of Super 8 found itself in that context: 'Experimentation had become stuck in the dead end of Structuralism, and in this way the "Underground Film" was resolutely murdered. I see my films as the alternative of the amateur as opposed to this academic death. [...] With the choice of a medium for the home, garden and the kitchen like Super 8 and with the use of the simplest camera techniques, I hope to reintroduce the innocence of the experiment.'[173]

On this expedition into what was for him still the unmapped territory of the Super 8 film, Jarman experimented with extremely diverse effects of light and colour and with different film speeds. Light took the place of the paint that had been applied to the canvas, and it was primarily the experimentation with this light and its more or less unpredictable influence on the exposed film

– such as mirrored light reflections or direct exposure to sunlight (e.g. in THE ART OF MIRRORS, 1973, or SEBASTIANE WRAP, 1975) – that were of central interest to him. And in this context it was above all the techniques listed below that he tried out:

- shooting with different filming speeds, and here the exploration of the 'single frame' technique is of particular interest. This is directly connected with the ...
- playback of these films at different projection speeds and the discovery of the 'slow down' effect in: ULLA'S FETE (1975), PICNIC AT RAE'S (1975/76), GERALD'S FILM (1976), THE FOUNTAIN (1978), JORDAN'S WEDDING and many other films
- refilming or repeated refilming of the visual material: the images of a Super 8 film projected on to a screen are refilmed with a Super 8 camera (e.g. in SEBASTIANE WRAP, 1975) or later also with a video camera or from a TV screen (WAITING FOR WAITING FOR GODOT, 1983)
- double and multiple exposures, e.g. in GARDEN OF LUXOR (1972)
- hand-painted, coloured filters: these were placed in front of the lens during the initial filming (e.g. in FIRE ISLAND, 1974)
- use of coloured paper as a filter: this was held in front of the lens during refilming

Single Frame & Slow Down

What are 'single frame' and 'slow down'?[174] These two techniques are among the most important explored by Jarman and are essentially based on experimenting with modified filming and projection speeds and the interaction between fast and slow motion. They initially originated out of simple economic considerations, which led him to develop a technique that made it possible to record over twenty minutes – instead of the standard three minutes – on a single Super 8 cartridge. The combination of single frame and slow down primarily appears in his home movies and was later also used in feature films, such as IN THE SHADOW OF THE SUN, THE ANGELIC CONVERSATION, IMAGINING OCTOBER and THE LAST OF ENGLAND. With his Nizo 480, Jarman filmed individual images in single-frame mode at a speed of 3–6 fps (frames per second) instead of the usual 24 fps. If a film shot in this way were projected at standard speed, the result would be a fast-motion effect: the progression of images would appear substantially accelerated (by a factor of around six to eight). However, a special Bolex projector made it possible for these Super 8 films shot in fast motion to be projected in slow-down mode at a reduced projection speed of around 3 fps, instead of 24 fps. This combination of single frame during shooting and slow down during projection restored a nearly normal tempo, and in the process it produced those series of distinct individual images that simultaneously seem to flow into one another in slow motion, 'like a series of moving slides'.[175]

In a further step, Jarman refilmed the Super 8 projections at normal speed with the Super 8 camera or, later, with a simple Olympus video camera (e.g. in THE ANGELIC CONVERSATION) that was connected to a U-matic recorder. In doing so, music was retrospectively added to a number of the Super 8 films, which had originally been shot without sound. The process of refilming made additional interventions in the appearance of the filmic images possible. However, neither in his home movies nor in his 'cinema of small gestures' did Jarman ever make use of technical devices like an optical printer or digital post-editing or anything of that kind. All of the corresponding effects were created either during the original shooting or during projection and refilming. As Jarman himself repeatedly describes, he made use of various coloured filters or experimented with the white balance of the video camera in order to influence and alienate the coloration of the film: 'In order to get unusual colours I fiddled around with the white balance button. Sometimes I put a piece of red paper in front of it, which gives the film a greenish tint, or a piece of green paper, which would give it a reddish tint.'[176] Finally, many films, including SEBASTIANE WRAP and PIRATE TAPE, were later transferred to 16 mm film for their public presentation.

In addition to these manipulations of coloration, it is primarily the change in the accustomed image quality caused by the refilming of the Super 8 films which substantially contributes to this alienation of the film images. Through the copying process these are invested with their characteristic, soft colours and contours and that lack of focus and grainy texture which associatively places them in the proximity of painted images. They are moving pictures that become visible in the form of their individual images through the combination of single frame and slow down. These individual images emerge for a fraction of a second before the eyes of the viewer. With their grainy textures, they are somewhat reminiscent of romanticising Impressionist or Pointillist paintings. The vigorous, strangely pulsating rhythm that Jarman has compared to the rhythm of a heartbeat emerges out of this constant, slow gliding of each individual image into the next. It massively influences viewers' ordinary perception and, with it, their sense of time: 'Shooting and projecting at three frames per second means that it is synchronised with the heart beat. Every time a frame goes through, you are forced to refocus slightly, which makes you really look at it.'[177] In this visual rhythm, the progressions of movements are broken up into their individual segments and intermediate layers become visible: the viewer's gaze can lose itself within the dream-like, meditative sequences of images to the extent that any 'real' sense of time disappears. This altering of perception can be observed particularly clearly in THE ANGELIC CONVERSA-TION, where the short sequences inserted at normal speed suddenly appear enormously fast and take on a special aura and dramatic quality because of this (see pp. 169 ff.).

However – in contrast to the slow-motion playback often used in music videos or commercials – in Jarman's films we are dealing with recordings in real time, with the documentation of time that was actually passing. Jarman does not expand a film sequence of three minutes to twenty minutes: twenty filmed minutes can actually be seen. He has emphasised this numerous times, for example, in a talk with Simon Field: 'With that way of filming with the Nizo-camera there is a cute observation which people attempted to do by stretching film in pop-promos. But it is not the same thing because the process is one which is quite different. It is not like to stretch the film in that sense. Because I got that twenty minutes.'[178]

'The filming, not the film.'[179]

For Jarman the concrete work on a film and the dynamic that develops during this collaboration with the other people involved – a dynamic that often follows a course of its own in unexpected directions – were substantially more significant than prospective considerations about the film as a finished product or speculative calculations aimed at reaching a specific target audience. The critics Keates and Romney ultimately characterise the individual aesthetic dimension of his films alternatively as 'Jarmanesque' or even in terms of the 'Jarman film', in the sense of an attempt to postulate the existence of an independent genre (see p. 98 f.). This is founded not least on precisely this way of working and a corresponding aversion against aesthetic fashions and whatever popular tastes happen to be dominant at a given time. The origins of this form of process-oriented work lie in Jarman's experiences with the Super 8 camera, which led to the first home movies and Super 8 films being created in shootings carried out in a spontaneous and improvised manner. At the same time, Super 8 provided him with extensive room for experimentation. This way of working was subsequently carried over into his 'cinema of small gestures', and it was also continued and further expanded during his work on feature films.

In this context it was primarily on three very different levels that the Super 8 camera opened up new freedoms for him: (physical) freedom while filming, independence from institutions and independence during production. In connection with his work on THE LAST OF ENGLAND, he describes this as follows: '[...] the Super 8 camera is free. 35mm is chained by money to the institutions. It could have been shot on 35mm, but economics have gutted mind from the format. My friends, the bluebells are flowering in the woods of Kent – now do you wait for someone to tell you you can film them? They'll have died before you get an answer. A 35mm crew will trample them to death. I can dance through them, throw my little camera in the air, turn somersaults. Fuck the crane and the track.'[180]

The Super 8 camera is small, easy to handle and simple to operate: it thus enables an impulsive and uncomplicated use and, with it, the greatest possible flexibility while shooting. On the technical side, preparations are as good as unnecessary and Jarman was able to concentrate entirely on the situation to be captured on film and on the results that he was aiming for. The medium could thus be handled in a manner whose simplicity recalls similarly impulsive possibilities in painting, and Jarman repeatedly emphasised its advantages: 'The great thing about Super-8 is that you can switch it on to automatic and get beyond all those technicalities.'[181] However, it was not just complex technical apparatuses that Jarman left behind in this way: he also left behind unwieldy institutional apparatuses like those of the film industry or of public and private financing. To the same degree that he could not imagine Francis Bacon being able to determine a year in advance what he would paint in the coming year (see p. 109), the Super 8 medium meant that Jarman had no need to bind himself to institutionally dictated guidelines – and the overt or covert attempts at exercising influence or censorship that accompanied them.

Filming without a Script

However, the extensive room for aesthetic and thematic autonomy that resulted was made possible only through an additional freedom – namely, in production. On the one hand it was economic restrictions that had led him to work with Super 8 film and, while doing so, to introduce techniques like the slow-down effect: 'Of course, there are good economic reasons, because you can make twenty minutes of film for nothing. You can make amazingly long films with no money.'[182] On the other hand it was precisely these economic circumstances that opened up this room for new freedoms by way of Super 8. The (relatively speaking) extremely low costs involved gave him the opportunity to set off on a filmic expedition – to begin production without a script that had been finished in advance and without the corresponding persuasion of potential investors. Where it was possible, he also utilised this method and its subversive power during later feature-film projects, and it led to the creation of films like THE LAST OF ENGLAND and THE GARDEN, which otherwise – particularly during the Thatcher era – would hardly have been given a chance to be realised.

Thus THE GARDEN, for example, was created from an abundance of Super 8 material that Jarman had shot over several weeks around his fisher's hut at the beach near Dungeness. As this initial material was being shot, the most basic outlines of the film did not exist yet – not to mention a script or even a 'story'. The motifs from the life of Christ began to become a concrete thematic dimension only after this initial phase of shooting. But even during the eight days of shooting that followed, during the completion of the film around the theme of the Gospel, Jarman's central interest lay in the unpredictability of the improvised, in capturing scenarios that developed out of situational events. Predefined images, shots or sequences had no place in the work on these films – in complete contrast to works like CARAVAGGIO or WITTGENSTEIN: '[...] making a film with no script you have to be on your toes: visual ideas develop as they run. [...] I have no idea how the scenes will look, and no wish to. Do I have sufficient confidence to let anything happen? As you light the Amaretti papers they flare up and disappear into the dark.'[183]

This filming without a script, a practice that originated in the early home movies, demands an extreme openness to chance occurrences and their unpredictable results. As previously discussed, Jarman understood chance as an 'extension of [his] life', which was diametrically opposed to the conventional situation on traditional film sets. Much like Harold Rosenberg's claim in connection with Action Painting (see p. 57), Jarman also wanted to place the process above the finished artwork and, in this way, to establish a direct link between art and life. By integrating the camera into his life, his everyday existence, he eliminated the artificial boundary between everyday situations and the filmic situation of a staged presentation. 'This is the secret of making small films; text and idea are definitely not fixed – FLOW WITH THE GLUE. This separates my work from the British television and features industry, where the people who make the films, directors and technicians, are paid in an hierarchical order, and brought together for money, not by a community of interest. Their work is adopted and adapted; [...] For me only film/makers who initiate and write their own work are of any value.'[184]

Filming as a Party

Jarman did not understand himself in terms of a director in the classic sense: he hated the hierarchical structures within the bloated apparatuses of the film industry. Instead he attempted to generate a creative environment, a community that made collective work on a film project possible. 'You should try and create an environment where people can be creative with people coming up with ideas. The chance for people to come together to make something is wonderful. There are certain shots that are impossible in my films because

I've never shouted through a megaphone, or used a walkie-talkie. I hate the feeling that I'm pushing people around. I always talk quietly to people. [...] I have an extreme aversion to authority – it's a reaction to my military background.'[185] These 'parties with friends', as he liked to refer to successful shootings, thus established a link between the private world and the public: 'My role was to find family within the films, that we found community within the filmmaking and if I tried to make a situation where everyone can come together for a few weeks and find something to work on which opened up avenues of different sorts of himself. That was the real purpose of filmmaking: to create community.'[186] This aspiration, which he had developed during his home-movie period by making the camera a part of everyday life, extends throughout all of his feature-film projects and emerges in particularly clear form in SEBASTIANE, THE ANGELIC CONVERSATION, THE LAST OF ENGLAND and THE GARDEN.

No Concern for the Audience

As steadfast as he was in this form of collaboration, he was equally uncompromising with regard to taking into consideration a potential target audience – this did not interest him while working on his films: 'Cinema audiences interest me no more than the tide of humanity that passes each day under my window in Charing Cross Road – I wish them well.'[187] Just as a great number of his home movies were originally created without any intention of a later public presentation, he did not consider the demands of potential viewers during the preliminary conceptual development or the concrete realisation of his later works and feature films. Based on the principle that this work emerges primarily out of an inner process within the artist and those involved in the given project, he did not orient himself according to possible tastes of audiences and target groups or other market expectations. The process of the film's creation and its results were always his main focus: it is not the film that is to find the audience but the audience that is to find the film. He expresses his wish for an active audience at a number of points in his writings. This audience is to leave stereotyped and familiar patterns of reception behind and instead to grasp the viewing of his films in the form of a stimulating process, an exciting journey, which can also provide inspiration for viewers to become active and creative themselves: 'The thing about the audience seems to me all wrong. In a sense I don't want an audience. I wish they'd all go away and do it themselves, which would allow the whole thing to collapse. No one should demand an audience whatsoever. Saying I'm working for an audience is a false promise ... I would encourage audiences to leave the cinema and get on with their own film. I would encourage everyone to become an artist because it is an inward journey and not an outward one. [...] What you should be looking at is the community of work, people working together. What is relevant is the collaboration in a fruitful way of a group of people.'[188]

Underground & Anger

This process-oriented way of working, this attempt to generate a creative working environment and community and in this way to establish a direct link between the artistic process and life, is to be seen in the context of contemporary tendencies of that time: the happening and Fluxus artists of the sixties and early seventies postulated that 'Art is life'. More and more, the urgent need to liberate art from its distanced and institutionalised spheres and to bring it into closer connection with life found expression in the increasingly overlapping fields of the visual and performing arts. This was both connected with the rejection of all limitations and hierarchical structures and characterised by a critical questioning of established concepts of art, of the division between artist and audience and also of the mechanisms of the commercial art market. By defining work on a film as a communal process, a 'party with friends', Jarman simultaneously deconstructed the antiquated image of the artist as the lone and visionary creative genius. And the significance for Jarman of close affinities to the vital realm of the 'underground' culture of that time gained a corresponding extension a few years later with Punk culture and the New Romantics: 'The sixties were to see major interventions by artists. David Hockney publicly acknowledging his sexuality from the beginning of his career; Kenneth Anger and Maya Deren's gift of the underground cinema; feature films like IL MARE;[189] Andy Warhol's sexual circus; Rudolph Nureyev's leap to freedom. [...] We joined THE UNDERGROUND. The underground, like the bars, was illicit. [...] at the first showing of Anger's SCORPIO RISING and FIREWORKS at Camberwell art school we expected a police raid.'[190]

These were not academic and theoretical experiments but works that emerged out of a lived underground – a scene that was closely linked with the cultural and gay subculture that had provided Jarman with the corresponding background coming from art school. With his reference to illicit bars, Jarman points to the close connection between these realms. At that time, openly and directly thematising homosexual ways of life was possible only from the marginal position of a socially subversive underground. In contrast to the analytical and theoretical avant-garde concepts of the structural film or the materialist film in the sixties and seventies, these are more anarchic, impulsive and transgressive. Thus it cannot come as a surprise that this theme remained just as invisible in the primarily conceptual work of the experimental avant-garde as in the mainstream films of Hollywood.

In *Now You See It* Richard Dyer points to the close links between homosexual film-makers, subculture and the works of the so-called underground film: 'Underground films were always recognised as a very gay tradition. [...] The concerns of the underground – with personal identity, with self disclosure, with gender roles, with subversiveness – have a particular urgency in a lesbian and gay context, and even more so in the context of the development of newly assertive gay identities in the period.'[191] In her article 'Promiscuous 8', Laura Hudson additionally refers to the special significance of the 8 mm and Super 8 formats in underground films.[192] She understands 'margin as site of resistance' and 8 mm film as a 'Tool of Defence', a medium capable of undistortedly and authentically reproducing ideas and experiences. Completely uncompromising without being bound to any specific conventions, here it appears as the ideal medium for expressing political and personal interests that are not represented by the mass media or the film industry: 'To tell personal stories. Although the status of 8mm fluctuates in the margins it is not necessarily a mode of film-making, or cultural engagement, which pushes sub-cultures further into the ghetto of disenfranchisement. It can be a powerful tool imbued with an authenticity that mainstream media can only allude to, a tool capable of conveying undiluted ideas and experiences, that can tap into and extend current resources without compromise and without being suffocated by conventions.'

Jarman himself also repeatedly talked about the spheres of influence of artists from the experimental underground and the Beat Generation of the fifties and sixties: 'I had grown up with Kenneth Anger and Andy Warhol, that was the cinema I saw in the 1960s as an art student.' Alongside the previously presented influences from painting and literature, in the area of film it was primarily Kenneth Anger, Maya Deren and Andy Warhol who lastingly occupied him and whose films – along with early works of the classical avant-garde – were shown and discussed in the context of art school and the emerging scene of London's off and art-house cinemas: 'I'm not certain what effect Andy had on my generation. Anger's films were more effective. Anthony Balch's film of Burroughs preceded the Factory. Warhol was a discovery of the *late* sixties. [...] I imagined Warhol had a greater influence on my work than he really had. My Super 8 of Andrew kissing his friends was a spoof. Anger, Burroughs, Ginsberg and Rauschenberg were the influences – Andy, the court jester.'[193] Inspired by Surrealism and films of the classical avant-garde, artists of the early underground, such as Maya Deren, Sidney Peterson or Kenneth Anger, developed films featuring a very personal expression. In their works of the forties and fifties the central focus is primarily on their own person, their search for themselves: 'The films from the late forties take the filmmaker as subject-matter, her or his inner life, revealed by dreams, released by ritual, universalised by myth.'[194] Entirely in the style of the home movies private spaces and flats become shooting locations, people from the film-makers' circle of friends are involved in the films themselves or help to complete their production.

In this context, several interesting formal and thematic parallels between Anger's and Jarman's works and their manner of working seem worthy of note. Kenneth Anger was born in Hollywood in 1930; he had already used his parents' home-movie camera to shoot his first short film, FERDINAND THE BULL, by the age of seven. Ten years later, FIREWORKS (1947) was created in his parents' flat over the course of three days, and it has since advanced to become a classic of underground film. All of the scenes in FIREWORKS were shot in a single take, and it was to remain the only film by Anger for which he composed a script. Anger had already become a disciple of the British occultist Aleister Crowley in his youth and was deeply influenced by his teachings about black magic and occultism. While Jarman was primarily interested in the symbolism of alchemy, the writings of C.G. Jung and the theoretical dimension of occult teachings, Anger was also fascinated by their direct practice. His filmic work is permeated with this aspect: numerous works take the form of a magically invoked merging of his dreams, desires, myths and visions. However, light, reflections of light and fire appear as central and repeatedly recurring elements in the work of both film-makers. Jarman had discovered by chance that directly shining a beam of light on to the film of a camera set on automatic exposure almost completely darkens the image and that this then returns back to its original state after the light source is removed. He utilises this effect of 'magical light' as well as the element of fire in a quotation-like manner, and he often deconstructs it through multiple exposures – in Anger's films, on the other hand, it plainly occupies a position of magic symbolism and symbolic power.

Like Jarman, Anger also places emphasis on an individually defined, conservative perspective and contrasts it with the pop culture emerging at that time: 'I am a conservative, meaning that I cherish things of value. This places me at the antipodes of a cheap hustler like Andy Warhol, who is the garbage merchant of our time.'[195] Anger was also highly interested in Ancient Egyptian culture, its symbolism and its monuments, such as the Pyramids and the statues of gods carved in stone. During the process of working on a film he was just as unconcerned about potential viewers as Jarman: 'But when I work on a film I don't think I could ever worry about whether people will like or understand it. When I really get into that creative thing of making a movie, it's just me, and the camera, and whatever else happens to be there.'[196] It is this direct relationship, this immediate connection between the person filming and the camera that enabled him to develop a similarly personal cinema whose thematic and aesthetic liberties were later also explored by Jarman: 'A freedom that is only possible through the artist's intimate view through the lens of his camera, in a word through "personal cinema".'[197]

The Artist's Intimate View

Within the two categories of 'private home movies' and 'Super 8 short films' (see p. 123), it is possible to identify five primary, substantial areas of thematic concentration:

- Theme 1: 'Family life'
  STUDIO BANKSIDE (1970/72), ULLA'S FETE (1975), SLOANE SQUARE,
  A ROOM OF ONE'S OWN (1975/76), PICNIC AT RAE'S (1975/76) and
  JORDAN'S WEDDING (1981), among others

- Theme 2: Journeys
  JOURNEY TO AVEBURY (1972), FIRE ISLAND (1974), GERALD'S FILM
  (1976), THE FOUNTAIN (1978), THE PANTHEON (1978) and PONTORMO
  AND PUNKS AT SANTA CROCE (1982), among others

- Theme 3: Staging/'Performance'
  GARDEN OF LUXOR (1972), TAROT (1972), THE ART OF MIRRORS
  (1973) and JORDAN'S DANCE (1977), among others

- Theme 4: Portraits
  ANDREW LOGAN KISSES THE GLITTERATI (1972), TAROT (1972),
  DUGGIE FIELDS (1975/76) and PIRATE TAPE (1982), among others

- Theme 5: Music
  BROKEN ENGLISH: THREE SONGS BY MARIANNE FAITHFULL (1979)
  and T.G.: PSYCHIC RALLY IN HEAVEN (1980/81), among others

This thematic classification is based on those films released or, alternatively, filmographically catalogued as of 2008 (when the German edition of this text was published); however, these make up only a small fraction of the complete existing Super 8 film material by Jarman. For this reason the list is to be seen neither as comprehensive nor as a rigid system but instead as an indication of the thematic diversity of his work: it is certainly open to diffuse boundary lines and overlapping. Thus in the following sections a few films and their contexts will be discussed as examples for the individual areas.

Theme 1: 'Family Life'

Although almost all of Jarman's Super 8 films display, to varying degrees, a private dimension – even if only because the film was shot in improvisation with friends – several films nonetheless place the 'documentation' of private events in the foreground. In those films that depict 'family life' in the expanded sense used here, people and places from Jarman's immediate surroundings form the centre of interest. These films consist of recordings of friends at celebrations or parties, but also of everyday living environments and situations. Like most of the films from the other four areas, these were originally shot without any intention to later publicly present them.

In the autumn of 1973 the writer Anthony Harwood, who was a close friend of Jarman, moved to New York and offered to let Jarman move into his flat in Sloane Square House, because it had become apparent that it was impossible to heat the gigantic warehouse spaces at Butler's Wharf in the winter and there was no warm water. Jarman was able to spend the following years on Sloane Square, but in 1976 he was forced to vacate the flat shortly after Harwood's death. Harwood had not paid the rent for months and Jarman, whose right to rent the flat had been granted by a court while Harwood was still alive, now found himself confronted with disproportionately high demands for back payments related to rent, repairs and court expenses. Above all, however, it is likely that the lifestyle and the fashion extravagancies of the flat's occupants were not entirely in keeping with the owner's taste, and she used the situation as a pretext to get rid of them. Thus, in June of 1976, Jarman organised a large removal party, decorated the walls of the flat with graffiti and invited his guests to take everything with them that wasn't nailed down. Together with his flatmate, the musician and later producer Guy Ford, he shot SLOANE SQUARE, A ROOM OF ONE'S OWN (also known under the titles SLOANE SQUARE and REMOVAL PARTY) on this occasion. The individual motifs and scenes come both from that large removal party and from the preceding years on Sloane Square.

In complete contrast to the combination of single-frame and slow-down techniques utilised in many of the other films, he shot large portions of SLOANE SQUARE in fast motion only, that is, using single frame. The camera was usually positioned statically at a fixed location in the room and set on a single-frame exposure with large intervals. A few shots were recorded – also in fast motion – with the hand-held camera quickly moving. The extreme time-lapse effect that condenses several hours or days into a few minutes can be observed not only in the people who momentarily appear and disappear in the image but also in the patches of sunlight and the shadows from the windows that rapidly progress along the floor. SLOANE SQUARE essentially consists of three parts. The first part of the almost ten-minute film had already been created in 1975: one year before Jarman moved out and during his work on SEBASTIANE. It was filmed entirely in black and white and shot mostly in fast motion. It is primarily people in a room that can be seen here. Jarman's friends and Jarman himself appear at particular locations inside the flat in the absence of any context and for fractions of a second; they enliven or disjointedly pass through the space and then occupy particular places just as quickly as they leave them again or, alternatively, disappear entirely. The second part is in colour and was created in 1976, shortly after Harwood's death and during the weeks preceding their moving out. Here, as opposed to the first part, what we see are static and fragmentary shots generally recorded at normal speed and featuring friends and individual objects: lips, eyes, hands, a neck, jewellery, a pencil, a key ring, etc. The images of the second part take a form that stands in contrast to the other two parts, like an attempt to try to hold on to those brief moments condemned to immediately disappear once more. The normal filming speed – accustomed in itself – seems far slower in comparison, and the fragmentary framings seem like attempts to preserve parts of those subjects and objects that fill the individual moments of the present and exist in an irrevocable process of disappearing. The third part, which is also in colour, is once again shot in fast motion: the entirely graffiti-covered walls and ceilings of the flat provide the background of the 'removal party'. The people who appear on screen for fractions of a second are replaced by household objects and other objects towards the end of the film. While the camera is initially still positioned statically at a single point in the room, as at the beginning of the film, it increasingly takes on a 'life of its own' during the third part, becoming an ever more rapidly and hectically moved hand-held camera whose time-lapse shots no longer record anything but segments, splinters of a fragmented and destroyed reality.

While the progression of motions are broken up into their individual seg-ments and intermediate layers are rendered 'visible' in the films combining the single-frame and slow-down techniques, the fast-motion recordings of Sloane Square create precisely the opposite effect: the intermediate tones of the sequences of motions are reduced to a minimum, the motions themselves seem disjointed and condensed. The fragmentary character of the distinct shots also becomes tangible to the viewer. They are fragmentary in the sense that they no longer suggest any closed continuity of progression.[198] Instead, individual images are filtered out of a continuous sequence in the manner of a stroboscope and recorded in the viewer's (filmic) memory. Recordings filmed using the two different techniques can be perceived as diametrically opposed, nonetheless, they are extremely similar in terms of their effect. In the sequences of Sloane Square the uniqueness, transience and irretrievability inherent to any specific situation or act – or, more generally, to every moment we experience – are rendered substantially more radically visible than in the combination of single frame and slow down. The absence of the information required to preserve the continuity of our perception causes precisely that in-visible 'micro-version of death', in which the subject freezes into an 'immortal' image, to become directly 'visible'.

Three other Super 8 films, namely, ULLA's FETE (1975), PICNIC AT RAE's (1975/76) and JORDAN's WEDDING (1981), document events that are absolutely classic home-movie themes: a garden party, a picnic and a wedding. All three films were recorded using Jarman's combined technique of single frame and slow down. ULLA's FETE was filmed in black and white and the other two films in colour; sound was added to all three after shooting.

Jarman shot ULLA's FETE, also know as ULLA's CHANDELIER, during a garden party organised by Andrew Logan and Luciana Martinez. The party was held to raise money for their mutual friend Ulla by auctioning off clothes and objects that they had brought with them. She had been caught by an attentive shop detective while trying to make off with a chandelier from Harrods and had been sentenced to a fine of several hundred pounds.

One year later, PICNIC AT RAE's was created on the occasion of a picnic organised by the London fashion designer Rae Mouse. Duggie Fields, Miss Gaby and Andrew Logan were among the guests.

In the third film, JORDAN's WEDDING, Jarman documents the 1981 wedding of Pamela Rooke, better known as the Punk icon Jordan, who also appears in his films SEBASTIANE (1976), EVERY WOMAN FOR HERSELF AND ALL FOR ART (1977), JORDAN's DANCE (1977) and B2 TAPE/FILM (1981/82) and, as Amyl, plays one of the leading roles in JUBILEE (1978). She began her career at Vivienne Westwood and Malcolm McLarens's legendary boutique Sex, in the punk and fashion scene of London's King's Road. Jordan had completed training as a ballet dancer as a child and teenager. As a young schoolgirl she had already begun experimenting with her outward appearance, which she increasingly stylised and refined. In the late seventies she finally reached the peak of her fame as the 'punk princess' Jordan – as she was referred to in the media – and she played a not insubstantial role in shaping the punk fashion trends of that time. 'Her life was a pas de deux with outrage', remarks Jon Savage in his extensive work on the history of the English punk scene, *England's Dreaming: Sex Pistols and Punk Rock*.[199] There we find an interesting remark from Jordan herself about the story of how she personally developed a closer connection with the gay subculture of that time: 'When I came up to London, I went to the Masquerade Club in Earl's Court, a gay club, which was outrageous even by today's standards. It was very difficult for a woman to get into those clubs, the male gay scene was very insular. They were very worried about women coming into their clubs and the only way you got in was by how you looked. If you looked crazy and outrageous you were all right. It so happened that I liked good dance music and the only places you could get that was those gay clubs. They played things like "Rock Your Baby", "Rock The Boat", lots of Bowie.'

Today, not only ULLA's FETE but also PICNIC AT RAE's seem like nostalgic historical accounts about the flower power generation of the late sixties and early seventies. A harmonious and peaceful ambience has spread among these gatherings' guests, whose carefree yearning for love, peace and happiness seems to implicitly reproduce that slogan of the period: make love, not war. The camera glides gently and indifferently past the guests; it follows a dance step or glides on to the next event and a new group of people. It gets lost in the trees and in the sky and dreams along with the dream of the guests. Through the lightness and freedom of its movement – so eminently important to Jarman – it underscores the light-heartedness that lay in these get-togethers. In contrast to the casually recorded scenarios of ULLA'S FETE, the people in PICNIC AT RAE'S are filmed from very close up. The camera could be described as scanning over the parts of their bodies, which appear onscreen in a fragmentary form. Because of the immediate proximity and presence of the camera, many of the protagonists in this film act out the familiar poses deliberately turned towards the camera and the staged gestures of classic private home-movie recordings. Here Jarman ventures to approach the individual guests so closely with his camera – participating in their immediate private sphere as an observer – that it would have been impossible to ignore him in many cases: an interaction with the person filming in the form of a smile, nod or raised glass is directly provoked. By contrast the 1981 film JORDAN'S WEDDING, which records the punk star's wedding, permits us to recognise surprising parallels to ULLA'S FETE, both in the manner of its shooting and in the atmosphere that it seeks to convey: in spite of the posed arrangement formed for the group photo and the bride and groom's kiss staged for the camera, the scenes here appear candid, as though casually recorded. Their protagonists seem spontaneous, and they hardly notice the presence of the camera. In no way do they represent the active, aggressive and provocative attitude of the punk generation of that time. On the contrary, the images in JORDAN'S WEDDING are defined by a lightness similar to that of ULLA'S FETE – not least because of the use of single frame and slow down. Jordan, all in white, is more reminiscent of a flower child of the late sixties than a punk diva of the eighties. And 'Waterloo Sunset', the song by The Kinks which Jarman later added to the film, completes this impression.

Theme 2: Journeys

In the thematic range of traditional private home movies, the motif of the journey is – along with that of 'family life' – among the scenarios most commonly recorded on camera. In Jarman's work we also find a number of home movies created during excursions to the surrounding English counties (JOURNEY TO AVEBURY and GERALD'S FILM) or during journeys and stays abroad, for example, in America (FIRE ISLAND) or Italy (incl. THE FOUNTAIN, THE

PANTHEON and PONTORMO AND PUNKS AT SANTA CROCE), and these can be identified with this thematic area in a narrower or more general sense.

The film JOURNEY TO AVEBURY was created in the summer of 1971, during a trip to the megaliths of a prehistoric temple complex near Avebury, in the County of Wiltshire. Jarman completed this early Super 8 film in the following year, and several years later he integrated it into the first part of IN THE SHADOW OF THE SUN (see pp. 162 f.). A slight fast-motion effect can be recognised on account of its being filmed using the single-frame technique; however, some of the shots were also recorded at normal speed. In contrast to many of the other home movies, the individual shots of JOURNEY TO AVEBURY, which are separated by emphatic cuts, are arranged or juxtaposed in such a way that they generate a clearly identifiable visual rhythm. The grainy images themselves depict a landscape at the height of summer in luminous colours: ripe cornfields swaying in the wind and lush green pastures with grazing cows. An expansive and rich landscape presents itself – with its isolated, lonely and only seemingly randomly arranged megaliths, which stand out darkly against the bright and warm sunlight. Finally, approaching banks of clouds intensify the horizontal structuring of the images and the impression of the landscape's gentle expansiveness, bound only by the horizon.

In this context it is interesting that Jarman also created a series of paintings entitled *Avebury Series* in the same period (see figs. 30a, b). However, the contrast between the images in the film (see fig. 31) and the images of this series could not be greater and illustrates what the medium of film – in the form of the Super 8 camera – meant for Jarman at that time: finding an adequate expression of his yearning for an irretrievably lost, harmonious past. This was an expression of his yearning for the bygone and lost beauty of a pristine, undestroyed nature and landscape able to lead him, in his memory, back home to the days of his childhood. These were images that it was impossible for him to convey by way of painting at that time. Like many of his paintings of the late sixties and early seventies, those of the *Avebury Series* are also dominated by severe geometries and a cool, detached emptiness: horizontal structural axes are interrupted by vertical lines suggesting a dimension of space. Here the landscape is reduced to a handful of dark parallel lines: it has nearly been annihilated, vanished. Torn out of the swaying cornfields, the stones find themselves arranged alone or in small groups along the horizontal axes, and they appear like quotations without footnotes before the light, monochrome background. They are the sole remaining, mute witnesses to the landscape of his memory.

A few years later, in October of 1976, Jarman spent a weekend at the Redcliffe Gardens in Essex with his friend, the photographer Gerald Incandela.[200] During this excursion they discovered an old Victorian boathouse next to a small, nearly dried-up pond in a forest clearing. Jarman had his Nizo with him and GERALD'S FILM was created spontaneously and without any prior plan-

Figs. 30a, b: Derek Jarman, *Avebury Series No. 4*, 1973

Fig. 31: Stills from the film JOURNEY TO AVEBURY, 1973

ning – likewise entirely in the tradition of the classic home movie. However, unlike JOURNEY TO AVEBURY, Jarman once again used the combined technique of single frame and slow down to make this film. In slow visual strides that merge into one another, the camera passes through a clearing and approaches towards a decrepit wooden building, which seems to be expending its last remaining strength in an effort to remain standing. The beams of the roof's visible framework extend up into the sky, and parts of the structure supporting the walls have become exposed. Jarman feels his way along what remains of the decaying surface with the camera – past the outer walls and into the house's interior – and he gradually begins to explore the life within it. Featuring a rhythmic, step-by-step movement forward, the images here once again display a grainy but simultaneously very soft texture. As in JOURNEY TO AVEBURY, these images stir associations with romantic motifs by the Pointillists and Impressionists of the preceding century through the blurred and merging colours, soft focus and diffuse textures so characteristic of this technique.

Soft, very light colours – a delicate green, wood covered in grass, sunbeams – fall into the house's interior through its windows and illuminate the overgrown floor, contrasting with the hard-edged and dark shadows. This results in a play and interplay of light and shadow, the sun's backlighting and the roof beams that stand out darkly before it. Gerald repeatedly appears on screen for a few moments and walks through the room in order to explore the house's interior. Jarman films him in front of the open fireplace and through the diamond-shaped window panes. And Gerald's clothing, his green felt hat and his scarf, fit into these surroundings in a manner that is no less perfect than it is coincidental. In *Dancing Ledge* Jarman later recalls: 'He looked like one of the workmen who might have built the place a hundred years ago, with the green felt hat from Pasolini's CANTERBURY TALES and the white scarf wound around his neck.'[201]

Jarman was fascinated both by the state of natural decay and the pristine quality simultaneously radiated by the remains of the old wooden building: 'It's something extraordinary, because it was completely undisturbed, not vandalized or something else you will expect – it wasn't at all, it was untouched!' GERALD'S FILM would also become a search for romantic images of a harmonious idyll that had ceased to exist for Jarman. He once again undertook an attempt to capture the passing and the past on film by means of images that arouse a sense of long-gone times, thus perhaps rescuing them from their final disappearance: 'I thought that this is very sad, but on the other hand here it is on the film and in a way it is still here.'[202] GERALD'S FILM is a film in memory of something unknown and nonetheless familiar, and the tender and delicate images created in the process seem to be not just a declaration of love to the long-gone time of the old boathouse's origins, but also to Gerald, who walks within this time once more in the film.

Unlike GERALD'S FILM and JOURNEY TO AVEBURY, which were both re-corded in England, the 1974 film FIRE ISLAND is one of the home movies that Jarman shot during his travels abroad. In the summer of 1974 he resolved to turn his back on England for a while, and he visited his friend Anthony Har-wood in New York. The four months that he spent there were his longest stay in this city. He took part in the excessive life that New York offered him, and he repeatedly talks about the intense impressions of this period at numerous points in his autobiographical writings. Fascinated by the gay nightlife and locations offering nameless, anonymous encounters, he immersed himself in a world of saunas and public cruising grounds, like those of the old piers on the Hudson River or the deserted beaches of Fire Island: 'I had a very wild summer [...] By the end of that summer I was living at night. I was on the verge of being trapped in this American dream of liberated sex. Out every night on the piers, or at the Continental Baths; out at Fire Island, sleeping rough and meeting people on the beach. This night-life was charged with an excitement far greater than drugs; as you stepped into the dark you entered the world of strangers, on the derelict piers you left the imprisoned daylight world behind. [...] Out at Fire Island the atmosphere was the same. The shrubs in the woods that lie along the shore were heavily scented, full of fireflies, silent floating will-o'-the-wisps. The silence and deep satisfaction of being alone and accountable to no one attracted me as much as the possibility of a chance encounter. I would spend every night wandering, then sit by the sea-shore watching the sun rising. This world had a purity that one never encounters in "civilised" surroundings. Living this way could preserve a cherished anonym-ity. As the decade wore on, I grew further and further away from the social events, the cocktail parties and openings, even my own studio. Out alone at night one was a traveller. Power, privilege, even good looks, certainly money, disappeared in that dark.'[203]

Fire Island is located around 45 miles from New York City, which can only be reached by ferry, and it serves as the weekend home and private beach of New York's upper class. On account of both its high-spirited private parties and the beaches and dune landscapes of its nature reserve, the island has tradi-tionally been and still remains a popular gay destination and cruising ground. For example, the gay travel guide *Spartacus* promises the interested traveller: 'Cruising: Anywhere and everywhere from the time you get on the ferry, but especially the west end of the boardwalk at The Pines and the "Meat Rack" and bushes between Cherry Grove & The Pines.'[204] In *At Your Own Risk* Jar-man remarks 'the lid was off; the dance was on', with regard to this new, liber-ating and unfettered sense of life that was striving to overcome him there – a sense of life whose intensity was completely inconceivable in the England of that time. The grand party of new-won freedoms and sexual emancipation from antiquated and limiting norms was in full swing. No one could imagine that it would only last a few more years and that soon, after the emergence of the first rumours and public announcements regarding a new 'mysterious plague' (see p. 67), it would come to an abrupt end in the early eighties.

The calm and static images of FIRE ISLAND, parts of which Jarman would also integrate into his later film IN THE SHADOW OF THE SUN, consist exclusively of shots filmed from fixed camera positions. By using coloured filters, which he held in front of the camera lens while filming, he immersed the recordings in an intense violet, dark blue or orange: except for the high, surging waves of the ocean, almost no movement can be made out. Occasionally the images are also fragmented through a reflective surface held horizontally in front of the lens, and they split to form an additional, reversed image that increasingly but irregularly becomes distorted towards its edges. The images allow us to vaguely make out those landscapes beyond their 'civilised' surroundings that Jarman writes about: empty, deserted, endless sandy beaches, pebbles and occasional tree trunks stretching up into the sky. Between them there are the monotonous, constantly returning, high waves of the ocean. The intense monochrome colour tones defamiliarise this place and distance it from its customary framework. The dark blue and the intense violet are nocturnal colour tones, between them – for very brief moments – there are images in a glaring, aggressive reddish orange: '[...] the colour of abundance and plenty. It gives delight and enlightens.'[205] Somewhere in the sand a young man poses, nude, the starfish in his hand balanced in front of his face. The emptiness and expansiveness of these images are associated with the feelings of liberty and freedom from obligation inherent to this form of cruising and anonymous encounters, but they are also images of loneliness, yearning and desire. ... Out alone at night one was a traveller ...

Theme 3: Staging/'Performance'

The circumstances surrounding those Super 8 films that can be grouped within the following three categories of staging/'performance', portraits and music differ substantially from the home movies of the two previous thematic areas. Where the films of the areas 'family life' and 'journeys' were characterised primarily by their improvisational and casual form of filming, which is also a distinctive feature of traditional home movies, a great number of the following Super 8 films are either recordings that were deliberately staged and structured for the camera and feature primarily performative elements (incl. GARDEN OF LUXOR, TAROT, THE ART OF MIRRORS and JORDAN'S DANCE) or they are selected events captured on film and then further processed (ANDREW LOGAN KISSES THE GLITTERATI, T.G.: PSYCHIC RALLY IN HEAVEN and PIRATE TAPE (W. S. BURROUGHS)).

The 1972 and 1973 films GARDEN OF LUXOR and THE ART OF MIRRORS are among the first of those meditative Super 8 films whose images produce the previously mentioned 'ambient tapestry of random images' (see p. 100), and they very consciously seek to distance themselves from any 'narrative' – and subsequently also interpretation. They are the first brief experiments whose aesthetic results would later stimulate Jarman to work on his 'cinema of small gestures', and they already challenge viewers to engage in that associative form of viewing which would become indispensable in the case of films like IN THE SHADOW OF THE SUN or THE ANGELIC CONVERSATION. In contrast to many of his home movies, both of these films were not filmed using the combined technique of single frame and slow down. However, they are characterised by their intensive use of superimposed images, multiple exposures and the refilming of multiple projections, as well as the use of coloured filters that immerse these filmic assemblages in monochrome colour tones, further alienating them.

GARDEN OF LUXOR (also known as BURNING THE PYRAMIDS or A GARDEN OF LUXOR) is named after the title of the postcard whose reproduction of the Pyramids underlies a large portion of the film's images. As in the case of numerous other short and feature films by Jarman, Christopher Hobbs designed the sets for this film, and he is himself present in a few shots.[206] Much like a leitmotif, the image featuring the Pyramids of Luxor repeatedly emerges, enters into the foreground or has the shrubs, leaves or flames of other images superimposed on top of it. There are images of a reclining youth in a sleeping pose, the close-up of a face, images repeatedly overlaid with flames, their light or the glow of their light. A horde of riders inserted from a fictional film races across the postcard's two-dimensional landscape of the Pyramids – as does an aimlessly wandering crowd. Their movement through space invests the images with a magical sense of depth. Through the use of coloured filters, the images are additionally immersed in intense tones of orange, blue or violet, and the multiple superimpositions cause a fantasy landscape to emerge to the accompanying meditative and monotone singing of Nico. The experimentation with light and colour and the images' kaleidoscope-like merging into and over one another creates effects that are so unpredictable and random that their aesthetic dimension became wholly identifiable only after the film material had been developed. And it repeatedly confronted Jarman with new and surprising results: 'July 1973, Shad Thames: The footage for THE ART OF MIRRORS came through the door this morning. It's some of the most unusual film I've ever seen. It will be impossible to edit as there is not a moment I'll want to lose – each reel is more surprising than the last. The mirrors flashing sunlight into the camera with the light meter set at automatic sends the whole film lurching into negative. Luciana Martinez and Kevin Whitney in black evening-dress are excellent. There's one shot of Luciana where the light falls through her mesh hat on to the blue triangular make-up which is wonderful. Gerald looks sinister in his paper-bag mask – the green filter takes less of the light than the heavy red, but you still need the sun to make it really sing. This is the first film we've made on Super 8 with which there is nothing to compare. The other super 8s of the last few months are still too close to 16 mm work; whereas this is something which could only be done on a Super 8 camera, with its built-in meters and effects. At last we have something completely new.'[207]

Compared to GARDEN OF LUXOR, the scenarios of the 1973 film THE ART OF MIRRORS (also known as SULPHUR) seem staged and substantially more based on a concept. In a tableau-like manner, two men and a woman (Gerald Incandela, Kevin Whitney and Luciana Martinez) stride through a space whose outlines are only vaguely discernible. The film is introduced by images of a roaring fire. In this work Jarman's interest is centred on his experimentation with sunlight reflected in a mirror: its focused beam of light is slowly swung into and back out of the camera lens. The 'magical light' in the form of a circular mirror is solemnly passed on from one person to the next in a manner reminiscent of a ritual; new groupings repeatedly form, shifting in the manner of a backdrop and then already disappearing once more in the next moment. On film the beam of light appears star-shaped and almost white. Through the automatic light meter, the film image is dramatically and almost entirely darkened by such extreme overexposure. It only slowly becomes lighter when the ray of light is moved out of the lens. A constant shift and strong contrast between gleaming white light and a bluish and dark, nocturnal black is the result. The Pyramids in fluorescent orange and the light of a flickering flame are inserted in between for fractions of a second.

A few years later Jarman would incorporate the images of the Pyramids and the fire, Gerald Incandela with the paper mask over his face and the reflections of the mirror as well as a few other sequences from both GARDEN OF LUXOR and THE ART OF MIRRORS into his film IN THE SHADOW OF THE SUN, which he completed in 1980 and which will be discussed in detail in the chapter on the 'cinema of small gestures'. The images of all three films are very concrete manifestations of Jarman's eminent interest in diverse texts on magic and alchemical teachings.

This interest had begun more or less by chance in the early seventies, with his reading of C.G. Jung's *Alchemical Studies* (volume 13 of the *Complete Works*). Even then, however, his interest was focused less on the level of content and metaphysics than on the aesthetic level, which seemed to open up a completely new, mysterious, enigmatic and romantic dream world to him: 'I stumbled into alchemy reading Jung's *Alchemical Studies* early in the 1970s. I don't know what made me pick it. Perhaps the fascinating illustrations of metals, kings and queens, dragons and serpents.'[208] Jarman subsequently read numerous original texts, such as *Hieroglyphic Monad* and *Angelic Conversations* by the astrologist and mathematician Dr John Dee, whose writings – together with Shakespeare's sonnets – provided the inspiration and material for THE ANGELIC CONVERSATION. He also read *Cause, Principle and Unity* (*Della causa, principio et uno*) by Giordano Bruno and texts by Paracelsus. He purchased a 1651 English first edition of Heinrich Cornelius Agrippa's *Of Occult Philosophy* (*De occulta philosophia*) for the ridiculous price of £5 at a flea market and later offered it to the British Library. Gaia Shaw has extensively studied Jarman's private library, and in her work *Queer Gravity* she notes that at that time he was also fascinated with emblem books from the same period: 'Their linear, black and white illustrations were available to the literate and illiterate middle classes, and the books were popular for their educational value. Emblems were visual representations that stood for associated ideas. The emblem unifies for us themes of pictures, alchemy and writing, and thus the public theatre where emblems were important to enriched imagery and poetic language.'[209]

The signs and symbols of alchemy and magic used by Jarman in his works are also to be read in this sense: as elements expanding his own poetic and metaphoric idiom. Jarman, who acquired substantial knowledge in this area through his years of studying these writings, is interested not in a precise filmic realisation of magical and alchemical ideas and theories but in their visual and aesthetic components, which could enrich and expand the realisation of his own ideas and visions. Or as Tony Rayns expresses it in his essay 'Credo of a Voyeur': 'He is not interested in the para-scientific aspects of alchemy, instead, he uses its language and symbols for his own romantic rhetoric.'[210]

It is not the individual images of his films that are to be read or deciphered primarily in terms of a magical, alchemical symbolic language. Instead, for Jarman, the process of filming became in itself an alchemical binding of light and material, whose results could be just as unpredictable and surprising as those appearing during the alchemical search for gold. In *Dancing Ledge* he writes: 'Film is the wedding of light and matter – an alchemical conjunction.' Later he also extended this connection, progressing from the original initial bond that emerges during filming to that involved in projection, in which light once again enters into a bond with the material of film: 'John Dee was involved in alchemy, and I once wrote that the cinema was the wedding of light and matter. I mean the film is matter and the light in the projector ... And it's an alchemical wedding in a sense as the joining of earth and fire. Water is not there, but it is an alchemical conjunction in its own way and I saw these parallels.'[211] This was a bond whose results he further transformed in his Super 8 films through the rerecording of images and their repeated refilming.

Theme 4: Portraits

It is above all the short Super 8 portraits of artist friends, such as Andrew Logan (ANDREW LOGAN KISSES THE GLITTERATI, 1972), Christopher
Hobbs (TAROT, 1972) or Duggie Fields (DUGGIE FIELDS, 1975/76), that can
be associated with this thematic area, but it also includes films like PIRATE
TAPE (1982), about the American writer William S. Burroughs. While the
images of the spontaneous and improvised recordings for PIRATE TAPE display
a great deal of restlessness and dynamism, the first three films are characterised altogether by planned and structured recordings, whose images appear
tableau-like and static: 'During the seventies I made a whole series of small
Super-8's of artist's studios. Duggie's was just one of them. I did Andrew's and
also Christopher Hobbs' [...]. I thought this one [DUGGIE FIELDS] is probably
one of the most interesting of them. I tried to make it as static as the paintings
were, in fact that the images of life fused with the images on the paintings as
much as possible. That was very easy because Duggie's room was so spectacu-
larly designed, it seemed like an extension of his work.'[212]

In 1972 Jarman shot the eight-minute film ANDREW LOGAN KISSES THE
GLITTERATI in Logan's studio. The artist's friends, including Gerlinda von Regensburg and Peter Schlesinger (the lover of David Hockney), stage a camp
revue of kisses in hilarious costumes and eccentric drag. Deliberately played
into the camera and filmed from static positions, each in a single shot, the
performers outdo one another with their exaggerated poses and theatrical gestures. The monotone, detached voice of Lou Reed in his song 'The Kids'
contrasts with the staged drama of the situation. The costumes as well as the
irony of the performance evocatively represent a celebrated atmosphere of the
seventies: camp and drag. It is to be remembered that 'drag' sought to also
be understood above all as a political statement at that time, and that it was
utilised within the emancipatory gay movement as a provocation against the
heterosexist normative world: 'Drag, radical drag. In the early seventies, we
celebrated the trannies of Stonewall. We all got into dresses. Good ones were
so cheap then: Balenciaga or Dior for less than a fiver. As Mrs. Hippy, a southern belle, I didn't get very far, but the dress gave me confidence and two years
later I won the Alternative Miss World.'[213]

The first of the Alternative Miss World Parties, which Jarman mentions
here and which have since become legendary, also took place in 1972 and
ANDREW LOGAN KISSES THE GLITTERATI is to be seen above all within the
context of this event initiated by Logan. Alternative Miss World seeks to persuade contestants of both sexes and from all age groups, including hopeful
talents, celebrated public figures and unknown individuals to create fanciful
outfits and to present themselves to the audience in them. The competitions
still continue to be held at irregular intervals lasting several years and generally

at unusual locations. Each of them is given a specific theme and the contest has already secured an established place for itself in the London avant-garde fashion scene and underground culture. As a sculptor, Logan looks at his parties 'like a very large piece of sculpture ... a surreal art event.'[214] Jarman, who took part in the competition as Miss Crepe Suzette, won in 1975 and captured the event on Super 8 in his film ANDREW LOGAN'S ALTERNATIVE MISS WORLD (contained in GLITTERBUG): 'March 1975, Butlers Wharf: Keith dyes my hair primrose with a black triangle at the back; it's very short, a crew cut. I've a massive wardrobe of costumes from the Super 8s, including the silver diamanté dress from IN THE SHADOW OF THE SUN and a troubadour dress and armour from the film we made last summer at Corfe. I have a head-dress made from a green rubber frog, with pearls and lashings of ruby and diamanté drops. This time I'm going to win. [...] In a brief speech as reigning Miss World, I offer my services formally to close bankrupt British industries in the coming year, by tying them up with pink ribbon.'[215]

The film DUGGIE FIELDS was created three years later and it is comparable to ANDREW LOGAN KISSES THE GLITTERATI in terms of the manner of its shooting. In keeping with the aspiration formulated above – according to which Jarman wished to use the recordings to more intimately grasp the static character of Fields's paintings – he again shoots the film in distinct, very calm shots from fixed camera positions, although he uses single frame and slow down instead of normal speed. However, the familiar effect resulting from this is scarcely perceptible in DUGGIE FIELDS, because only occasional and very limited motion occurs. Both films are in colour and the Rolling Stones song 'You Can't Always Get What You Want' was added to DUGGIE FIELDS after shooting. Recorded in Duggie Fields's studio, the primary focus is on the works of the London Pop Artist: his paintings, collages, sculptures and objects. What we see are works of bold Pop Art – full of quotations or ironical inscriptions (for example, the caption 'hand-painted'), 'revised' works of Classical Modernism and Surrealism (Mondrian and Dalí) incorporated in a quotation-like manner, and collages of playing cards and pin-up photos from magazines of the fifties and sixties – but also sculptures and everyday objects, such as ashtrays. Duggie Fields himself is present only for brief moments and in immediate proximity to his works. Jarman has integrated him subtly, statically posing in and around his own art.

In September of 1982 William S. Burroughs, whose work *Naked Lunch* was still banned in England during the sixties, came to London for the event 'The Final Academy', organised by the B2 Gallery. Jarman and Genesis P-Orridge – performer and musician from Throbbing Gristle and Psychic TV, among other groups – collected Burroughs at Heathrow Airport, and Jarman began to film Burroughs during the taxi journey to London. Over the next few days he and his Super 8 camera followed 'everyone's literary big daddy',[216] a name Jarman also used for the established cult author, as he made his way through London and during his public readings. The images of the resulting film, Pirate Tape (W. S. Burroughs), were shot in colour and single frame/ slow motion and differ from the two previously discussed portrait films for a number of reasons. On the one hand, unlike Logan or Fields, Burroughs was not a part of Jarman's closer circle of friends and was instead admired by Jarman because of his literary works. On the other hand, Pirate Tape is once again shot with Jarman's characteristic home-movie aesthetic, featuring images that slowly and gradually merge into one another. No staged settings and no scenes deliberately played into the camera are to be found here, instead, Jarman tries to use his gaze through the camera to gain a – vague and simultaneously very subtle – closer grasp of the person to be portrayed. The progress of this approach is very slow and, to the same extent, the person of Burroughs stands in the foreground and is the focal point.

To be precise the film consists of two parts: the first part shows Burroughs during his arrival in London and during his tours through the city. In an endless loop his hoarse voice constantly repeats the text 'Boys, school-showers and swimming-pools full of them', underlaid with the industrial music of Genesis P-Orridge (Psychic TV). In *Dancing Ledge* Jarman describes Burroughs as an eccentric, unapproachable and even directly stand-offish figure, with whom it was impossible to have a conversation: 'WSB emerges tortoise-like to greet his audience. He stoops like a cadaver in the catacombs of Palermo and talks of mummies and immortality. To speak to him is almost impossible, as he is always on the move in little erratic circles. At rest he retires into himself and puts out a signal, "Leave me alone".'[217]

The images of Pirate Tape represent precisely this unapproachability and aloofness: after Burroughs exits the taxi, for the first few minutes of the film his silhouette appears only in fragmentary form among other passers-by or is overlaid with multiple other images that are almost completely disintegrated and now consist only of their coloured textures. It is only after half of this first part that the images of him increasingly become more concrete and the figure of this old man with a cane, who appears somewhat lost and gives passers-by his autograph, shifts more visibly into the foreground. The first part ends with a close-up of Burroughs swinging his cane and attempting to cross a street. The second part of the film is very short. Following a black screen that lasts several frames, it begins with a new piece of music by Psychic TV, but without spoken text. The transition from the first part is formed by a close-up. Fading in out of the bright light of a spotlight, it shows Burroughs for just under two minutes during one of his public readings in London. Filmed against the light of the spotlight in a profile close-up seen from the left and from behind, we see him bent over one of his texts while reading. And although it is filmed from extremely close-up, the glaring backlight and the melodious, monotone music make him appear as unapproachable and distant as during his walks through the bustling streets of London. This very personal way of more closely grasping Burroughs and the mysterious and enigmatic aura that he had skilfully built up and maintained over the years is also to be found in a nuanced form in Jarman's other portrait films: they are never concretely biographical and factual but, instead, always diffusely fragmentary and personal. Developed out of highly specific and very immediately present life contexts that always also stand in contact with those of Jarman, they all seem to fulfil – in a figurative sense – that aspiration expressed during his work on DUGGIE FIELDS, 'that the images of life fused with the images on the paintings as much as possible.'[218]

Theme 5: Music

In the mid-eighties Jarman began to shoot music videos for songs by the Pet Shop Boys (incl. 'It's a Sin', 'Rent' and 'Being Boring') and The Smiths (incl. 'The Queen Is Dead' and 'Panic'). However, it was less a personal interest in also working in the area of music promotion than primarily financial reasons that led him to do so. The strict demands of the music industry regarding image, running time, sequences of cuts and the number of cuts felt just as limiting to him as the extensive technical complexities bound up with a production of this kind. Here again, Jarman was interested above all in the subject of the depiction, in the people in front of the camera and in the appropriate possibilities for them in the performance that he was attempting to organise.

However, he began to become particularly fascinated with the almost endless possibilities offered by the editing and processing of video material and, in this context, especially by the transfer of Super 8 material to video, its further editing in this medium and its retransfer back to 16 mm or 35 mm film. He compares the colour palettes of video editing programs with the palettes of a painter. They enabled him to achieve new, seemingly unlimited forms of colour definition and superimposing images: 'By the early '80s it was possible to transfer Super 8 footage to highband, edit in video, and re-transfer the lot back to 35 mm film, the gauge of the feature. You could achieve effects on video which would have cost a fortune on film, and all the time the technology was improving; it was impossible to tell now if the image on your TV was generated in Super 8. Blown up to 35 mm, the quality is something quite new, like stained glass, the film glows with wonderful colours. The video gives you a palette like a painter, and I find the result beautiful.'[219] Music functioned, so to speak, as a medium for transitioning between his Super 8 material, video and film. Jarman transferred the technique of video processing into the realm of film, and in THE LAST OF ENGLAND and THE GARDEN it became the central form of editing the images and the dominant aesthetic component. On the other hand, projections of his early home movies shown at live concerts of the Pet Shop Boys had also led him to pursue attempts to link some of the early home movies (STUDIO BANKSIDE and A GARDEN IN LUXOR) – in an unmodified form and without any additional processing – with songs by the Pet Shop Boys ('Being Boring' and 'Violence') in the form of music videos.

Separately from this, Jarman had already shot several independent short music films with his Super 8 camera in the early eighties, that is, several years before his later involvement with the field of music videos. These had then been transferred to 16 mm or 35 mm film. BROKEN ENGLISH: THREE SONGS BY MARIANNE FAITHFULL (1979) and T.G. PSYCHIC RALLY IN HEAVEN (1980/81) are among the home-movie and Super 8 films that I would like to classify among and subsequently discuss as part of this fifth area of 'music'.

On 23 December 1980 the group Throbbing Gristle could be seen and heard at the London disco Heaven with their experimental, electronic tapestries of sound. The year before, Throbbing Gristle had produced the soundtrack for Jarman's Film IN THE SHADOW OF THE SUN and Jarman, who had already been interested in the industrial music of Genesis P-Orridge, Psychic TV and Throbbing Gristle for several years, filmed their performance that evening with his Super 8 camera. Because the group's stage presence was very static, he tried to use camera movements to generate dynamic sequences of images: 'I threw the old Nizo Super 8 about in time to the music, at "stop frame". The band is restrained, almost static on stage. Genesis P. Orridge stands on the spot in his combat-grey; Peter Christopherson adjusts the controls, twiddling a few knobs here and there.'[220] Using his now proven technique, Jarman once again repeatedly refilmed the material recorded using single-frame exposure and added audio to it in the form of three pieces of music ('Slug Bait – Brighton', 'Maggot Death – Studio', 'Maggot Death – Rat Club') from Throbbing Gristle's first LP, *2nd Annual Report*, released in 1977.

Jarman himself sees this film as marking his arrival at an end point on his filmic Super 8 expedition, as he states in *Dancing Ledge*: 'This work takes experiments with superimposition and refilming, begun in 1972 with IN THE SHADOW OF THE SUN, as far as I can go.' And T.G. PSYCHIC RALLY IN HEAVEN genuinely does resemble an atomisation of images: there are almost no more objectified entities. Recognisable, identifiable and interpretable images and sequences are broken up into rhythmically pulsating textures of colour immediately after they emerge. They fall apart, dissolve and merge together with images laid (layered) above and below them, whose textures do not seem any less abstract. Jarman has negated the static quality of the stage show through the movement of the camera. Through the intensive processing of the film material he has drawn closer to the atonal, associative sound formations of Throbbing Gristle in a form whose individual visualisation of the sound seeks to merge the tones and the images together on a common level. Within the rapid succession of light and dark, rhythmic flashes and pulsating coloured textures of light and shadow, there are objectified images – like the silhouette of a musician or his face – that briefly emerge for a few moments at irregular intervals, only to immediately be swallowed up once more by the pulsating textures of colour. The group's performance recedes entirely into the background, and the transposition of T.G.'s tones and sequences of tones into images is emotional and of the same genius as their source. In the description of Steve Jenkins: '[...] the film's visual surface appears to bleep, moan and pulse along with its soundtrack. This denial of the visual pleasure afforded by most concert films – a privileged view of the stars – in turn draws attention to the soundtrack's content. "Music" vanishes, replaced by a mutant collage of sounds [...].'[221]

The film BROKEN ENGLISH: THREE SONGS BY MARIANNE FAITHFULL was created one year earlier. To be precise, the film actually consists of three independent films that merge seamlessly into one another, each of them accompanying a song by Marianne Faithfull: 'Witches Song', 'The Ballad of Lucy Jordan' and 'Broken English'. Neither the music nor its filmic transposition could stand in greater contrast to T.G. PSYCHIC RALLY. Some of the sequences to the Marianne Faithfull songs appear to be just as concrete as the images to the music of Throbbing Gristle are abstract. Nonetheless, the images here also attempt to directly – in some cases perhaps somewhat too directly – convey the individual musical intentions: these very concrete stories have been translated into images that are equally concrete and also narrative. This has sometimes earned Jarman criticism and the accusation that he offers viewers a series of déjà-vu experiences by means of relatively trivial posturing. In a critique for the BFI *Film Bulletin*, Cynthia Rose writes: 'The main fault of Derek Jarman's film is its uninventive reliance on a more or less explicit translation of the lyrics to screen images in all three songs. [...] Though the editing is fast and slick, this approach brings nothing new to the music; rather, it makes the simplicity of the lyrics seem pedestrian.'[222] And links of word and image as direct as, for example, the appearance of the fire coinciding with the word 'fire' in 'Witches Song' or the orange tinting of the film images to the words 'the world turned to orange' in 'The Ballad of Lucy Jordan' do in fact seem somewhat lacking in fantasy. Still, this was a common and oft-used stylistic device in the early days of music-video production, and its purpose was to help the publicised song to achieve a greater degree of recognisability through such extremely direct text-image associations. However, precisely in the context of Jarman's works, it is in fact surprising to suddenly find such concrete links between text and image. Particularly in THE BALLAD OF LUCY JORDAN the room provided for free association and interpretation seems extremely limited, because instead of opening up the text, the images attempt to illustrate and comment upon it.

However, in BROKEN ENGLISH and WITCHES SONG I feel that associative and indirect elements dominate: the visual compositions develop freely and are substantially less strictly linked to the given text.

WITCHES SONG is shot in colour and black and white at normal filming speed, and aesthetically it is the video which is most strongly based on Jarman's earlier Super 8 films. It contains elements – like the experimentation with sunlight reflecting in a mirror, the man with the paper mask, several protagonists wearing artistic masks and a 'magical dance' around a campfire – which are already familiar from JORDAN'S DANCE, THE ART OF MIRRORS and IN THE SHADOW OF THE SUN and are placed within a new context here. But the main shooting location, the Surrey Docks, is itself a wasted industrial landscape in the Docklands that recalls similar settings from earlier Super 8 films. The film is introduced by black-and-white footage and it is rung in with the sounds of church bells: St Paul's Cathedral, Marianne Faithfull walking through the streets of London, a man dressed in black with a paper mask stepping in front of her and leading her into another world of colour and – simultaneously – a world of magic. Creatures wearing carnivalesque make-up or masks and dressed in fanciful costumes reflect the sunlight in circular mirrors and welcome her to a dance together around a large, roaring fire. Here again, fire is a central element and is shot in close-up, in between there is the man with the paper mask observing the situation. The dance develops into a ritual reminiscent of a wedding: a priest blesses a couple, they place rings on one another's fingers, the couple kisses and begins to make love in the light of the flames. They are watched by the masked figure, who is surrounded by the other figures, some of whom are allegorical, such as Death or the Devil. Gradually everyone involved leaves the place where these events occur and, with the last bars of 'Witches Song', the first images to 'The Ballad of Lucy Jordan' begin.

Of the three films, this is the one that most immediately and directly transposes the lyrics into corresponding images illustrating the content. The images are in black and white with a handful of inserted shots either recorded in colour or tinted after being recorded. Marianne Faithfull strolls through the streets of London. Her face is lit with glaring light and she seems absent-minded and lost in thought. The first melancholy bars of 'The Ballad of Lucy Jordan' begin, occasionally overlaid with the noise of traffic, children's voices and other sounds. She lets everything go on around her, and in her mind she reviews bygone years. As a kind of 'flashback', the following images that are inserted and superimposed directly illustrate the thoughts formulated in the song's lyrics. However, in this context it is interesting that this directness of the 'narrative' still remains intact despite the many multiple superimpositions of the film's images, which seem to merge into one another much like a collage. The use of this technique is incapable or scarcely capable of opening up room for independent associations in this film: second for second, often bar by bar, the corresponding images are made to accompany the concrete passages in the lyrics in such a way that the room which the superimpositions open up for viewers' own associative images and connections are immediately negated again and the potential room for freedom provided by the dissolves becomes nothing more than a seamless transition. The melodrama already present within the lyrics of this ballad about the seemingly wasted life of a 37-year-old woman evaluating her past invests the absence of a corresponding abstraction in the song's visual transposition with still more force. The ballad ends with an instrumental conclusion and Marianne Faithfull finds herself on Piccadilly Circus, at the foot of the statue of Eros: she circles around it and a close-up of Eros forms the transition to the third and final song.

'"Broken English" is the most successful of the three songs. We used old footage of Stalin and Hitler, cut together so that they smile and wave to each other in a ballet of destruction. There's footage of Mosley, and video material that the Oval Co-op have given me of the police at Lewisham. The film starts with the Bikini H-bomb explosion monitored on a space-invaders machine; and ends with the destruction in slow motion of the huge concrete swastika that crowned the Nuremberg stadium.'[223] In complete contrast to the soft transitions and dissolves in THE BALLAD OF LUCY JORDAN, BROKEN ENGLISH is characterised by hard cuts and the deliberate juxtaposition of very different visual material. Here Jarman uses original material from newsreels and wartime documentary footage, and he mounts the images of military parades, mass unrest, battle scenes, streams of refugees and book burnings alongside those of Hitler, Stalin, flags with swastikas and demonstrations of the radical-right British National Front to form a brutal collage. On an associative level, this massive confrontation within the visual material leads to new connections, whose semantic significances can be reminiscent of John Heartfield's political collages in terms of their subversive effect. In both cases the intended messages are provided with their radicalism and draw the necessary attention to themselves through the element of 'shock', which is created through the combination of radical opposites. Introduced by the atom-bomb explosion, in BROKEN ENGLISH the madness of the images of feverish violence is further intensified through the inserted shots of a rock 'n' roll dance contest, and they find their apocalyptic conclusion in the explosion of the swastika on the stadium. In between, overlaid with the marching little monitor men of a Space Invaders arcade game, we repeatedly see a close-up of Marianne Faithfull, her monotonous voice demanding: 'Don't say it in Russian, don't say it in German, say it in broken English ...'

Although it may not become obvious upon first viewing the film, in BROKEN ENGLISH: THREE SONGS BY MARIANNE FAITHFULL Jarman has succeeded in not only arranging three thematically very different songs into a sequence but also in uniting them into a whole through the figure of Marianne Faithfull. Her walk through London, from St Paul's to the Statue of Eros on Piccadilly Circus and finally on to the amusement arcade, provides the framework and the moments linking the individual videos. This journey carries her off into the world of her own songs and subtly attempts to take the viewer with her.

[6]

'Cinema of Small Gestures': Super 8 as Feature Film

THE AESTHETIC RESULTS THAT Jarman was able to achieve with his home movies and short Super 8 films form the foundation and point of departure for his efforts to further expand and intensify his exploration of this medium. The freedoms opened up during the filmic process and through the extremely limited financial demands of production provided ideal conditions for him to continue with this work and to further pursue his ideas about developing the Super 8 format into a recognised professional medium within the field of film. Jarman's attempt to create moving images with a minimum of technical, organisational and financial requirements is somewhat reminiscent of Jean Cocteau's emancipatory demand that film 'will only become an art when its materials are as inexpensive as pencil and paper', thus simultaneously liberating it from the covert censorship of material constraints and restrictions.

In numerous essays and notes Cocteau deals with the theme of the material and institutional constraints to which film productions are generally subject and also with their rules, which repeatedly and strongly limit experimentation and creativity. He had already formulated his concept of free and artistically self-determined work on film decades before the introduction of the Super 8 format. In this context he had also pointed out the potential of a less expensive medium – in his case, the 16 mm format – which could enable young, still-unknown film-makers to realise their own plans and experiments with greater autonomy and without concern for the demands of the market. No one 'in 1948 would pay out an amount equivalent to that million francs, to let a young film-maker do what he wished, without any material, artistic or moral constraint [...] In my view, 16mm film is the only means of solving the problem [...].' And many details in the accounts of his own improvisational way of working with this medium display parallels to that of Jarman: 'When I use it, 16mm film, which I have just shot in my garden, takes things to extremes. Liberated from any material considerations, since I was using Kodak reversible film and since what normally amounts to five million francs cost me five thousand, I made a film which was not in the slightest a film. I invented it as I went along, improvising minute by minute and using the people who happened to be spending Sunday with me in the country as actors. The result was a series of fairly ridiculous, and unusable scenes; yet this complete freedom to say whatever came into my head gave them a power that would be impossible to obtain if it were a question of bankrupting a film company.'[224]

These were among the reasons why Super 8 film established itself in the sixties and seventies – particularly in the areas of experimental and avant-garde film – as the most common and popular format. However, most of the works created are short films. By contrast Jarman's idea was to further extend the possibilities of this format of the artistic realm in the direction of feature films, also in terms of approaching their running times. This preceded other similar efforts in an entirely different area, namely, that of the Cinéma Vérité. This term was coined by Edgar Morin and Jean Rouch to refer to a specific style of documentary film in which the interview format is a central element and production is based on the use of light and flexible film equipment by a usually two-person crew for camera and sound. In her essay 'Promiscuous 8' Laura Hudson points out that Super 8 combined with audio could provide the ideal conditions for developing a cinema that might come closest to those ideas formulated in Cinéma Vérité. Richard Leacock was a pioneer of Cinéma Vérité, and he had already worked together with the Scottish documentary film-maker Ruby Grierson in the thirties. In the sixties, together with other well-known film-makers like Jean Rouch and Chris Marker, he undertook an attempt to establish Super 8 as a viable alternative in the practice of documentary film. However, the format never became generally accepted – aside from a few exceptions, such as the American documentary film-maker Bill Stamets, who saw Super 8 as the only possibility for developing the subjective components of a documentary film and creating a 'personal vérité'. The reasons for this lack of acceptance are similar to those in the case of fictional and feature films: '[...] the lack of serious consideration by curators, theorists, teachers and audiences and the current difficulties in distributing and exhibiting 8 mm exclude it from any place in the media dialogue. Few filmmakers work exclusively in 8 mm however. What 8 mm has, above all other amateur formats, is the possibilities to be incorporated into any other media. It is infused with a promiscuous nature which has the ability to transcend the limitations imposed upon it.'[225]

Cinéma Vérité was concerned above all with the simplicity and directness of the filmic process and a theoretical and practical investigation of the reproduction and documentation of categories like 'reality' and 'truth'. By contrast Jarman's claims upon this format were primarily related to his striving for independence and autonomy in his working process, a demand that in his case (as in that of Cocteau) derived from the way in which he worked as a fine artist, specifically as a painter. On an aesthetic level it was precisely the 8 mm format's 'promiscuous nature' – as Hudson has so aptly characterised this material's openness to further processing – with which Jarman began to experiment on many levels. As described above, the superimpositions and transformations of images in his earliest Super 8 films and the 'cinema of small gestures' are characterised above all through refilming by means of a Super 8 camera and through a subsequent transfer to the 'presentation formats' of 16 mm and 35 mm. In his later films THE LAST OF ENGLAND and THE GARDEN, which grew out of the concept of the 'cinema of small gestures', he pushes this 'promiscuity' in the form of multiple material metamorphoses even further, apparently to its absolute limits: the material shot on Super 8 is transformed on video, digitally edited and finally transferred to 35 mm. The boundaries are blurred and have become nearly invisible. It is primarily the following films that are subsumed under Jarman's 'cinema of small gestures':

- IN THE SHADOW OF THE SUN,
- THE ANGELIC CONVERSATION and
- IMAGINING OCTOBER.

The first two will be discussed in detail in the course of this chapter. The impulses behind their creation have private dimensions comparable to those of his home movies and short Super 8 films. In the case of IN THE SHADOW OF THE SUN these largely take the form of fragments and parts of earlier home movies. The origins of THE ANGELIC CONVERSATION lie in a weekend excursion to the County of Dorset with two friends ('Family life') and IMAGINING OCTOBER was created during a stay in the Soviet Union ('Journey'). At the level of content, the images of these Super 8 films have – sometimes radically – cast aside the innocence of his early, personal home movies by evoking direct associations of varying intensity with themes like sexuality, violence and power. Through their handling of these themes they also open up a level that is political (understood in a broader sense). Subject matters that had already been omnipresent since 1976 in his feature films SEBASTIANE, JUBILEE and THE TEMPEST are now also clearly formulated and become directly visible on Super 8 film in the 'cinema of small gestures'.

On a technical level, Jarman's 'cinema of small gestures' continues, further develops and links together all of those techniques that he had examined in his short Super 8 films: the single-frame technique, the slow-down effect, refilming and repeatedly refilming visual material, double and multiple exposures and the use of coloured filters (see pp. 124 ff.). However, the slowing of the sequences of images brought about through the combination of single frame and slow down does more than just relativise the seemingly objective sense of time and its progression: the impression of segmentation that is created in the process very consciously draws viewers' attention to each individual gesture and to otherwise imperceptible details. The space opened up by the interruption renders their history visible – their inherently passing nature and the way in which they immediately become past. For viewers, who thus find themselves in the role of secret observers, they are made sensible, tangible: 'The single frame makes for extreme attention, a concentration that is voyeuristic. Time seems suspended. The slightest movement is amplified. This is the reason I call it "a cinema of small gestures".'[226]

The rhythmically pulsating images merge into one another and are repeatedly overlaid with other images, sometimes multiple images. Jarman once referred to the sound collages in THE LAST OF ENGLAND as a palimpsest.[227] This term is borrowed from the Greek and essentially means 'scraped off again' – referring to ancient and medieval manuscripts on which the original texts have been removed through washing or erasing and then replaced by newer texts. Today a palimpsest's layers of writing can again be deciphered by means of fluorescence photography. The term palimpsest can be very aptly applied to the superimposed images of Jarman's films, which are created through multiple exposures and refilming. It is able to provide a more concrete designation for the results than the terms collage or assemblage, which are derived from fine art: the individual visual layers of these films can no longer be specifically distinguished or identified, instead, they permeate one another. The filmic images display a transparent character that is similar to that of superimposed tones and sounds. They are not mounted above and next to one another and they do not cover each other, instead, they always maintain that transparency which permits traces of 'what lies beneath' to be revealed.

At that time Jarman seemed convinced that he would be able to contribute to a repositioning of the medium of Super 8 film at the level of a professional film format by focusedly continuing with this work and testing and exploiting the possibilities which opened up. Thus, in a handwritten note referring to his two films IN THE SHADOW OF THE SUN and PSYCHIC RALLY IN HEAVEN, he remarks: 'These films are a small part of a much larger body of work in Super 8, which James [Mackay's] Dark Pictures is gradually going to make available in 16 mm during the next few years, as funds become available. The future of Super 8 is enormous. The effects of IN THE SHADOW OF THE SUN for instance cost £100 and are unrealizable on large gauges. The cameras are now much more sophisticated than the Nizo 480 which was used for these early films [...] S-8 translates ideally into video – At the moment the problem with S-8 distribution is the lack of sophisticated modern equipment in universities & regional cinemas. If this was remedied the necessity to blow the films up for institutions would disappear.'[228] At the same time, however, it was also clear that the 'cinema of small gestures' would always remain a small-scale cinema. Regarding his feature films, his audience's continuous interest in them was more important to him than a one-off commercial success that would allow a film to just as rapidly disappear into oblivion. In the same sense, he wanted to appeal to small circles of viewers in small cinemas with his Super 8 films and the 'cinema of small gestures', in the manner of a travelling exhibition: 'I like it best when they are shown in a small auditorium to a small, intimate audience. You don't enjoy a sunset accompanied by a whole crowd either.'[229]

In the Shadow of the Sun

In the Shadow of the Sun is the first project in this series of 'sunsets' in Jarman's 'cinema of small gestures'. It is impossible to identify a precise point in time when this film, which was originally entitled English Apocalypse, was made. Instead, it was a work in progress that went on for several years and began in 1972, during a journey to the megaliths at Avebury. In addition to images from Journey to Avebury, it also contains parts of the films Garden of Luxor and Tarot (The Magician), which were also shot in 1972. Jarman recorded the majority of the film in 1973, and it is present within The Art of Mirrors as an independent work. One year later, during his stay in America, Jarman finally created the last images for it on Fire Island, although only a small portion of these are taken from his film of that name. He subsequently used his Nizo 480 to refilm the images of the different Super 8 films, which were projected on top of one another with two projectors; in doing so, he experimented with a series of filters in various colours.

The first public screening of In the Shadow of the Sun was held in the mid seventies at London's ICA. Finally, in 1980, it became possible to present the film to a larger audience during its screening at the Berlinale. However, Jarman was faced with the problem that much of the film had suffered quite a lot in the course of its frequent playing during previous years, and transferring it to a new copy by means of an optical printer was beyond his means at that time. Nonetheless, through the intervention of the Internationales Forum des Jungen Films and the support of the Freunde der Deutschen Kinemathek – that is, the Berlinale forum and the friends of the German film museum in Berlin – it became possible to rescue the copies and to transfer the entire film on to a 16 mm copy. During screenings of his Super 8 films, Jarman usually played music cassettes to accompany them, because the films did not have a soundtrack of their own. Thus the Super 8 version of IN THE SHADOW OF THE SUN was originally shown with the music of Berlioz's *Grande Messe des Morts*; when the 16 mm version was created, it could finally be provided with a soundtrack specifically composed for it by Throbbing Gristle.

The Origins of the Images

The superimposed and seemingly interwoven, grainy images and fragments of images are in colour. The original sources of the images are sometimes scarcely identifiable, because of the numerous superimpositions and refilmings. The images are dominated by those characteristic, bold tones of red, orange and violet produced using filters. They were created in combination with the single-frame and slow-down technique, but the differences in their reduced speeds vary to an extent that is sometimes perceptible: with the numerous superimposed layers of images, this opens up new impressions of movement and spatial depth. Jarman borrowed only part of the images of IN THE SHADOW OF THE SUN from previously familiar sequences out of the individual short films mentioned above; he primarily made use of unpublished raw material created while shooting the films. For example, JOURNEY TO AVEBURY consists exclusively of calm, static shots featuring only a handful of very sparingly employed pans and zooms. On the other hand, IN THE SHADOW OF THE SUN presents us largely with dynamic images, which have been filmed with a restless hand-held camera and seem to advance towards or proceed past the eyes of the viewer. The landscape is passed through at a rapid speed and the point of view of the camera is no longer static, but instead constantly changing. Because they sometimes independently progress in entirely different directions, the movement inherent to these images substantially contributes to the film's idiosyncratic effect of space and depth. This idiosyncrasy derives from the fact that both the dimension of space and the sense of depth can never really be delineated, 'got hold of' – instead, they once again find themselves in a state of metamorphosis or dissolution immediately after their apparent formation. It is a transparent and permeable depth that can associatively be best compared with overlapping sounds, which convey this impression of a spherical space without concrete boundaries.

Another repeatedly recurring motif comes from GARDEN OF LUXOR: the Pyramids, which are also superimposed with other motifs. What is remarkable about these sequences is that they already consist of superimpositions of multiple 'visual layers' in GARDEN OF LUXOR, and in IN THE SHADOW OF THE SUN they are once again fragmentarily interwoven with additional images.

The only film that Jarman shot explicitly in preparation for IN THE SHA-
DOW OF THE SUN is TAROT (also known under the title THE MAGICIAN). Christopher Hobbs, who did the sets for many of Jarman's Super 8 and feature films,
plays the role of a magician and is filmed in his small rented room in Islington,
which – according to Jarman – represented a little *Gesamtkunstwerk*: 'He lived
in one room of trompe l'œil grandeur in a decayed terrace house in Islington,
where the water splashed through the rafters and the garden was overgrown
by an enormous sleeping princess rose bush. We filmed Christopher as the
magician for IN THE SHADOW OF THE SUN in this room, looking like an extra
from IVAN THE TERRIBLE in purple velvet with gold embroidery and a bulky
fur collar among his crystal cabinets and seventeenth-century hangings.'[230]
Finally, another short sequence of outside shots filmed in the same year, on the
terrace next to Butler's Wharf, was inserted in between this footage, and parts
of this are also to be found once more in IN THE SHADOW OF THE SUN. TAROT
is surely the Jarman film that features the most explicit allusions and references to magic and occultism; nonetheless – not least on account of Hobbs's
opulent appearance – the impression that it leaves behind is a rather camp one
with an ironic wink. It is only with its processing and superimposition for IN
THE SHADOW OF THE SUN that the footage achieves its metamorphosis from
staged hocus-pocus into more penetrating, enigmatic and mystical images. All
too 'representational' visual messages – like the sequences in which Hobbs lays
out the tarot cards, opens a mysterious little box with an old key, conjures up a
rising cloud of white smoke by clapping his hands together or passes through
and illuminates the room with an old seven-branched candelabrum in his
hand – are deconstructed. The material is integrated into the 'alchemical' process of the film's creation, overlaid with images from FIRE ISLAND or THE ART
OF MIRRORS and fused into a new collective image that seems to repeatedly
rearrange itself, like the constantly changing images of a kaleidoscope.

THE ART OF MIRRORS was completed in 1973; while it was not specifically
shot in preparation for IN THE SHADOW OF THE SUN, a substantial portion of
its images have become a part of it. As described above (see pp. 145 ff.), THE
ART OF MIRRORS is the first film in which Jarman deliberately experiments with
randomly created combinations of images. It is the first film on Super 8 that
he could no longer compare with any of his other works, because – through his
experiments with coloured filters and the repeated refilming – he had caused
something 'entirely new' (Jarman) to emerge in an unpredictable manner. In
this sense, the film is certainly to be understood in terms of a preparatory
work for IN THE SHADOW OF THE SUN. Jarman has adopted the two central
motifs of fire and light from it: the flames – of a bunch of burning roses,
among other things – and the 'magic light' in the form of sunlight reflected in
a mirror. The figure with the paper mask also reappears here: directly before
the fragments from FIRE ISLAND, we see Gerald Incandela passing through an

imaginary space with a mask and mirror. Here the reflections of the mirror are additionally overlaid with roaring flames. Jarman repeatedly takes up the motif of the reflected light that seems to burn a white disc into the images of the film: it is combined with the landscape images from the journey to Avebury and with shots from THE ART OF MIRRORS and from FIRE ISLAND, among other things. An exact distinction is no longer possible: the light emerges from the background and sometimes simultaneously penetrates through the various overlapping and superimposed images. This can also be recognised particularly clearly in the images of Fire Island. The material is not identical with the sequences used in FIRE ISLAND, but it also differs in terms of its aesthetic dimension. The images of the deserted beach and the dune landscapes in FIRE ISLAND are defined by dark and sometimes almost ominous colours. Here, on the other hand – not least because of the superimpositions and the insertion of the white ray of light – bold and glaring colours dominate: in addition to pink and orange, particularly an intense midnight blue and a glowing, fiery red. Additionally, in IN THE SHADOW OF THE SUN it is not Fire Island's significance as a gay meeting place but the unusual name of the island that was decisive for these sequences having found their way into this film. In *Dancing Ledge* Jarman notes: 'I've filmed the final section of IN THE SHADOW OF THE SUN out at Fire Island, more for the name than its reputation [...].'[231]

Silence is Golden

Jarman has divided this film into four sections: 'The first section is based on a journey to the standing stones at Avebury in Wiltshire, coupled with two fire mazes. It contains a man who points, another who takes photos, a third in bondage, and animals – dogs and a sacred cow. There are burning roses which occur throughout the film. The second maze is circular – Ronde de la Mort – in which a couple dances in the flames which devour the whole landscape and the great standing stones. A third and final image of Narcissus, a mirror which flashes the sun into the camera so that the image explodes and reinvents itself in a most mysterious way. [...]

'The second section is an invocation. Black and white masked figures walk through the flames. A magician finds the key to a cabinet of secrets. Now we are in the kingdom of the other sea [...]. Atlas supports the world lost in the galaxies. Dancing at the edge of time. [...]

'The third section contains the typewritten messages. The images are evanescent. [...]

'In the final section the images fade into blank footage where the atoms dance, punctuated by explosions, and a figure listens to a message on a shell:

SLNC
IS
GLDN.'[232]

However, the four-part division that Jarman carries out here is a primarily theoretical one and only very vaguely recognisable in the film, for example, in the images from the journey to Avebury at the beginning or when the 'atoms dance' at the end. All of the other motifs – such as the images of the typewriter, the flames, the burning roses, the masked figures, the circles of flames, the picture of the Pyramids, etc. – cannot really be assigned to the individual sections as independent themes. Instead they can be identified at numerous different points in the film, usually with other motifs superimposed on top of them, and they can no longer be isolated within this collage of images. The theoretical structuring in terms of 'content' has thus once more been undone through the actual montage of images and the superimpositions, and it is ultimately not to be significant for the experience of viewing the film. As previously mentioned, Jarman's reading of C.G. Jung's *Alchemical Studies* was of substantial significance for him in this context and at this time. However, elements of magic or alchemy are to be sought and interpreted not so much directly in the images of the film, but instead in the nature of the film itself – in its material as a complete, aesthetic product. After all, Jarman saw the formation of the images as a kind of alchemical process with a more or less uncertain outcome. Jung's studies were merely the stimulus and the key for the images that Jarman then created: 'Jung's *Alchemical Studies* and *Seven Sermons to the Dead* provided the key to the imagery that I had created quite unconsciously in the preceding months; and also gave me the confidence to allow my dream-images to drift and collide at random.'[233] It is quite true that meaning – in the sense of a specific content, not to mention a 'story' – is not intended here. however, it is no less true that viewers are to permit themselves to become immersed within that 'ambient tapestry of random images' and to combine their own associations into a personal meaning.

At this point, at the latest, it becomes clear that this film's images rigorously resist a content- and narrative-based approach to their understanding. Moments and individual images can be situationally grasped, but when an attempt is made to construct a larger, general 'semantic context' out of them, they disintegrate just as quickly as they had formed before viewers' eyes and in their minds. They can be more closely grasped only by way of a subjective and associative level of interpretation that discerns new connections with each viewing and forms new symbols out of these: 'The film was structured around a series of cryptic phrases which appear briefly in the film as Penny types them with one finger – these are some of them:

SLNC

IS

GLDN.'[234]

However, when viewing the film, even the semantic connections between the sequences of letters pressed on the keyboard of the typewriter cannot be deciphered and remain entirely hidden to viewers. The paraphrase employed by Jarman, 'SLNC IS GLDN', becomes the second part of the saying 'speech is silver, but silence is golden' when its missing vowels are added, and it is able to fittingly represent this claim in IN THE SHADOW OF THE SUN.

Through the absence of the vowels – those central elements needed to invest language with its voice, communicability and tonal individuality – Jarman transforms the phonetic representation of this saying into a pictorial representation. Much like an ideogram, it can only produce meaning again when it is seen as a whole. Looked at individually, they are isolated groups of letters that can no longer be deciphered. Jarman's idiosyncratic adaptation can certainly be interpreted as a direct reference to a questioning of statements produced through writing and language, of the significance associated with them and of their dubious claim to unambiguousness. Indeed, with 'SLNC IS GLDN', a 'cryptic phrase' emerges which realises its own message about remaining silent in a form so rigorous that it silences itself. Jarman has also integrated this phrase into several other works. He begins the script that he published in volume 12 of *Afterimage* for his unrealised film NIJINSKY'S LAST DANCE with the encrypted form of the two combinations of letters 'SLNC GLDN': here the phrase serves as the title and is supplemented by its written-out form.[235] We also find the words 'SILENCE IS GOLDEN' in encrypted form in one of his *Black & Gold Paintings: Silence*, which he created in 1986 (see fig. 32). They are scratched into the layer of paint covering the three black shards of glass which extend outwards from the shattered, gold-coloured plate of glass that forms the background of this three-dimensional combine. In the lower right corner of the work we find a supplementary text, which has also been scratched into the black paint and invites us to grant the visions of our own dreams an appropriate amount of room: 'The dreams that possess you can blossom and bless you.'[236]

The four-part structure outlined by Jarman is scarcely perceptible while watching the film; nonetheless, a compositional division into several succinct sections can be recognised, and it clearly influences viewers' associative experience of the sequences of images. It is primarily two motifs that underlie the superimposed and rapidly changing images and accompany the film over extended stretches: in the first twenty minutes it is the moving images of the landscape footage created while journeying to Avebury. These images' warm tones of yellow and orange are now visible only in the form of frag-

Fig. 32: Derek Jarman, *Silence*, 1986

ments 'interwoven' with other motifs. Not only do they repeatedly overlap with very concrete flame motifs – through their pulsating, warm colours they also themselves produce the impression of roaring flames and firelight, which penetrate through the other seemingly transparent images. It is only for brief moments that the Avebury images can also be recognised without superimposed material, as independent landscape images. These moments of 'pure', original, unedited images are so remarkable because they are framed by the superimposition of a 'magical', very bright and circular area of light, which is created through mirror reflections and which seems to burn through the soft colours in the form of white light. The shots of Fire Island form the second motif, which follows the Avebury images from the middle of the film onwards. In any case this transition is not gradual and is, instead, to be perceived as a definitive break in the film: only the white circle of reflected light, which seems to burn its way into the centre of the images, remains and connects the two parts. The first images of the grass and dune landscape of Fire Island are immersed in a bold red and are linked with a sequence from TAROT. The yellow and orange tones of the Avebury images have disappeared: from now on, glowing tones of red dominate. These derive from the Fire Island material and were produced by means of colour filters. Additional motifs featuring concrete references or allusions to elements of magic or alchemy become visible through the sequences from TAROT, as well as the images of the Pyramids and circles of flames. The last concrete, 'representational' image from IN THE SHADOW OF THE SUN – a figure in a white robe wearing a death's-head mask and slowly turning towards the viewers before the background of the images of the Pyramids – dematerialises. It dissolves into pulsating, grainy and completely abstract textures of colour in dark violet and midnight blue – these are interrupted only for brief moments by whitish grey flashes of light. They are the dark tones of colour from FIRE ISLAND and that fourth and final section described by Jarman, 'where the atoms dance, punctuated by explosions'. But the youth listening to a mysterious message from a seashell has vanished, become invisible:

SLNC
IS
GLDN.

The Angelic Conversation

'Love is too young to know what conscience is,
Yet who knows not conscience is born of love?'[237]

Simultaneously an observation and a question, these lines from Shakespeare's Sonnet 151 reflect upon the relationship between love, innocence and conscience, and we find them placed before the opening images of the film. The Angelic Conversation is a remarkable love story about the searching, meeting and parting of two young men. What makes it so remarkable is that Jarman has succeeded in using the existing visual material to construct a gay love story that, in its lightness and in terms of its self-concept, neither deals with this theme in a problematising light nor situates it within a directly violent context. The film clearly stands far beyond the bounds of that 'tradition' of 'celluloid closet' productions (Vito Russo), which has grown rankly since the invention of film: at best this self-proclaimed moral authority pleads for compassion for homosexual desire, but it generally deals with it judgementally, and in many cases condemns it. Above all, however, this was also one of the first films – apart from the problem-oriented material by gay film-makers of the fifties to the seventies – that was thus able to capture what Jarman referred to as a secure place within a heterosexually dominated and not infrequently heterosexist (filmic) society: 'Gay film-making has often presented itself as a problem which makes it safe in the heterosexual world – "poor things they have such terrible lives". Most of the first gay films were to do with completely thwarted situations e.g. Jean Genet's Chant D'Amour – a perfect image for that period: the 1950s. Films like Sebastiane, Ron Peck's Nighthawks and Taxi zum Klo were all so anguished. I wanted to make a film which didn't have that violence. In a sense the narrative feature films have absorbed the violence. The Super-8 camera allows you to get away from that.'[238]

The Angelic Conversation is a very gentle film. At the same time, however, this is not in order to disregard images of hostility and violence, but in an attempt to clearly position them – in that outside world that actually has and is the problem: through its heterosexual norms. In themselves, the two protagonists' encounters and their developing relationships with one another emerge in complete carefreeness and ease. For this reason, however, a central question emerges all the more forcefully out of the background: Why do these 'poor things [...] have such terrible lives'? However, the search for concrete answers to this question also remains futile. Jarman only counters it with a few images of hope: shrubs blossoming in bright colours, which will someday overgrow the insignias of power and control as well as the repression that go with them.

The History of the Film's Creation

If we take a somewhat closer look at the history of its creation, then THE ANGELIC CONVERSATION is – strictly speaking – a traditional home movie. Its origins lay in an idea that had been present in Jarman's mind for some time: filming a gay love story based around several of Shakespeare's sonnets. The film was to break with that problematic thematic tradition criticised by Jarman and to convey images that are as carefree as they are tender. Jarman developed neither a script nor a general concept for approaching the film. Instead, the film's images were created spontaneously and situationally: here, just as in his short home movies, filming with the Super 8 camera became 'an extension of [...] life'.[239] The two protagonists were not casted actors either, instead, they were – to a certain extent – chance acquaintances whom Jarman had met in London's gay club scene. Jarman had already been noticing the archaeology student Paul Reynolds for some time at various parties, and he spontaneously agreed to Jarman's offer to film him. At that point in time, during the initial recordings with Paul, everything else – the love theme, Shakespeare and the sonnets – was still completely unclear. But then one evening they both met Philip Williamson, the second person involved in the film: '[...] Paul said, "He looks great." I said, "Why don't we put him in the film, shall I go over?" It was a sort of dare! I said "Let's make the film a love story, because then it will be commercial."'[240] Philip was also immediately interested in contributing to a film. In the summer of 1984, during a holiday of several weeks that Jarman spent with the two of them in the County of Dorset, the first shots of Paul and Philip together were finally spontaneously created at Dancing Ledge, a coastal region on the Isle of Purbeck: 'As always, I had my Super 8 camera with me and we played around with it. [...] The boys fell in love during the holiday and asked me to record a love scene with them. I was able to construct a film around this scene, and I had finally found a hook on which I could hang the wonderful sonnets by Shakespeare, *The Angelic Conversations*.'[241] Jarman recorded the central love scenes and the fight scene at home, both in Super 8 and in video; the fight scene (see also pp. 183 f.) was filmed as a single shot. The material with Philip was created on the coast of Dorset, at Winspit and Dancing Ledge, that impressive and simultaneously mysterious coastal landscape where Jarman also shot sequences from JUBILEE and the final scene of THE LAST OF ENGLAND. Most of the material with Paul was recorded on the Isle of Grain, a peninsula to the east of London, at the mouth of the Thames. The shots with Philip at the window of the old house were created at Montacute House, an elegant Elizabethan villa in Somerset.[242]

The images of THE ANGELIC CONVERSATION slowly glide from one to the next and were also created using the combined technique of single frame and slow down, which Jarman had utilised in his early home movies and short

Super 8 films. The sequences in colour are repeatedly interrupted by mono-chrome or black-and-white shots. However, in contrast to Jarman's early home movies, it was now no longer a Super 8 camera but a video camera that was used to refilm the projected images. Jarman subsequently also made use of video technology for editing and for the production of the master tape, as he describes in detail in an interview with Simon Field and Michael O'Pray: 'The film was generated on Super-8 and a VHS video camera linked to a U-matic deck. The Super-8 footage was transferred through that video camera by projection on a wall at about 3 frames per second. The resulting U-matic was time-coded by Research Recordings onto VHS video cassettes. We did a preliminary edit, here in my flat, on VHS with a simple camera, home movie editor with two decks and a television set. We chopped it together. Then using the time-coded VHS we edited the U-matics and put them onto 1 inch tape. That tape became the master tape. This is all silent at this stage. And then the whole thing was transferred to 35 mm film. That's the steps for the image.'[243]

The slow-motion sequences that characterise the entire 78-minute film as-sociatively recall paintings set in motion, the images of a painter. They magic-ally draw the viewer's gaze into the depths of the action and to individual details that often remain unseen and hidden in film images projected in real time. Viewers' eyes, their perception, become increasingly accustomed to the slow motion, and within the film they find themselves in a time that is altered in terms of its structure and significance. As has already been described in the previous chapter (see p. 126), Jarman likens the rhythm of the images pul-sating and advancing from one into the next with the rhythm of a heartbeat. In the process, the relative and relativising aspect of time becomes a central element: '[...] it is like an heartbeat. I think that in that film time actually is suspended, that's why it is so successful.'[244] Through the almost medita-tive state generated by this extended viewing in single frame and slow down, our perception of time and its relationship to movement and plot takes on a different, previously unknown and unaccustomed dimension. The visual dissection of gestures and movements render these visible in the form of small and infinitesimal elements; interstices open up and draw the focus of the gaze to themselves. Those few sequences in the film which are presented to the viewer at normal speed thus appear all the more immediate and, in terms of their visual effect, more forceful – almost violent. These deal with only three motifs: the ablution, brief portions of the wrestling match and the love scenes.

However, it is not just the viewers who set out on a visual voyage of discov-ery while watching THE ANGELIC CONVERSATION, working on this film also became an expedition into unknown territory for Jarman himself. 'I was ex-ploring a landscape I had never seen on film: areas of psyche that hadn't been projected before. I have seen very few films on male love which are gentle, they usually have a violent subtext – the violence you have to traverse before you make peace with yourself. [...] THE ANGELIC CONVERSATION is a journey of discovery, my journey of discovery through the summer of '84.'[245] The point of departure in the history of this film's creation thus consisted of the filmed 'events' and the plan to employ these to realise the idea of making a film related to Shakespeare's sonnets. The actual film finally emerged out of Jarman's sorting through the filmed material. Like the majority of his home movies, it was originally without sound: 'It was really a silent film. All the things that happen in that film were things that happen in "home movies", like down on the beach swimming, walking through the landscape, going to the stately home. [...] The drama is restored by the sonnets.'[246] With regard to its two protagonists, the film remained non-verbal, without dialogue – but nonetheless not silent. The band Coil composed a soundtrack specifically for the film, and the music by Benjamin Britten (the 'Sea Interludes' from *Peter Grimes*) as well as countless sounds from Jarman's archive – such as the constantly recurring ticking of a clock or the rolling of the ocean and crying seagulls, which he recorded while shooting on the coast, among other places – result in a perfect tapestry of sounds added to the images after their filming. Finally Jarman integrated fourteen of Shakespeare's sonnets into this, in the form of the actress Judi Dench's recitation. He initially had all of the sonnets recorded, and he arrived at the final selection for the given passages in the film only while adding the film's soundtrack. The completed version then contained the following sonnets in this order: 57, 90, 43, 53, 148, 126, 29, 94, 30, 55, 27, 61, 56 and 104.[247] With the exception of Sonnet 148, all of the texts in THE ANGELIC CONVERSATION are from that portion of the sonnets addressed to a young man. Jarman has joined the sonnets with the film images into an associative whole. The texts do not provide a commentary on the images, nor do the images illustrate Shakespeare's texts, instead, a network has been created in which all of the elements appear interwoven with one another.

The images of the film were created in improvisation, more or less without a predetermined concept; by contrast, the elements of sound and language were carefully selected and structured. In his article 'Innocence and Experience', Mark Nash ultimately arrives at a very apt characterisation of the associative sequences of images in THE ANGELIC CONVERSATION by grasping the film in terms of a 'meditation': 'THE ANGELIC CONVERSATION is a meditation on passages from Shakespeare's sonnets. It is a meditation on light, cinema, desire, death.'[248]

Shakespeare's Sonnets[249]

As much as Shakespeare's sonnets have already been researched, puzzled over and written about, their background nonetheless remains obscure and uncertain: neither the historical situation within which they were written nor an exact dating of their creation are considered to be even remotely known or proved. In reading the sonnets, of which there are 154, it also becomes apparent that they are evidently not arranged in any planned sequence that could reveal a direct and immediate interconnection between them. The only thematic categories relate to the addressees of the texts: sonnets 1 to 126 address a young man. It is considered probable, but not certain, that only one individual is involved. Sonnets 127 to 154, on the other hand, are addressed to a 'Dark Lady'. Jarman deliberately chose to have the sonnets recited by a female voice, that of Judi Dench, in THE ANGELIC CONVERSATION. On the one hand, this prevented the text from being attributed to one of the two male protagonists as a monologue and, on the other hand, it integrated the element of 'the feminine' into the film: '[...] I wanted a woman's voice so that there was no confusion. If I had used a man's voice it would have seemed that one of the young men was talking about the other. One of them would have had the dominant voice, and I didn't want that to happen, so the voice became that of an observer, leaving the imagery autonomous. It also established the feminine in the film, which otherwise would have been lacking. It completed it.'[250] It may seem problematic to employ the term 'the feminine' in THE ANGELIC CONVERSATION in such a general and indistinct form and as a counterpoint to models of masculinity that have already been deconstructed anyway. Nonetheless, an entirely different association also strikes us in a very immediate manner: the voice of Judi Dench as the representative of the Dark Lady, who remains invisible. It is namely through her presence that the film opens up the wide realm of what fluctuates between the sexes: this is one of the characteristic elements of Shakespeare's sonnets and will be further discussed below. After the film's completion, Jarman has thus enabled viewers to associate one of the two protagonists (namely Philip – through his fan he seems more to occupy the role of an observer) with the Dark Lady of the sonnets and to become her.[251]

Except for Sonnet 148, all of the sonnets in THE ANGELIC CONVERSATION are from the first group. Still, the identities of their addressees are both unknown and uncertain. And finally, the dedication added at the beginning of the sonnets has also provided further material for speculation. Not only is the identity of 'Mr. W.H.' uncertain, this is also true of his role: is he the young man to whom the love poems are dedicated or only a friend who has handed the sonnets on to their publisher? In his foreword to an edition of the sonnets,[252] the writer W.H. Auden sides with the protagonists of the position which assumes that 'Mr. W.H.' is not the addressee but only the individual who passed the sonnets on.

However, at the point where questions about the possible identity of the individuals end, an additional – equally uncertain and in part also questionable – field of speculation begins: that regarding Shakespeare's sexual orientation. After all, he dedicated more than eighty per cent of his love poems to a young man. Aptly and with a somewhat ironic undertone, Auden describes the reactions. While these varied, they were agitated in every case and hysterical in some: 'Confronted with the extremely odd story they tell, with the fact that, in so many of them, Shakespeare addresses a young man in terms of passionate devotion, the sound and sensible citizen, alarmed at the thought that our Top-Bard could have had any experience with which he is unfamiliar, has either been shocked and wished that Shakespeare had never written them, or, in defiance of common sense, tried to persuade himself that Shakespeare was merely expressing in somewhat hyperbolic terms, such as an Elizabethan poet might be expected to use, what any normal man feels for a friend of his own sex. The homosexual reader, on the other hand, determined to secure our Top-Bard as a patron saint of the Homintern, has been uncritically enthusiastic about the first one hundred and twenty-six of the sonnets, and preferred to ignore those to the Dark Lady in which the relationship is unequivocally sexual, and the fact that Shakespeare was a married man and a father.'[253] In recent years the latter reading has, in a certain sense, also found its way into discussions within the fields of gender studies and queer studies. In the course of efforts to break up established categories of sexual desire, the question repeatedly arises in this context: does it make sense to continue to pursue laboured attempts at determining sexual orientation? Furthermore, in Shakespeare's time these had not yet even been given a name or exist in the definitively polarising form of 'heterosexual'–'homosexual' that is familiar to us. As interesting as conjectures of this kind may be for Shakespeare scholarship and historically or biographically oriented works, they are ultimately of very marginal relevance for actual readings of the texts, which permit substantially more multifaceted interpretations and perspectives. Precisely that which is ambivalent, fluctuating between genders, can be experienced in the sonnets in terms of an extension. This extension does not wish to see the subjects of desire immediately, compulsorily and directly divided up among long-familiar categories. It might thus be able to help situate declarations of love like those in the sonnets on a more universal level that would – at some point in our reading – make the explicit question about the object of devotion's gender seem obsolete. Kate Chedgzoy has occupied herself extensively with the question regarding Shakespeare's identities, and in her work *Shakespeare's Queer Children* she finally succinctly summarises the discussion regarding his sexual orientation: 'Perhaps the question that really needs to be asked is not "Was Shakespeare gay?", but rather, "Why do we care whether Shakespeare was gay – what does Shakespeare's sexual identity matter to us?"'[254]

It is under precisely these premises that Jarman's exploration of this material is also to be understood. Entirely in the sense of the 'strategy of naming' discussed in Chapter 2 (see pp. 38 ff.), it was not the explicit question about his sexual orientation that interested Jarman but, instead, the various nuances in homosexual desire's thematisation in Shakespeare's work. In this way, the 'Top-Bard' is removed from his position of unquestionability; at the same time, however, the strategies for the denial and avoidance of taboo thematic areas within the traditional, bourgeois reception of culture are unmasked through the progressive transposition. This is precisely that form of deconstruction which is to be found in Jarman's thematic exploration and reworking of all of his 'classic' themes, from THE TEMPEST to EDWARD II: 'Taking the private world out into the public is all based upon my upbringing as a painter. I reproduce those attitudes within the film. [...] We do have a private world which people don't come into. It comes back to sexuality, which is why it is so important for the films. And that is why there is a tentative attempt to reclaim Shakespeare for a homoerotic tradition. That is my political stance. It's a minority group. It cuts across all political groupings.'[255]

Under Attack

THE ANGELIC CONVERSATION was completed in 1985, exactly in the middle of Margaret Thatcher's second term of office, and the images of the film are to be seen in the immediate context of the period in which they were created. Only a few years after the first cases of Aids in the UK became public (in July of 1982 Terrence Higgins had become the first British person to die of the disease), the UK found itself in a phase of more and more rigid censorship and repressive executive measures and changes to laws. THE ANGELIC CONVERSATION appeared in the midst of a social ice age, whose law-and-order politics brought about the emergence of an emotional vacuum that left no room to breathe for groups and individuals considered undesirable in terms of social policy. Both the perplexity and uncertainty connected with HIV and Aids and the predominantly negative attitude towards homosexuals, who simultaneously represented the 'primary risk group' for the disease, generated an intolerable climate of repression defined by a total lack of perspectives in its early years. Those first years of the Aids crisis – in combination with old-fashioned concepts of morality and anachronistic laws, some of which had their origins in the nineteenth century or earlier – led to occasionally extreme societal reactions towards homosexuals and/or others seen as potential Aids risk groups in the eyes of the general public. Richard Davenport-Hines analyses many of these events in his study *Sex, Death and Punishment*.[256]

Thus in 1985, for example, the Bloomsbury bookshop Gay's the Word faced charges on the basis of a customs act from 1876 (!). In addition to medical books about HIV and erotic literature, the books listed in the process also included works by Jean Genet, Kate Millett, Jean-Paul Sartre, Edmund White, Tennessee Williams and Oscar Wilde. The only common denominator among the books which were seized was their content's connection with homosexuality. HM Customs and Excise considered them to be indecent and the depiction of male nudity inherently obscene. The seizures were not reversed until a year later and only after a determined defence campaign, which pointed out that the charges were in violation of directives of the European Union. Until the seizures were reversed and the charges against Gay's the Word were dropped, all American and Continental gay newspapers and magazines were banned in the UK. At that point in time, it was above all access to the current state of information on the topic of Aids which became significantly restricted in this way.

It was also in 1985 that the Regents Park Clinic, the first private clinic for venereal diseases, planned an advertising campaign in London's taxis. However, the Metropolitan Police allowed this only on the condition that the phrase 'sexually transmitted diseases' be replaced by 'personally transmitted diseases'. They argued that the originally selected description would be 'not nice for families'. It was only after extensive hesitation that the Yellow Pages declared they would be prepared to include an insert from the clinic; several magazines resisted persistently. This general anti-sexual attitude, which worked in part with completely irrational taboo zones (e.g. protecting families from the fact that there are sexually transmitted diseases), predictably became significantly more intense when dealing with groups of people who were already looked down upon by society anyway. When a gay-and-lesbian club in Taunton requested telephone repairs in December of 1986, a whole group of British Telecom employees arrived: three technicians, a supervisor and a manager, all of whom were wearing rubber gloves to protect them from a potential infection with Aids. At the last minute, however, they had finally backed down from their original demand for protective masks and an individual contact person at the club who would be able to present them with a negative HIV test.

Nonetheless, the government made no attempts of any kind to counter situations like these. On the contrary: within this social context, Lord Halsbury tabled a bill in December of 1986 that was intended to prohibit local authorities from providing financial or other assistance to anyone endorsing or promoting homosexuality or teaching its acceptability in a school.[257] The text was drafted by Lord Campbell of Alloway, a conservative barrister '[...] who feared that "positive images" of homosexuality "involve a direct attack on heterosexual family life" by undermining "paternalistic disciplines" [...]'.[258] This was the preliminary draft bill of what became law as 'Clause 28', which was passed by the House of Commons in 1988 with a majority of 53 votes (254 to 201). The censorship measures of Clause 28 had repercussions not just for educational institutions but also for numerous groups who were thus prohibited from talking about homosexuality in a non-negative form, not to mention endorsing it. The interpretation of the provisions was extended to written materials in libraries and thus to all literary works that occupied themselves with homosexuality in any form that was not negatively judgemental. Thus it can hardly come as a surprise that in 1989 an opera house in Glyndebourne was ordered to remove Benjamin Britten's *Death in Venice* from the programme of performances for schools, because the work could be in violation of this law. Nonetheless, coverage in the media was divided, because there was a desire to concentrate on 'more important' questions, for example, whether the sonnets of Shakespeare or the novellas of Ronald Firbank should be removed from public libraries ...

Without the widespread panic- and fearmongering surrounding Aids and HIV and the associated vague notions and prejudices against so-called 'risk groups', the enforcement of laws of this kind would have been substantially more difficult to legitimate. In the words of Davenport-Hines: 'The recrudescence of such vicious nonsense would have been impossible without HIV. Inside and outside Parliament HIV was the pretext for the Halsbury campaign.' Every one of the Halsbury debates dealt with the male homosexual way of life, which evoked corresponding fears and the prejudices linked to them. Davenpoprt-Hines presents the example of one of those unspeakably inflammatory newspaper articles from the British tabloids, whose themes and front pages Jarman also thematised and dealt with in many of his works (the 'newspaper baby' in THE LAST OF ENGLAND, paintings of the *Queer Series, At Your Own Risk*, etc.):

'Under the headline
LABOUR'S CASH AIDS THE NEW BLACK DEATH,
Lord Wyatt of Weeford asserted with almost total inaccuracy in the
News of the World (9.11.86),
The start of AIDS was homosexual love-making.
Promiscuous women are vulnerable, making love to
promiscuous bisexuals.
Then they pass AIDS on to normal men.
Yet some Labour councils encourage AIDS with grants
to homosexual centres ... They also encourage children
to experiment with sex.
This is murder.'[259]

Thus it can actually no longer really be surprising that such a flood of misinformation and inflammatory reports surrounding the Halsbury Clause transformed the fears regarding HIV and Aids into concrete and massive anti-gay violence among certain segments of the population: in the period directly before May of 1988, when the regulation was passed, gay bashers terrorised patrons at the Vauxhall Tavern, a gay pub. A gay man was stabbed while waiting for a bus at King's Cross, shots were fired into the overfilled Apprentice Pub in London, there was an attempted bombing at a lesbian-and-gay disco in Leeds and arsonists lit a meeting hall in Milton Keynes on fire directly before a meeting of opponents of Clause 28. In December of 1987, arson caused £20,000 of damage to the offices of the magazine *Capital Gay*. In the same week, a canister of poison gas was thrown into a gay bar in Cheltham, and forty guests had to be taken to the hospital. The Reading Matters bookshop in Haringey, which had been the target of numerous erroneous and libellous newspaper reports, received arson and bomb threats as well as death threats against its employees. The drag performer Terry Latour's flat was targeted with an incendiary device after he had received anonymous phone calls and been reviled as a 'gay bastard'. Finally, the regional authority of Strathclyde threatened students' unions that they would cut off their funding if they did not distance themselves from gay-and-lesbian organisations and end their campaigns for equal rights for homosexuals.

Even the media themselves – particularly television companies like Channel 4, but also the BBC – were not spared from demands for stricter laws and censorship. Thus, after the broadcast of Derek Jarman's film SEBASTIANE, calls were made for the imposition of new pornography laws for television. An episode of the television series Two OF Us, which was broadcast before midnight, could be shown only after the removal of a scene in which two boys kiss: 'New legislation on private videos, or the proposed fiscal controls over satellite television, provide other examples of an impetus to codify and regulate the distribution of all sexual images. The notion accepted by Wolfenden, and enjoyed by the British in the 1960s, that what one thought and did in one's own home was not a matter for state intervention, is being eroded. Privacy is being abandoned. [...] Erotic images are equated with "sick" pornography, or are said to be a danger as they incite people to sex which is no longer "safe".'[260]

In the autumn of 1990, twenty-three years after the passage of the Sexual Offences Act (see pp. 88 f.), the British government additionally saw fit to put all of those timid liberal tendencies still surviving in society back in their place with a new, concrete reference to this act and passed the so-called 'Clause 25' (later renamed 'Clause 29'). The proposed law was passed by Parliament as a part of the Criminal Justice Bill: it contained no new regulations of any kind with regard to homosexuals, but it nonetheless very emphatically pointed to existing criminal legislation and applicable laws and called on the courts to hand out more severe sentences for sexual offences that were already punishable. Situated on the same level as rape and incest, we find the so-called 'victimless crimes', and this was directed specifically towards the homosexual portion of the population: any man who flirted or held hands with another man in public, let others use his bedroom (!) or shared it with more than one person or with a man under 21 could be sentenced to up to five years of imprisonment. The private sphere, which had hitherto seemed to be protected, was thus exposed. The number of convictions rose significantly and, under these circumstances, any discussion about harmonising the homosexual age of consent became a far-off prospect.

Jarman experienced this period of directly tangible repression and unequal restrictions of personal freedoms – combined with the general political climate under Thatcher's government – as a threatening, war-like state, whose apocalyptic metaphors find their visual pendant in THE LAST OF ENGLAND, among other works. THE ANGELIC CONVERSATION is also to be seen as very concretely situated within this context. However, the central theme here is the realisation of a love story between two men in tender, non-violent images before the backdrop of a heavily armed, violent and hostile society.

A Dream World

As complex as the associative visual structure of THE ANGELIC CONVERSATION may appear, it is nonetheless still possible to identify essentially four large thematic sections inscribed into the film in the form of a structure that is not readily apparent. I will use the following keywords to refer to them:

- search
- rite
- love
- memory

As has already been mentioned, the reasons why the film is so remarkable include the fact that it does not directly thematise violence and that it no longer deals with homosexuality on a problematising level. Instead, violence and violent elements, metaphors and insignia of power emerge extremely subtly – though from all sides – out of the scenarios and on to the surface, where they seek their way into the viewer's consciousness: 'THE ANGELIC CONVERSATION is a dream world, a world of magic and ritual, yet there are images there of the burning cars and radar systems, which remind you there is a price to be paid in order to gain this dream in the face of a world of violence.'[261] The fact that Jarman interpreted the realm of magic – with its secrecy and clandestine quality – as a metaphor for the situation in which homosexuals found themselves is revealing for the viewing and interpretation of THE ANGELIC CONVERSATION, but also for other films by Jarman that play with rituals and elements of magic. For him it is no coincidence that a whole series of homosexual film-makers, from Cocteau to Kenneth Anger, work with elements of magic and alchemy in their films: 'I think of the area of magic as a metaphor for the homosexual situation. You know, magic which is banned and dangerous, difficult and mysterious. I can see that use of magic in the Cocteau films, in Kenneth Anger and very much in Eisenstein. Maybe it is an uncomfortable, banned area which is disruptive and maybe it's a metaphor for the gay situation.'[262]

The first images of the film show a young man (Philip) sitting at the open, barred window of an old villa in Somerset and longingly looking out at the garden, the light, the sun. This scene is repeated at several points in the film. On the one hand it radiates a sense of calm, serenity and a touch of melancholy. On the other hand, however, it is underlaid with the sound of a relentlessly and loudly ticking old grandfather clock, which permits associations with passing time and the irretrievable moments implied by it, as well as with the disturbing ticking of a bomb that could go off at any time. The images are accompanied by the voice of Judi Dench, who begins her recitation of Sonnet 57:

> Being your slave, what should I do but tend
> Upon the hours and times of your desire?
> I have no precious time at all to spend,
> Nor services to do till you require.
> Nor dare I chide the world-without-end hour
> Whilst I, my sovereign, watch the clock for you,
> Nor think the bitterness of absence sour
> When you have bid your servant once adieu.
> Nor dare I question with my jealous thought
> Where you may be, or your affairs suppose,
> But, like a sad slave, stay and think of naught
> Save where you are how happy you make those.[263]

The second protagonist (Paul) emerges out of the darkness like an apparition, absorbed in thought and holding a round mirror in his hand, which reflects the light of the sun. With the ticking of the clock still present, the gigantic rotating dishes of a radar station threateningly force their way between the two. Bearing heavy burdens on their backs, an aimless and laborious search among impassable, rock-strewn surroundings begins. The landscapes of the County of Dorset, the coast of Dancing Ledge and the Isle of Grain become an (emotional) no-man's-land, a barren landscape of stone, sand, rocks and rubbish, 'brought to life' only by the two searchers and accompanied by the words from Sonnet 90:

> Then hate me when thou wilt; if ever, now;
> Now, while the world is bent my deeds to cross,
> Join with the spite of fortune, make me bow,
> And do not drop in for an after-loss.
> Ah, do not, when my heart hath 'scaped this sorrow,

Come in the rearward of a conquered woe;
Give not a windy night a rainy morrow,
To linger out a purposed overthrow.
If thou wilt leave me, do not leave me last,
When other petty griefs have done their spite,
But in the onset come: so shall I taste
At first the very worst of fortune's might,
    And other strains of woe, which now seem woe,
    Compared with loss of thee will not seem so.

Much as in THE LAST OF ENGLAND, Jarman's recurrent longing for a 'lost landscape' penetrates through these landscape images to reach the surface. This longing has survived total commercialisation, overbuilding and the construction of ever more roads and motorways: 'In the short space of my lifetime I've seen the destruction of the landscape through commercialisation, a destruction so complete that fragments are preserved as if in a museum.'[264] However, in THE ANGELIC CONVERSATION these landscapes are, above all, a visual metaphor for the societal context: that social and emotional no-man's-land in which homosexual desire, life and love found themselves in the United Kingdom of the eighties. The two appear as prisoners, monitored by the ceaselessly rotating radar dishes: 'Destruction hovers in the background of THE ANGELIC CONVERSATION; the radar, the surveillance, the feeling one is under psychic attack; of course we are under attack at the moment.'[265] The environment appears hostile, without illusions and empty. As they make their way through the 'public' landscape of the stony wasteland during their search, we repeatedly see Philip in the protected, 'private' interior space of the Elizabethan villa, longingly gazing out the window. Sonnet 43 captures this longing in words:

When most I wink, then do mine eyes best see,
For all the day they view things unrespected,
But when I sleep, in dreams they look on thee
And, darkly bright, are bright in dark directed.
Then thou, whose shadow shadows doth make bright,
How would thy shadow's form form happy show
To the clear day with thy much clearer light,
When to unseeing eyes thy shade shines so!
How would, I say, mine eyes be blessèd made,
By looking on thee in the living day,
When in dead night thy fair imperfect shade
Through heavy sleep on sightless eyes doth stay!
    All days are nights to see till I see thee,
    And nights bright days when dreams do show thee me.

The two figures' seemingly endless search shifts from the surface, from the outside, to the underground, to the inside of some sort of cavernous labyrinth. In the dark and murky passages, only the torches they carry before themselves shed light on their surroundings. Now and then a 'magical' Bengal flare abruptly immerses the walls in glaring light; in between, there are close-ups of roaring flames. Paul repeatedly sends out light signals with the reflecting mirror, and the darkness is ruptured for the first time by a brief sequence showing Philip before a blossoming dog-rose shrub. The two seem to be approaching one another, an opening becomes visible at the end of the labyrinth, daylight penetrates into its interior – repeatedly interrupted by a short sequence which symbolises direct desire for the first time and shows one of the two as a torch-bearer with exposed torso. These images are already from the material of the second part: the ablution. Before succeeding in climbing out of the darkness and into the open air to the words of Sonnet 148, there is a short but fierce battle with one's own gigantic shadow, a wrestling with oneself – before a smoking, orange-red background thickened by the gold-coloured smoke continually pouring into it:

> O me, what eyes hath Love put in my head,
> Which have no correspondence with true sight!
> Or, if they have, where is my judgment fled,
> That censures falsely what they see aright?
> If that be fair whereon my false eyes dote,
> What means the world to say it is not so?
> If it be not, then love doth well denote
> Love's eye is not so true as all men's no.
> How can it? O, how can Love's eye be true,
> That is so vexed with watching and with tears?
> No marvel then though I mistake my view;
> The sun itself sees not till heaven clears.
>   O cunning Love, with tears thou keep'st me blind,
>   Lest eyes well-seeing thy foul faults should find.

The path out of this shadow zone of rocks and darkness leads into the open air, into the light, to the shores of the sea. For a few brief moments we once again see Philip sitting at the window of the Elizabethan house and melancholically gazing out into the open air. Blossoming flowers and a deep-blue sky are visible for a few seconds, in a shot inserted like a foreign body. This is followed by a purifying bath in the ocean, which is accompanied by Benjamin Britten's 'Sea Interludes' (from *Peter Grimes*) and forms the prologue to the second part of the film: '[...] the ritual washing of the tattooed man who looks like a king or prince, the giver of rings, carrying his crown, and sceptre. At the time I was thinking of the Anglo-Saxon poem *The Wanderer*; service willingly given, not exacted. There is no compunction in the scene.'[266] And it is precisely this which also seems to be one of the most immediate associations of the images that follow: no longer permitting any feelings of guilt to emerge on account of social norms, no longer permitting one's conscience to be defined from without, purifying oneself of imposed prejudices and the pangs of conscience deriving from them – having oneself celebrated and crowned.

Christopher Hobbs, in the role of a magician, opens the ceremony by mesmerisingly rotating a golden, gleaming sphere in his outstretched hands. The bell sound of little chimes rings quietly in the background, recalling a church ceremony. Together with the magician, the two protagonists reverently kiss the sphere, and the ablution and veneration begins. In contrast to the preceding images, the ones here are projected at normal speed: Philip holds two torches and Paul is almost affectionate in washing the body of the tattooed man. The tattoos are the history that this body has thus far been able to narrate; they are inextinguishable. He is adorned with pearls, sceptre and crown to the words of Sonnet 94:

> They that have pow'r to hurt and will do none,
> That do not do the thing they most do show,
> Who, moving others, are themselves as stone,
> Unmovèd, cold, and to temptation slow;
> They rightly do inherit heaven's graces
> And husband nature's riches from expense;
> They are the lords and owners of their faces,
> Others but stewards of their excellence.
> The summer's flow'r is to the summer sweet,
> Though to itself it only live and die;
> But if that flow'r with base infection meet,
> The basest weed outbraves his dignity:
>   For sweetest things turn sourest by their deeds;
>   Lilies that fester smell far worse than weeds.

It is a solemn, reverent celebration of the male body, which is followed by a kind of self-purification: Philip lies in the gentle current along the seashore, scooping up water with a shell and pouring it over his body. The images are once more in single frame and slow down, overlaid with brief inserted sequences showing Paul surrounded by torches and roaring flames. The scene of self-purification exudes a great inner calm, comparable to the calm that lies in the exhaustion which follows a long journey or hike.

Finally, the third part of the film, 'love', is introduced with the final lines of Sonnet 55 – the two protagonists have found one another:

> So, till the judgment that yourself arise,
> You live in this, and dwell in lovers' eyes.

The two protagonists first draw closer to one another physically by way of a wrestling match: it is a struggle with oneself and with the other. The black-

and-white images are in single frame/slow motion and were shot in a single take: 'Virtually one take. We didn't rehearse it. The fight sequence and love sequence were both done in one day. They gave us the centre of the film.'[267] As has already been suggested in the discussion of the 'motif of wrestling' (see pp. 77 ff.), the images of this wrestling match convey not so much elements of violence and fighting as the two protagonists' initial, tender drawing closer to one another, which is more reminiscent of a trance-like dance than a fight. The extreme slowing of the images' progression means that their movements, the touch of their bare upper bodies and also their embraces seem very close, almost tender. The eight-minute sequence conveys to its viewers a sense of a meditative and timeless depth. This is finally very suddenly interrupted by the images of the actual love scenes, which are projected in real time. Because the viewers' perception had become accustomed to the uniformly slowed rhythm of the film, the movements in these scenes now have a far more immediate and intense effect. While the images of the wrestling match remained – with only a few exceptions – in black and white, the images of the subsequent love scene's four sequences are entirely in colour. The two protagonists' gestures and embraces radiate a sense of great intimacy and security, and they convey an infinite calmness, which has finally emerged after their wanderings and their struggles. These scenes are interrupted only by brief inserted shots showing the two in black and white and slow motion, and they are accompanied by the text of Sonnet 27:

> Weary with toil, I haste me to bed,
> The dear repose for limbs with travel tired,
> But then begins a journey in my head
> To work my mind when body's work's expired;
> For then my thoughts, from far where I abide,
> Intend a zealous pilgrimage to thee,
> And keep my drooping eyelids open wide,
> Looking on darkness which the blind do see;
> Save that my soul's imaginary sight
> Presents thy shadow to my sightless view,
> Which like a jewel hung in ghastly night,
> Makes black night beauteous and her old face new.
>   Lo, thus, by day my limbs, by night my mind,
>   For thee, and for myself, no quiet find.

These images conclude with a fanfare, which introduces an almost ten-minute collage of affectionate encounters between the two. In contrast to the preceding sequences, these are once again in slow motion and largely in black and white. Both men now wear black suits and these are images that can, in a certain sense, be associated with 'everyday life' – simply being in love and living. In between there are images of a boy who, like an angel, watches over the two of them. For a few seconds the image of the ceaselessly rotating radar dish is once again inserted, but it has lost its menacing power. Surrounded by a thick wreath of flowers, it disappears into the background, vanishes into insignificance: 'THE ANGELIC CONVERSATION is gentle. There is that hovering, external violence, but at the end of the film it's cauterised by the blossom, which obliterates the radar. The blossom takes over.'[268]

The film's final sequences initially take up motifs from the first part of the film again: Paul with two torches in his hands, the steep coast along the sea, Philip in the impassable rocky landscape and on the shore with the shell in his hand – in between, a blossoming flower once more, for fractions of a second. Their paths separate again. These are the images of memory – images that are reflected in the words of Sonnet 56:

> Sweet love, renew thy force; be it not said
> Thy edge should blunter be than appetite,
> Which but today by feeding is allayed,
> Tomorrow sharp'ned in his former might.
> So, love, be thou; although today thou fill
> Thy hungry eyes even till they wink with fullness,
> Tomorrow see again, and do not kill
> The spirit of love with a perpetual dullness.
> Let this sad int'rim like the ocean be
> Which parts the shore where two contracted new
> Come daily to the banks, that, when they see
> Return of love, more blest may be the view;
>   Or call it winter, which being full of care,
>   Makes summer's welcome thrice more wished, more rare.

The film ends in an English landscape garden. Philip passes through the garden with a fan in his hand. Absorbed in thought and filled with pleasant memories, he comes to a pond filled with water lilies: 'The lily-pond is a wishing-well; Philip sees memory in it at the end of the film.'[269] Paul is somewhere else within this garden: repeatedly kissing a blossoming branch, he once again finds the images of their purifying bath before his eyes for a few brief moments. He deeply breathes in the scent of the blossoms, and this is accompanied by the words of the final sonnet, Sonnet 104:

> To me, fair friend, you never can be old,
> For as you were when first your eye I eyed.
> Such seems your beauty still. Three winters cold
> Have from the forests shook three summers' pride,
> Three beauteous springs to yellow autumn turned
> In process of the seasons have I seen,
> Three April perfumes in three hot Junes burned,
> Since first I saw you fresh, which yet are green.

Ah, yet doth beauty, like a dial hand,
Steal from his figure, and no pace perceived;
So your sweet hue, which methinks still doth stand,
Hath motion, and mine eye may be deceived;
    For fear of which, hear this, thou age unbred:
    Ere you were born was beauty's summer dead.

What emerges is not only the two protagonists' dreams of and longings for one another, but more so their wish for more humane, peaceful surroundings: 'In all home movies is a longing for paradise', Jarman has noted in connection with his earliest Super 8 films.[270] It is a longing for immortalisation and eternity. In THE ANGELIC CONVERSATION, dreams are subjected to permanent surveillance. However, it is not only the wreath of flowers around the radar that symbolises hope. Particularly the garden, where Jarman chooses to have the film end, is a direct expression of hope: 'The word paradise is derived from the ancient Persian – "a green place". Paradise haunts gardens, and some gardens are paradises.'[271] Years later, at a point in time when Jarman was already severely ill, he laid out a garden of his own at Dungeness. The coastal landscape resembles that wasteland, that impassable terrain, familiar to us from THE ANGELIC CONVERSATION – but he nonetheless caused the most wonderful plants and flowers to blossom among the stones and rocks.

[7]

Farewell to Super 8

ON 22 DECEMBER 1986, one year after completing THE ANGELIC CON-VERSATION, Jarman learned that he was HIV-positive: 'My body was thrown into the struggle, bringing me into a spotlight in a way I never expected or wanted. On 22 December 1986, finding I was body positive, I set myself a target: I would disclose my secret and survive Margaret Thatcher. I did. Now I have my sights on the millennium and a world where we are all equal before the law.'[272] For Jarman the topic of Aids had already been omnipres-ent for years on account of numerous infections and deaths among his im-mediate circle of friends and acquaintances. However, the knowledge of his own infection brought about fundamental changes, for example, the direct politicisation in the themes of his remaining films as well as his direct polit-ical involvement in the gay rights movement. While sexuality had been just one element among many (though a very central one) in his work up to that point, it now became the basis of his work as a film-maker and artist: some-times as a politically conceived statement and sometimes as a very personal sharing of a momentary feeling – or, in most cases, both.

However, 1986 would become a decisive year not only because of his defining diagnosis with HIV, but for other reasons as well: in the summer of that year, Jarman finally succeeded in completing his film CARAVAGGIO after seven years spent working on this project, and its production was now ensured through the British Film Institute. It was to become his first feature film shot on 35 mm film. On the other hand, it was in the same year that he began shooting THE LAST OF ENGLAND, the film with which he would bid farewell to the 8 mm format. Only a few years before, Jarman had still been determined to professionalise the use of the Super 8 format in feature films, but after THE LAST OF ENGLAND he turned his intense attention to his work with 35 mm film, and he used Super 8 only selectively (e.g. in WAR REQUIEM and THE GARDEN). In several interviews given years later, he explained this turning away from 8 mm film through precisely that shift in content from the 'documentation' of private events or associative sequences of images to 'concrete' themes, whose appropriate formal realisation now provided the focus of his interest. In THERE WE ARE JOHN, one of his last interviews, he declared with regard to THE LAST OF ENGLAND: 'I mean it doesn't actually tell you about the reality of this place; it was much more a mental journey. And bits of it are rather good, but it gets up and down. You can't possibly make a film which is consistent with a Super 8 camera. It's too complicated.'[273] In an interview with Chris Lippard given a few months prior to this, he describes this turning away from 8 mm film in a very similar fashion: 'You can't go any further. You can do it in a different way, but those films went as far as they could go and I became more interested in the formal aspects again, as in WITTGENSTEIN and in EDWARD II; it became more interesting to deal with those problems.'[274] This focus on formal elements, such as light, colour, symbolic 'costumes', etc., becomes particularly apparent when we call to mind the visual realisation of films like EDWARD II or WITTGENSTEIN, for example, in contrast to comparable early 16 mm films like SEBASTIANE, JUBILEE or THE TEMPEST. However, parting with the 8 mm concept did not mean parting with the home movie and the concepts of the 'cinema of small gestures'. On the contrary: for Jarman, work on 35 mm productions still meant the collective realisation of a project, and it meant working with friends – perhaps more so than ever.

Since his earliest films, he had worked together with a steady circle of friends, which continually grew over the course of time: the best-known is surely the actress Tilda Swinton, who played leading roles in the films CARAVAGGIO, THE LAST OF ENGLAND, THE GARDEN, EDWARD II and WITTGENSTEIN, but there are also actors like Spencer Leigh (CARAVAGGIO, THE LAST OF ENGLAND and THE GARDEN) or Nigel Terry (CARAVAGGIO and EDWARD II). Christopher Hobbs designed the sets for JUBILEE, CARAVAGGIO and EDWARD II; Simon Fisher-Turner was responsible for the music and sound design of THE LAST OF ENGLAND, THE GARDEN and EDWARD II and for the compositions in BLUE. The producers James Mackay and Don Boyd are also to be mentioned: Jarman produced numerous films with the two of them (incl. BLUE, THE GARDEN, THE LAST OF ENGLAND and THE ANGELIC CONVERSATION).

Jarman's concept of the 'cinema of small gestures' is also indirectly present in all of his other works. In THE GARDEN, however, in the form of Super 8 material transferred to video, digitally processed and finally transformed on 35 mm film, he realised this concept once more – directly and pushed to what seem to be its ultimate limits: 'The smallest gestures are amplified on film: a shaking hand holding the camera can make an earthquake, a speck of dust becomes a beam in the eye, a scratch a super-highway. In epic film – except in the hands of a master like Eisenstein – all is lost: a half-smile, a nod, a frown, are invisible in the juggernaut moves of the camera. THE GARDEN is a simple domestic drama, a document. No fiction. The smallest gestures.'[275]

The theoretical impetus, philosophy and working method of his 'cinema of small gestures' thus remain an element of all his other films. However, THE ANGELIC CONVERSATION and THE LAST OF ENGLAND are definitively his last two feature films to be shot on Super 8 and then subsequently transferred to video and copied on to 35 mm film. They are also the last of his films to be of significance to the group of the Romantic Aesthetics, which was emerging at that time in the UK. Along with the film-maker, painter and video artist John Maybury, this group's members included Michael Kostiff, Cerith Wyn Evans, Daniel Landin, Sophie Muller, Richard Heslop and Steven Chivers, among others. From the late seventies to the mid-eighties, they were loosely connected with one another in London. The Romantic Aesthetics or the New Romantics, as they were also called, were young artists who were experimenting in crossovers between various media, such as Super 8 film, 16 mm film, video and digital. They rejected the established and overly theoretical British avant-garde as well as their teachers, such as Peter Gidal or Malcolm Le Grice. They thus sought to implement their art in the midst of life: their installations, films and performances were presented in discos, night clubs or galleries – no longer under the exclusion of the general public, as in academic discussion clubs or small art-house cinemas. Exposure to a wide audience and innovative aesthetic experiments were no longer to be mutually exclusive – an aspiration that first very clearly revealed itself in the commercial music-video branch: 'The irony is that so much of what we see on MTV comes directly from the avant-garde. Either the European film avant-garde of the twenties or the American avant-garde of the forties, fifties and sixties. A five-minute chunk of the avant-garde is revealed in every half hour of MTV. This has not remained without implications for the rest of television, particularly advertising. On a television show about the history of abstract film, Malcolm Le Grice recently complained that MTV has stolen the avant-garde's images and thus degraded them. It hasn't earned anything better.'[276]

Jarman's influence on this group is recognisable through his understanding of himself as a painter, his work with Super 8 film, the idea of the home movie and the concept of the 'cinema of small gestures' – but above all through his friendship with several of the artists, his personal support and a few projects together. Thus, for example, he realised the project THE DREAM MACHINE (16 mm, 33 min., colour) together with Evans, Maybury and Kostiff. Each of the people involved provided their own short filmic contribution to this associative and meditative short-film project about the life and work of William S. Burroughs and Brion Gysin. In addition, John Maybury designed the sets for JUBILEE and also contributed to several of Jarman's later films.

Just like Jarman, the New Romantic film-makers were not interested in theoretical constructs and ideological and political confrontations but in film-making per se. The effect of the films was observed and studied using the audience itself, on location in the clubs; the academic circle of the London Film-makers' Co-operative had lost its significance. Maybury – who had already made a name for himself through his ironic and subversive works, which repeatedly feature a clearly 'camp' and/or gay context – has very aptly described this: 'From 1982 I showed my films at the London Film-makers' Co-op and also used their cutting rooms. Later I was denied access for a few years, because the women that were doing the Co-op at that time found my films sexist. They said my actresses wore too much make-up; they said the fact that it was applied just as thickly to the male actors did not refute their criticism. I felt like Andy Warhol, as a Pop Artist facing Abstract Expressionism. For me, making art was not so burdened with problems. I didn't sit in front of the optical printer, instead, I brought my films to Boots, a pharmacy chain. For me, that was film-making.'[277]

As different as the film-makers subsumed under the term New Romantics were in terms of their aims and results, it is nonetheless possible to discern a not insubstantial common denominator among them. They no longer occupied themselves with film-theoretical constructs and the writing and publication of texts, like the formalists, for instance: 'instead they made – also often indirect – reference to a web of texts, films, music and painting belonging to a tradition that placed its focus on the image. Associations, quotations and feelings have taken the place of purism and the autonomy of the formalistic film.'[278] It was not just Maybury and Evans who confronted this tradition with unstable, hand-held cameras, simple editing and the use of music cassettes at film screenings – because it was simply too complicated to get good audio on Super 8 film. At the level of improvisation, Jarman's way of working was adopted and set forth by a new generation of film-makers. Above all, however, it is also inherent in terms of aesthetic and thematic links: associative sequences with intense visual effects penetrate to the surface, sexual fantasies and homosexual desire become central themes and are realised in often ironic and theatrical scenarios, or, in the words of Michael O'Pray: 'Theatricality, "amateurish" home movie quality, special attention to the *mise en scène* and the theme of sexuality, a radical identification with the world of homosexual experience, these characteristic elements of Jarman's work are palpable in these new films.'[279]

While a young new generation of film-makers was discovering the freedom of improvisational possibilities in the medium of Super 8 film, the concrete communication of direct statements was becoming more and more important for Jarman – not least because of the ever more dramatic developments in the Aids crisis in the mid-eighties, but above all on account of his own direct affliction. Jarman's turning to an intensive occupation with what he calls 'consistent' works was intimately connected with his desire for directly formulated statements, which he wished to convey through the media of film and painting. His experiences related to the knowledge of his own HIV infection, the deaths of countless close friends and acquaintances, his own illness, the political situation around him and his seemingly inescapable powerlessness in the face of all of this were too intense. Thus it is also no surprise that Jarman shifted from the apolitical onlooker at political gay emancipation events of the seventies to being at the centre of a newly formed queer movement in the late eighties and early nineties. He participated in discussions and demonstrations of ACT UP, actively resisted discriminatory statements by politicians or the British tabloid press and integrated elements of this activism in many of his new works, such as the images of a gay demonstration by OutRage! in EDWARD II or the inflammatory front pages from the tabloid press in some of his paintings from the *Queer Series*.

Working on the basis of his own personal experiences, he now bundled his strategy of the autobiographical together with the strategy of naming. Central thematic areas like sexuality and power and their links to society and politics no longer rest behind his works like a private foil: they are explicitly thematised. He deliberately selected the themes of his late films (EDWARD II and WITTGENSTEIN) in direct connection with these links and their political relevance. Where consistent messages once again fail in the context of his very personal confrontation with disease, dying and death (THE GARDEN) or images seem completely inadequate on account of the personally experienced tragedy, which is not at all communicable in its actual dimensions (BLUE), he continues to develop new means of realisation corresponding to his themes. Parallel to this, he once again began to direct intense attention to painting. More than ever – as his central medium of expression, as his 'lifeline' – this once again took over that function of 'self-defence' that it had served in his early years. This first becomes apparent in the small-format *Black & Gold Paintings* and the numerous combines and assemblages – those works created at Prospect Cottage in Dungeness during the first years after he learned of his HIV infection. The messages of the late large-format paintings of the *Queer Series* and *Evil Queen Series* then force their way to the surface: immediate, direct and demanding. The confrontation with disease, dying and death as well as their direct connections with life, with his own story, becomes the central theme of these works. With their forceful and expressive application of paint as well as the inscriptions in and on their surfaces, they battle not only against hopelessness, sadness and anger but also a little against the inescapability of our own mortality.

[8]

Never Go to Hollywood

IN A PERSONAL CONVERSATION during the early nineties, Jarman once mentioned that, years before – after the premiere of his first feature film SEBASTIANE (1974) – it had become clear to him that he would presumably never be able to expect a career in Hollywood:

'After the screening of SEBASTIANE at the Locarno Film Festival I realized that I'll probably never go to Hollywood ...'. The scandal at Locarno and at various other premieres was too great, the reactions too intense to the images of the unaccustomedly open depiction of homosexuality in the context of this myth of a Christian martyr. Jarman's place was and remained elsewhere: throughout all the years between SEBASTIANE and BLUE – painting, filming and writing from self-determined niches in self-assured subversiveness against prejudice and hypocrisy.

Only a few days after Derek Jarman's death on 20 February 1994, the Hollywood film PHILADELPHIA, featuring Tom Hanks and Denzel Washington in the leading roles, had its European premiere. Over twelve years after the outbreak of Aids, this was to be the first film in the history of Hollywood to venture to openly confront the themes of Aids and homosexuality, and it did so with a thoroughly emancipatory aim.

See fig. 33 >

Fig. 33: Derek Jarman eulogy and advertisement for the film PHILADELPHIA.
Reproduction of a page from the magazine magnus, Berlin, April 1994

[9]

Notes

2. Somewhere Over the Rainbow – Childhood Images

1   Derek Jarman, *Chroma: A Book of Colour – June '93*, London, 1994, p. 146.
2   Derek Jarman, *Dancing Ledge*, London, 1984, p. 40.
3   See, e.g. the following works by Derek Jarman:
      Dancing Ledge, London, 1984, pp. 40 f., 186.
      The Last of England, London, 1987, pp. 108, 235.
      Modern Nature: The Journals of Derek Jarman, London, 1991, pp. 18 f.
      Chroma: A Book of Colour – June '93, London, 1994, p. 67.
4   Derek Jarman, *Dancing Ledge*, London, 1984, p. 41.
5   Derek Jarman, *Modern Nature: The Journals of Derek Jarman*, London, 1991, p. 68.
6   Both of the two different years of 1928 and 1929 are indicated at different points.
      1928 in: Derek Jarman, *Modern Nature: The Journals of Derek Jarman*, London, 1991,
      p. 68, or alternatively,
      1929 in: Derek Jarman, *The Last of England*, London, 1987, p. 117.
7   Derek Jarman, *The Last of England*, London, 1987, p. 118.
8   Ibid., p. 131.
9   Ibid., p. 107.
10   Cited in: Ibid., p. 128.
11   See: Derek Jarman, *Modern Nature: The Journals of Derek Jarman*,
      London, 1991, p. 264.
12   Derek Jarman, *Dancing Ledge*, London, 1984, p. 231.
13   Benjamin Britten was commissioned to compose *War Requiem* for the reconstruction of
      Coventry's St Michaels Cathedral, which had been destroyed during the Second World
      War. The work was first performed in 1962 in the rebuilt cathedral, which stands beside
      the medieval ruins. For the performance Britten demanded a Russian soprano, a British
      tenor and a German baritone. He had interwoven the texts of the Latin mass with texts
      from Wilfred Owen's poems. During the First World War, Owen was a soldier for only four
      months, including five weeks at the front. All of his texts are from this brief period. Owen
      was killed seven days before the end of the war. Jarman's film is accompanied by the original
      recording of the premiere at St Michaels Cathedral. The soloists are: Galina Vishnevskaya,
      soprano; Peter Pears, tenor; Dietrich Fischer-Dieskau, baritone. See also: Ruth Ballenger,
      Musical Expression in Selected Texts from Benjamin Britten's War Requiem <http://www.
      calstatela.edu/centers/Wagner/requiem.htm> [accessed January 1998].
14   Derek Jarman, *War Requiem: The Film*, London, 1989, p. 14.
15   Ibid., p. 9.
16   Derek Jarman, *At Your Own Risk: A Saint's Testament*, London, 1992, p. 17.
      Modern Nature: The Journals of Derek Jarman, London, 1991, p. 57.

17   See: THE GARDEN from 38'30". Jarman also utilises the rotating globe as a metaphor in other semantic contexts in JUBILEE, CARAVAGGIO and THE LAST OF ENGLAND (see also p. 45).

18   Derek Jarman, *The Last of England*, London, 1987, p. 21.
      See also: *Dancing Ledge*, London, 1984, pp. 49 f.
      Modern Nature: The Journals of Derek Jarman, London, 1991, pp. 50 f.

19   Derek Jarman, cited in: *Viennale Katalog 1988*, Vienna, 1988, p. 36. Only a German translation was published in the catalogue; the English version here is a retranslation of that source: "Wie Kafkas Gefangener ist Tucker auf ewig ein Flüchtender, in Wartezimmern, in den Korridoren der Schule, im Krankenhaus, im Büro, immer auf der Flucht vor der Wirklichkeit seiner Homosexualität, in eine Anzahl von Verkleidungen gezwungen, welche die Armut der Seele des kleinbürgerlichen Lebens überdecken sollen. Tagsüber der effizient arbeitende, unterdrückte Büroangestellte, in seinem Anzug; in der Nacht das Leder und die Ketten des Sado-Masochisten.'

20   Derek Jarman, *At Your Own Risk: A Saint's Testament*, London, 1992, p. 18. See also: ibid., pp. 30–31, and Derek Jarman, *Dancing Ledge*, London, 1984, p. 50: 'By sixteen I was fully aware of my sexual orientation but imagined, and probably even hoped, that I'd grow out of it.'

21   Derek Jarman, *The Last of England*, London, 1987, p. 22.

22   Richard Davenport-Hines, *Sex, Death and Punishment: Attitudes to Sex and Sexuality in Britain Since the Renaissance*, London, 1991, pp. 266 f.

23   Alfred C. Kinsey et al., *Sexual Behavior in the Human Male*, Philadelphia, 1948, 1998.
      Alfred C. Kinsey et al., *Sexual Behavior in the Human Female*, Philadelphia, 1953, 1998.

24   'Die Zahlen und Tatsachen dieser Statistiken fielen wie eine Atombombe in eine friedlich schlummernde Herde. Sie riefen Empörung, Erschrecken und Verwunderung hervor und schockierten die ganze Welt.' C. Kallwitz, *Das Sexualleben des Mannes nach den Ergebnissen des Kinsey-Report*, special series of the journal *Liebe und Ehe*, 7 (1951?), Regensburg and Vienna, 1951(?), p. 6.

25   See: Richard Davenport-Hines, *Sex, Death and Punishment: Attitudes to Sex and Sexuality in Britain Since the Renaissance*, London, 1991, p. 300.

26   Ibid., p. 300.
      Cesare Lombroso (1836–1909) was an Italian psychiatrist who considered all forms of deviance to derive from the excessive or reduced development of specific parts of the brain; he saw homosexuality as a form of psychological hermaphroditism. Max Nordau (1849–1923) was a Hungarian doctor who carried out a critique of civilisation. He lived in Paris from 1880 onwards, and he founded Zionism together with Theodor Herzl. In 1892 he published *Entartung* (trans. as *Degeneration*, 1895); his theories in this area are partially based on those of Lombroso and attribute the rise in instances of degeneracy to nervous disorders, among other things.

27   Ibid., pp. 307 and 308.

28   Derek Jarman, *At Your Own Risk: A Saint's Testament*, London, 1992, p. 22.

29   See: Richard Davenport-Hines, *Sex, Death and Punishment: Attitudes to Sex and Sexuality in Britain Since the Renaissance*, London, 1991, p. 320; Peter Tatchell, 'Private Exchanges', in: *Gay Times* (May 1997), London, 1997, pp. 38 ff.

30   See: Richard Davenport-Hines, *Sex, Death and Punishment: Attitudes to Sex and Sexuality in Britain Since the Renaissance*, London, 1991, p. 322.

31   Derek Jarman, *The Last of England*, London, 1987, p. 108.

32   'My father was an enthusiast, not an official photographer. The war footage lacks an element of propaganda.' Derek Jarman in: *The Last of England*, London, 1987, p. 205.

33   Derek Jarman, *Dancing Ledge*, London, 1984, p. 114.

34   Notes regarding the list of 8 mm scenes in THE LAST OF ENGLAND:
      Scene 1:   For quotation, see: Derek Jarman, *The Last of England*, London, 1987, p. 200.
      Scene 4:   Jarman calls this scene 'Sunday Lunch', see: Derek Jarman, *The Last of England*, London, 1987, p. 176, and *Dancing Ledge*, London, 1984, p. 114.
      Scene 5:   See: Derek Jarman, *Dancing Ledge*, London, 1984, p. 183.
      Scene 12:   See: Derek Jarman, *The Last of England*, London, 1987, p. 178.

Scene 13: Among the total of 139 shots, 114 contain hard cuts und 24 contain dissolves. For quotation, see: Derek Jarman, *The Last of England*, London, 1987, p. 212.

Scene 15: For quotation, see: Derek Jarman, *The Last of England*, London, 1987, p. 178.

Scene 16: For quotation, see: Derek Jarman, *The Last of England*, London, 1987, pp.118 f.

35 The unemployment rate climbed from 1.2 to 3.0 million during this period of time!

36 Derek Jarman, *The Last of England*, London, 1987, p. 181.

37 Ibid., pp. 190 f.

38 Ibid., p. 215.

39 Ibid., p. 211.

40 See: Chris Lippard, 'Interview with Derek Jarman', in: Chris Lippard (ed.), *By Angels Driven: The Films of Derek Jarman*, London, 1996, pp. 161–169.

41 Voice-over in THE LAST OF ENGLAND at 11'45". Text from: Derek Jarman, *The Last of England*, London, 1987, pp. 159 f.

42 Derek Jarman, *At Your Own Risk: A Saint's Testament*, London, 1992, p. 18. For the juxtaposition of headlines from the tabloids and the gay press, see: ibid., pp. 91 ff. For the scene with a baby in THE LAST OF ENGLAND, see: THE LAST OF ENGLAND at 73'55" and the photograph in: Derek Jarman, *The Last of England*, London, 1987, p. 171.

43 Paintings from this series featuring cover pages of *The Sun* include: *Blood* (1992), *Letter to the Minister* (1992), *Time* (1992) and *Toxo* (1992).

44 Roger Wollen, 'Facets of Derek Jarman', in: Roger Wollen (ed.), *Derek Jarman: A Portrait*, London, 1996, pp. 15 ff.
Several paintings from the *Queer Series* are (among other places) documented in:
Derek Jarman: Queer, ed. by Manchester City Art Galleries, Manchester, 1992.
Derek Jarman: Queer, ed. by Martin Baier, Cinemarstall e.V., Potsdam, 1993.
Derek Jarman: Evil Queen; The Last Paintings, Withworth Art Gallery, University of Manchester in collaboration with Richard Salmon Ltd., Manchester, n.d.
Roger Wollen (ed.), *Derek Jarman: A Portrait*, London, 1996.

45 Derek Jarman, *At Your Own Risk: A Saint's Testament*, London, 1992, pp. 4 and 20.

46 Martin Frey, 'Echoes of Past: Eine Rückschau auf das Leben und künstlerische Schaffen von Derek Jarman', in: *Filmkunst: Zeitschrift für Filmkultur und Filmwissenschaft*, 46.143 (3rd quarter of 1994), Vienna, 1994, p. 40. '[deren] Ausgangspunkt stets das Fühlen und Denken seiner eigenen Person, die persönliche, oftmals autobiographische Auseinandersetzung mit seiner Umgebung [...]'.

47 Les Levine, 'Post-larmoyante Kunst', in: Eleonora Louis and Toni Stooss (eds), *Die Sprache der Kunst: Die Beziehung von Bild und Text in der Kunst des 20. Jahrhunderts*, Vienna, 1993, p. 318.

48 Derek Jarman, *At Your Own Risk: A Saint's Testament*, London, 1992, p. 27.

49 Ibid., p. 26.

50 Kate Chedgzoy, *Shakespeare's Queer Children: Sexual Politics and Contemporary Culture*, Manchester and New York, 1995, p. 182.

51 Derek Jarman, *At Your Own Risk: A Saint's Testament*, London, 1992, p. 31.
For an explanation of the concept of Heterosoc, see also: William Stewart, *Cassell's Queer Companion*, London and New York, 1995, p. 117: 'Heterosexual society, and the institutions it has spawned. With the sinister undertones of Orwell's *1984* [i.e., through the term of Engsoc introduced by Orwell], the word implies the coercive methods that society uses to force people into heterosexuality and to suppress those that refuse.'
Painting as 'self-defence': 'At fourteen I paint in self-defence.'
See: Derek Jarman, *Dancing Ledge*, London, 1984, p. 50.
Painting as a 'lifeline': 'I see painting as a lifeline.'
See: Derek Jarman, *The Last of England*, London, 1987, p. 39.

52 Derek Jarman in: Simon Fraser, 'The Jarman Collage', in: *Rouge*, 6 (April – June 1991), London, 1991, p. 28.

3. Go West! Influences from Painting and Literature

53   Derek Jarman, *Dancing Ledge*, London, 1984, p. 54. See also: Derek Jarman, *At Your Own Risk: A Saint's Testament*, London, 1992, pp. 37 ff.

54   John Clellon Holmes, 'This Is The Beat Generation', *The New York Times Magazine*, New York, 16 November 1952, cited after: <http://www.charm.net/~brooklyn/Texts/ThisIs-BeatGen.html> [accessed March 1998].

55   Allen Ginsberg, *Snapshot Poetics: A Photographic Memoir of the Beat Era*, San Francisco, 1993, p. 7.

56   Regarding the terms counterculture, subculture and underground, see:
Dick Hebdige, *Subculture: The Meaning of Style*, London and New York, 1991, p. 148:
'The term "counter culture" refers to that amalgam of "alternative" middle-class youth cultures – the hippies, the flower children, the yippies – which grew out of the 60s, and came to prominence during the period 1967–70.
'As Hall [Stuart Hall et al. (eds), *Resistance Through Rituals*, Hutchinson, 1976] have noted, the counter culture can be distinguished from the subcultures we have been studying by the explicitly political and ideological forms of its opposition to the dominant culture (political action, coherent philosophies, manifestoes, etc.), by its elaboration of "alternative" institutions (Underground Press, communes, co-operatives, "un-careers", etc.) [...] Whereas opposition in subculture is, as we have seen, displaced into symbolic forms of resistance, the revolt of middle-class youth tends to be more articulate, more confident, more directly expressed and is, therefore, as far as we are concerned, more easily "read".'

57   Allen Ginsberg, *Howl and Other Poems*, San Francisco, 1997, p. 9.
Here the sequence of scenes in THE LAST OF ENGLAND
(begins: 6'30" / duration: *c*.35", 3 shots)

Audio	Image
[...] We heard prophetic voices:	Junkie
'I saw the best minds of my generation destroyed	Junkie
by madness, starving hysterical	
naked' (quotation from Howl)	Super 8 fragment
	Scene 1: Jarman's mother
Not with a bang but a whimper ...	Super 8 fragment
	Scene 1: Jarman's mother
...and gathered everything you threw	Panorama shot:
out of your dreamhouses [...]	Jarman in ruins

58   Derek Jarman, *Modern Nature: The Journals of Derek Jarman*, London, 1991, p. 56.

59   Derek Jarman, *At Your Own Risk: A Saint's Testament*, London, 1992, p. 83.

60   Derek Jarman, *A Finger in the Fishes Mouth*, Nr. Bridport, Dorset, 1972. The cited poems are found under their given numbers in this (unpaginated) work.

61   'Talking Cinema: Derek Jarman in Conversation with Simon Field', Audio Tape No. 1496, Institute of Contemporary Arts (ICA), London, 1987. Simon Field was director of the cinema at the ICA, and in 1996 he became head of the International Film Festival in Rotterdam.

62   *A Finger in the Fishes Mouth* also contains a separate text about the Lower East Side: 'Manhattan Lower East Side', Poem no. 10.

63   David Groff and Richard Berman (eds), *Whitman's Men: Walt Whitman's Calamus Poems Celebrated by Contemporary Photographers*, New York, 1996, pp. 53 f. (reprint from: Walt Whitman, *Leaves of Grass*, 1860.)

64   Ibid., p. 71.

65   See: Derek Jarman, *At Your Own Risk: A Saint's Testament*, London, 1992, p. 106.

66   Gay Liberation Front (GLF): A radical gay-and-lesbian organisation founded in New York and other American cities in 1969, directly after the events surrounding Stonewall. The first meeting in the United Kingdom was held in October of 1970 at the London School of Economics. One year later the meetings already included up to 500 participants. The

GLF presented a radical critique of society, dominant gender roles and the mechanisms of discrimination linked to them.

67 Derek Jarman, *At Your Own Risk: A Saint's Testament*, London, 1992, p. 63.

68 Derek Jarman, *The Last of England*, London, 1987, p. 140.

69 THERE WE ARE JOHN ... DEREK JARMAN IN INTERVIEW, August 1993, UK, 1994, 16 mm and VHS, b/w, 31 min., dir. by Ken McMullen, interview by John Cartwright, prod. by Sarah Barry (The British Council).

70 On this topic, see: *Derek Jarman: Evil Queen; The Last Paintings*, Withworth Art Gallery, University of Manchester, in collaboration with Richard Salmon Ltd., Manchester, n.d. In a television interview with Corny Littmann, Jarman explains the history of these paintings' creation with reference to, among other works, the painting *Bubble and Squeak*: premiere, Showbiz '93 of 6 Nov 1993, PORTRAIT DEREK JARMAN VON CORNY LITTMANN, Germany, 1993, *c*.25 min.

D.J.: 'Karl painted them. I sit in this chair and give him instructions like 'dip your hands in a little yellow' and such. We develop them together.'

C.L.: 'So you serve as the director?'

D.J.: 'Yes, because I don't have the strength anymore myself.'

C.L.: 'That really is interesting, to paint as a pair ... one painter, one director.'

D.J.: 'Yes, it is like film-making. I have already been working that way for years now and find it very satisfying.'

(D.J.: 'Karl hat sie gemalt. Ich sitze in diesem Stuhl und gebe ihm Anweisungen wie "Tauch deine Hände in ein bißchen Gelb" oder so. Wir entwickeln das gemeinsam.'

C.L.: 'Sie führen also Regie?'

D.J.: 'Ja weil ich selbst nicht mehr genug Kraft habe.'

C.L.: 'Das ist ja interessant: zu zweit zu malen ... ein Maler, ein Regisseur.'

D.J.: 'Ja, das ist wie Filmemachen. Ich arbeite jetzt schon seit Jahren so und finde das sehr befriedigend.')

71 Derek Jarman, *Modern Nature: The Journals of Derek Jarman*, London, 1991, p. 61.

72 Derek Jarman, *At Your Own Risk: A Saint's Testament*, London, 1992, p. 37.

73 See: Derek Jarman, BFI-Special Collection, Item 99: unpublished typescript, London, n.d., p. 2.

74 On this topic see: Emmanuel Cooper, *The Sexual Perspective: Homosexuality and Art in the Last 100 Years in the West*, London, 1987.

75 Derek Jarman, *The Last of England*, London, 1987, p. 41.

76 Wolfgang Max Faust, *Bilder werden Worte – Zum Verhältnis von bildender Kunst und Literatur*, Cologne, 1987, p. 48. Cited in: Toni Stooss, 'Am Anfang', in: Eleonora Louis and Toni Stooss (eds), *Die Sprache der Kunst: Die Beziehung von Bild und Text in der Kunst des 20. Jahrhunderts*, Vienna, 1993, p. 11. '[...] als notwendiger Bestandteil des Bildes, nicht als bildfremde Aufschrift, als hinzugefügter Kommentar oder als eingeschriebener Titel'.

77 Toni Stooss, 'Am Anfang', in: Eleonora Louis and Toni Stooss (eds), *Die Sprache der Kunst: Die Beziehung von Bild und Text in der Kunst des 20. Jahrhunderts*, Vienna, 1993, p. 8. 'Mit dem Kubismus, dem Futurismus, dem Dadaismus und vor allem auch mit dem Werk Duchamps werden die Grundlagen dafür geschaffen, daß sich Literatur und bildende Kunst zwanglos nähern, daß die einstmals aufgestellten Grenzen zwischen visueller Repräsentation und verbaler Äußerung sich zusehends verwischen.'

78 Derek Jarman, *Chroma: A Book of Colour – June '93*, London, 1994, p. 6.

79 Derek Jarman, *Dancing Ledge*, London, 1984, p. 60.
Comments regarding 'The New Generation Show' can be found in, e.g.:
Derek Jarman, *Dancing Ledge*, London, 1984, p. 75, and
Derek Jarman, BFI-Special Collection, Item 99:
unpublished typescript, London, n.d., p. 1.

80 Related references can be found in, e.g.:
Derek Jarman, *Dancing Ledge*, London, 1984, p. 70;
The Last of England, London, 1987, pp. 46 and 52; *Modern Nature: The Journals of Derek Jarman*, London, 1991, pp. 113 f., 137 and 156; *At Your Own Risk: A Saint's Testament*, London, 1992, p. 42.

81   Karin Thomas, *Bis Heute: Stilgeschichte der bildenden Kunst im 20. Jahrhundert*, Cologne, 1981, p. 255. 'In der Fortführung surrealistischer Automatismusvorstellungen manifestiert das Bild des prozessualen Action-painting die reale Identifikation von Kunst und Leben im Malakt, indem das Kunstwerk als dramatisches Selbstzeugnis, als spontanes Herausfließen der sich entäußernden, inneren Bewegung, die absolute Befreiung von allen ästhetischen Denknormen vollzieht.'

82   '[...] Harold Rosenberg's concept of action painting prominently published in "Art News" in 1952 [Harold Rosenberg, 'The American Action Painters', in: *Art News*, 51 (December 1952), pp. 22–23]. Rosenberg stressed process and activity over and above the finished product (which he described as a residue) as the essence of Abstract Expressionism.' Cited in: Walter Hopps, *Robert Rauschenberg: The Early 1950s*, Houston, 1991, pp. 161 and 169.

83   The iconography of Rauschenberg's paintings here uniformly follows that in: Walter Hopps, *Robert Rauschenberg: The Early 1950s*, Houston, 1991.

84   Armin Zweite, 'Kunst sollte kein Konzept haben: Anmerkungen zu Rauschenbergs Werk in den 50er und 60er Jahren', in: Armin Zweite (ed.), *Robert Rauschenberg*, Cologne, 1994, p. 42.
'Es sind, wie wiederholt betont wurde, offene Kunstwerke, und man darf in diesem Rahmen darauf hinweisen, daß Umberto Ecos richtungsweisendes Buch "Operta aperta" 1962 in Mailand erschien. Das "offene Kunstwerk" ist zu verstehen als ein Feld interpretativer Möglichkeiten bzw. als Konfiguration von Unbestimmtheiten, die den Betrachter zu einer Reihe veränderlicher Interpretationen veranlaßt und ihn so zu einer Art Coproduzent des Werks macht.'

85   Takashi Asai (ed.), *Derek Jarman: The Exhibition of Derek Jarman; Luminous Darkness*, Tokyo, 1990, n.p.

86   Eleonora Louis and Toni Stooss (eds), *Die Sprache der Kunst: Die Beziehung von Bild und Text in der Kunst des 20. Jahrhunderts*, Vienna, 1993, p. 10. 'Dabei ist es wichtig festzuhalten, daß mit dem Vordringen von geschriebener Sprache, von Elementen des Typographischen ins Bild, von Anbeginn auch das Vordringen von "Alltag" einhergeht.'

87   See, e.g. Derek Jarman, *Dancing Ledge*, London, 1984, pp. 67 ff.: 'Life was to change for ever after my return from America in the autumn of 1964. By October I had discovered my first gay pub – the William IV in Hampstead [...]'; or Derek Jarman, *The Last of England*, London, 1987, pp. 46 ff.: 'After I returned from America I discovered a new world.'

88   Derek Jarman, 'Jarman on Hockney', in: *Gay Life*, 29 (October 1988), Manchester, 1988, p. 31.

89   Derek Jarman, *At Your Own Risk: A Saint's Testament*, London, 1992, p. 46.
Derek Jarman, BFI-Special Collection, Item 99: unpublished typescript, London, n.d., pp. 2 f.

90   Regarding this, see also: Derek Jarman, *Dancing Ledge*, London, 1984, p. 70:
'By example he was a great liberating force, reaching far beyond the confines of the "art world": his work paved the way for the gay liberation movement at the end of the decade.'

91   Derek Jarman, 'Jarman on Hockney', in: *Gay Life*, 29 (October 1988), Manchester, 1988, p. 30.

92   Adhesiveness: 'a term employed in the now archaic pseudo science of phrenology – the study of human character based on the shape, size, and contours of the skull. [...] Adhesiveness could thus give form and legitimacy to the passionate same-sex friendships experienced so often by men and women in Anglo-American cultures throughout the nineteenth century.' David Groff and Richard Berman (eds), *Whitman's Men: Walt Whitman's Calamus Poems Celebrated by Contemporary Photographers*, New York, 1996, pp. 7 f.

93   Peter Webb, *Portrait of David Hockney*, London, 1988. The quotations are from the text accompanying fig. 35 and from the text on pp. 34 and 24.

94   Derek Jarman, 'Jarman on Hockney', in: *Gay Life*, 29 (October 1988), Manchester, 1988, p. 31.

95   Derek Jarman, *The Last of England*, London, 1987, p. 42. Regarding this, see Jarman's observations in: Derek Jarman, *Dancing Ledge*, London, 1984, p. 72, and Derek Jarman, BFI-Special Collection, Item 99: unpublished typescript, London, n.d., p. 2.

96 Valentine F. Hooven, *Beefcake: The Muscle Magazines of America 1950–1970*, Cologne, 1995, pp. 46 and 50.
Physique Pictorial: The magazine appeared from 1951–1990. It was founded in Los Angeles by Bob Mizer (1922–1992) and originally served the function of a model catalogue for his agency Athletic Model Guild. Because of the great demand, however, it was already being distributed in America and Europe in 1952 as a regularly issued magazine. In 1957 two drawings by Tom of Finland also appeared there for the first time (vol. 7, no. 1, Spring 1957). In 1997 a complete reprint of every issue was published by the Verlag Benedikt Taschen, Cologne.

97 *Physique Pictorial*, 10.3 (January 1961), p. 31, in: *The Complete Reprint of Physique Pictorial: Vol. I – III*, Cologne, 1997, vol. II. This statement is repeated in similar versions under photos in other issues.

98 Regarding the connections between Hockney's paintings and the photographs in *Physique Pictorial*, see also: Peter Webb, *Portrait of David Hockney*, London, 1988, pp. 55 ff.

99 Paul Melia, 'DH on Drawing', interview with David Hockney, London, 14 December 1994, cited from: <http://www.zen.co.uk/home/page/paul.m/dhchat.html> [accessed June 1998].

100 Emmanuel Cooper, *The Sexual Perspective: Homosexuality and Art in the Last 100 Years in the West*, London, 1987, p. 229.

101 Dawn Ades, 'Web of Images', in: The Tate Gallery (ed.), *Francis Bacon*, London, 1985, p. 22.

102 Wrestling motif in SEBASTIANE: at 20'15", 26'45" and 60'30".

103 Wrestling motif in THE ANGELIC CONVERSATION: from 46'12" to 54'10". Sonnet 55, see: William Shakespeare, *The Sonnets and Narrative Poems: The Complete Non-Dramatic Poetry*, New York, 1986.

104 Wrestling motif in EDWARD II: from 24'37" to 25'14".

105 Derek Jarman, *Chroma: A Book of Colour – June '93*, London, 1994, p. 57.

106 Derek Jarman in: BLUE, 1993, 35 mm, colour, 74 min.

107 Derek Jarman in: THERE WE ARE JOHN ... DEREK JARMAN IN INTERVIEW, August 1993, UK, 1994, 16 mm and VHS, b/w, 31 min., dir. by Ken McMullen, interview by John Cartwright, prod. by Sarah Barry (The British Council).

108 Sidra Stich, *Yves Klein*, Stuttgart, 1994, p. 69. '[Klein war] nicht der einzige, der sich vom Selbst als Subjekt der Kunst abwandte. Der "Tod des Autors" war *das* Thema der Nachkriegsavantgarde. Noch bevor Roland Barthes dieses Phänomen 1968 formulierte, konnte man es bereits in den Stücken von Samuel Beckett und Eugène Ionesco, den Romanen von Alain Robbe-Grillet, den Filmen von Jean Luc Godard und François Truffaut sowie in der Musik von John Cage und Pierre Schäffer beobachten.'

109 Pierre Restany, *Yves Klein: Fire at the Heart of the Void*, New York, 1992.

110 Hannah Weitemeier, *Yves Klein 1928–1962: International Klein Blue*, Cologne, 1994, p. 58. 'Der Effekt einer entmaterialisierten Silhouette verstärkt sich durch die verschwommene Transparenz des technischen Mediums zu illusionistischer Schwerelosigkeit.'

111 Regarding this, see: Pierre Restany, *Yves Klein: Fire at the Heart of the Void*, New York, 1992, pp. 10 f.

112 Hannah Weitemeier, *Yves Klein 1928–1962: International Klein Blue*, Cologne, 1994, pp. 39 f.

113 Axel Müller, 'James Turrell: Twilight Arch', 1991, informational sheet of the Museum für Moderne Kunst, Frankfurt am Main.

114 Derek Jarman, *Dancing Ledge*, London, 1984, p. 74.

115 In France the complete prohibition of all homosexual acts was revoked in 1789, in the course of the French Revolution. In Austria it was revoked in 1971.

116 Jeffrey Weeks, 'Capitalism and the Organisation of Sex', in: Gay Left Collective (ed.), *Homosexuality: Power and Politics*, London and New York, 1982, p. 18.

117 Simon Fraser, 'The Jarman Collage', in: *Rouge*, 6 (April – June 1991), London, 1991, p. 30.

118 Derek Jarman, *The Last of England*, London, 1987, p. 47, and Derek Jarman, BFI-Special Collection, Item 99: unpublished typescript, London, n.d., p. 2.

119 Tony Rayns, 'Credo van een Voyeur', in: Stichting Ambassade (ed.), *De Jonge Romantici en Derek Jarman in de Britse Film*, catalogue of the festival 'The Romantic Aesthetics', Amsterdam, 1986, p. 46: 'Terwijl voormalig akademie-klasgenoot David Hockney met zijn ,male-art' het feest van de jaren zestig uitbundig vierde, had Jarmans schilderwerk geen enkel raakvlak met zijn homoseksualiteit.'

120 Derek Jarman, *The Last of England*, London, 1987, p. 54.

121 Ibid., p. 39.

4. Beware of Definitions: Demarcation of the Rhetoric of Film Theory

122 Michel Archimbaud, *Francis Bacon: In Conversation with Michel Archimbaud*, London, 1993, p. 43.

123 Claude Monet recorded this statement in 1926, a few months before his death, in a letter to Evan Charteris, in which he criticises and rejects the painter John Singer Sargent's (1865–1925) theoretical discussion of the term Impressionism. Cf.: Martha Kapos (ed.), *Impressionismus*, Cologne, 1994, pp. 30 and 320. English translation cited in: Steven Z. Levine, 'Monet's Series: Repetition, Obsession', in: *October*, 102 (Summer 1986), pp. 65–75.

124 P. Adams Sitney, *Visionary Film: The American Avant-Garde 1943–1978*, New York, 1979, pp. 369 f.

125 This statement is not to be understood as posthumous and interpretive, instead, it is related to Jarman's own assessment, after BLUE, that he would probably no longer be able to realise another feature-film project on account of his poor state of health.

126 THERE WE ARE JOHN ... DEREK JARMAN IN INTERVIEW, August 1993, UK, 1994, 16 mm and VHS, b/w, 31 min., dir. by Ken McMullen, interview by John Cartwright, prod. by Sarah Barry (The British Council).

127 Gray Watson, 'An Archaeology of Soul', in: Roger Wollen (ed.), *Derek Jarman: A Portrait*, London, 1996, p. 35.

128 P. Adams Sitney, *Visionary Film: The American Avant-Garde 1943–1978*, New York, 1979, pp. VII–IX.

129 'Talking Cinema: Derek Jarman in Conversation with Simon Field', Audio Tape No. 1496, Institute of Contemporary Arts (ICA), London, 1987.
     On his isolated position as a film-maker – also within the so-called 'New British Cinema' of the eighties, see, e.g.:
     Derek Jarman, *Dancing Ledge*, London, 1984, p. 234.
     Derek Jarman, *The Last of England*, London, 1987, pp. 82 and 85 ff.
     'Discussion with Derek Jarman', in: Jonathan Hacker and David Price, *Take 10: Contemporary British Film Directors*, Oxford, 1991, pp. 248–260.

130 Michael O'Pray, *Derek Jarman: Dreams of England*, London, 1996, pp. 9 and 62.

131 Chris Lippard, 'Introduction', in: Chris Lippard (ed.), *By Angels Driven: The Films of Derek Jarman*, London, 1996, p. 3.

132 Tracy Biga, 'The Principle of Non-Narration in the Films of Derek Jarman', in: Chris Lippard (ed.), *By Angels Driven: The Films of Derek Jarman*, London, 1996, p. 23.

133 Peter Tscherkassky, *Film und Kunst – Zu einer kritischen Ästhetik der Kinematografie* (doctoral thesis, University of Vienna), Vienna, 1986, pp. 122 ff. 'Der Avantgardefilm sondert sich von den gesellschaftlichen Wirkungszusammenhängen ab, er entzieht sich dem Verwertungsprozeß von Industrie und Sozietät, der an einem spezifisch codierten, historisierbaren Gebrauch des filmischen Ausdrucksmaterials geknüpft ist. [...] Die Subversion dieser Filme ist die Negation der Sinnetze, wie sie die Texte des narrativen Kinos zu weben pflegen.'

134 THERE WE ARE JOHN ... DEREK JARMAN IN INTERVIEW, August 1993, UK, 1994, 16 mm and VHS, b/w, 31 min., dir. by Ken McMullen, interview by John Cartwright, prod. by Sarah Barry (The British Council).

135 Derek Jarman, *The Last of England*, London, 1987, p. 136.

136 Richard Porton, 'Language Games and Aesthetic Attitudes: Style and Ideology in Jarman's

Late Films', in: Chris Lippard (ed.), *By Angels Driven: The Films of Derek Jarman*, London, 1996, pp. 135 ff. *Five Faces of Modernity* cited in: ibid. (Matei Calinescu, *Five Faces of Modernity: Modernism, Avant-Garde, Decadence, Kitsch, Postmodernism*, Durham, NC, 1987).

137 Lawrence Driscoll, '"The rose revived": Derek Jarman and the British Tradition', in: Chris Lippard (ed.), *By Angels Driven: The Films of Derek Jarman*, London, 1996, pp. 65 ff. Driscoll borrowed the title 'The rose revived' from a pub found near the RAF station at Abingdon, where Jarman's father was stationed during the war.

138 Jonathan Keates, 'The Art of War: War Requiem', in: *Sight and Sound* (Spring 1989), London, 1989, pp. 133 f. Jonathan Romney, 'Edward II', in: *Sight and Sound* (November 1991), London, 1991, pp. 154 f.

139 Derek Jarman, *Dancing Ledge*, London, 1984, p. 129.

140 Ibid, p. 129.

141 *Wittgenstein: The Terry Eagleton Script; The Derek Jarman Film*, London, 1993, p. 118, and WITTGENSTEIN, 1993, 35 mm, 70 min., see at 46'.
In the texts of *On Certainty*, Wittgenstein notes: '... A meaning of a word is a kind of employment of it. For it is what we learn when the word is incorporated into our language.' See: Ludwig Wittgenstein, *On Certainty*, Oxford, 1969, § 61.

142 Richard Porton, 'Language Games and Aesthetic Attitudes: Style and Ideology in Jarman's Late Films', in: Chris Lippard (ed.), *By Angels Driven: The Films of Derek Jarman*, London, 1996, pp. 137 f.

143 Tracy Biga, 'The Principle of Non-Narration in the Films of Derek Jarman', in: Chris Lippard (ed.), *By Angels Driven: The Films of Derek Jarman*, London, 1996, pp. 12 ff and 22.

144 Gray Watson, 'An Archaeology of Soul', in: Roger Wollen (ed.), *Derek Jarman: A Portrait*, London, 1996, p. 37.

145 Roger Wollen, 'Facets of Derek Jarman', in: Roger Wollen (ed.), *Derek Jarman: A Portrait*, London, 1996, pp. 15 ff.

146 David Hawkes, '"The shadow of this time": The Renaissance Cinema of Derek Jarman', in: Chris Lippard (ed.), *By Angels Driven: The Films of Derek Jarman*, London, 1996, pp. 103 f.

147 Ibid., p. 105.

148 Richard Porton, 'Language Games and Aesthetic Attitudes: Style and Ideology in Jarman's Late Films', in: Chris Lippard (ed.), *By Angels Driven: The Films of Derek Jarman*, London, 1996, p. 138.

149 William C. Wees, *Light Moving in Time: Studies in the Visual Aesthetics of Avant-Garde Film*, Berkeley, Los Angeles and Oxford, 1992, p. 81.

150 Peter Sloterdijk, *Kopernikanische Mobilmachung und ptolemäische Abrüstung*, Frankfurt am Main, 1987, p. 30. 'Auseinanderbrechen des alteuropäischen Wahrheitsbegriffs. Wieder sehr grob gesprochen, meint dies, daß die drei Dimensionen des klassischen Wahrheitsraumes in unversöhnbare Richtungen auseinandertreiben. Das Wahre verliert tendenziell seine Beziehung zum Schönen und Guten, das Schöne emanzipiert sich mit grandiosem und bedrohlichem Eigensinn von Gutheit und Wahrheit, und das Gute wird vollends zu etwas, das zu schön wäre, um wahr zu sein.'

151 Frederic Jameson, *Postmodernism; or, The Cultural Logic of Late Capitalism*, Durham, NC, 1991, p. 31.

152 Karola Gramann, 'Tapetenwechsel: Interview mit John Maybury', in: *Sound & Vision – Musikvideo und Filmkunst*, exh. cat., Deutsches Filmmuseum Frankfurt am Main, 16 December 1993 – 3 April 1994, Frankfurt am Main, 1993, p. 35. 'Wer 1983 mit zwölf Jahren begonnen hat, Videos zu sehen, versteht heute wahrscheinlich viel mehr von der Montage als einem Mittel, Bilder zueinander ins Verhältnis zu setzen, als ein Filmwissenschaftler, der sich zwanzig Jahre lang mit Eisenstein auseinandergesetzt hat. Denn diese Kids waren einem unbarmherzigen Bombardement von Bildern ausgesetzt, die alle drei Minuten völlig neue Anforderungen stellten.'

153 Derek Jarman, *The Last of England*, London, 1987, p. 81.
154 Thus, for example, the production costs for JUBILEE were £50,000, for THE TEMPEST £150,000, for THE LAST OF ENGLAND £240,000 and for WITTGENSTEIN less than

£200,000. For his early projects he received grants of, for example, £1,000 for Sebastiane, £6,000 for The Tempest and £8,000 for Jubilee. The costs for his home movies and Super 8 films were naturally substantially lower, consisting of only £4,700 for Imagining October (27 min.), for example.

155 Chris Lippard, 'Interview with Derek Jarman', in: Chris Lippard (ed.), *By Angels Driven: The Films of Derek Jarman*, London, 1996, p. 163.

155A Jonathan Hacker, 'Discussion with Derek Jarman', in: Jonathan Hacker and David Price, *Take 10: Contemporary British Film Directors*, Oxford, 1991, p. 253. (At this point in time the costs of his further films, such as Edward II, Wittgenstein and Blue, were not yet included in the sum of £1 million named by Jarman.)

156 Holger Reichert, 'Film und Kino: Die Maschinerie des Sehens; Die Suche nach dem Ort des Betrachters in der filmtheoretischen Diskussion' (thesis, University of Vienna), Vienna, 1993, p. 56.

157 'Discussion with Derek Jarman', in: Jonathan Hacker and David Price, *Take 10: Contemporary British Film Directors*, Oxford, 1991, pp. 249 f. Regarding this, see also: Derek Jarman, *The Last of England*, London, 1987, pp. 167 and 196 f. Derek Jarman, *Dancing Ledge*, London, 1984, pp. 196 f.

158 William C. Wees, *Light Moving in Time: Studies in the Visual Aesthetics of Avant-Garde Film*, Berkeley, Los Angeles and Oxford, 1992, pp. 53 f.

159 Peter Tscherkassky, *Film und Kunst – Zu einer kritischen Ästhetik der Kinematografie* (doctoral thesis, University of Vienna), Vienna, 1986, p. 10.

160 Holger Reichert, 'Film und Kino: Die Maschinerie des Sehens; Die Suche nach dem Ort des Betrachters in der filmtheoretischen Diskussion' (thesis, University of Vienna), Vienna, 1993, p. 6.

161 Ibid, p. 66.

162 Paul Feyerabend, *Wissenschaft als Kunst*, Frankfurt am Main, 1984, p. 80.
'Darstellungen dreidimensionaler Gegenstände auf einem Blatt Papier sind wie Karten oder Modelle, um sie zu verstehen, bedarf eines Schlüssels.'
'Der archaische Künstler hatte die Fläche, auf der er malte, so behandelt, wie ein Schreiber ein Stück Papyrus behandeln würde; sie *ist* eine wirkiche Fläche, sie soll auch so *gesehen* werden [...] Die folgende einfache Zeichnung z.B. könnte drei Wege darstellen, die sich an einem Punkt treffen. [...]
'Der Künstler dagegen, der sich der Perspektive bedient, betrachtet die Fläche und das was er darauf setzt, als *Reize*, die die *Illusion* einer Anordnung von dreidimensionalen Gegenständen hervorrufen. Diese tritt auf, weil das menschliche Bewußtsein fähig ist, aus geeigneten Reizen illusorische Erfahrungen herzustellen. Jetzt wird die Zeichnung als Ecke eines Würfels gesehen, der sich entweder auf den Beschauer zu erstreckt oder von ihm weg (und dann von unten gesehen wird), oder auch als Ebene, die über der Papierfläche schwebt und eine zweidimensionale Zeichnung dreier sich treffender Wege enthält. [...]'
Paul Feyerabend, *Against Method*, 3rd ed., London, 1993, pp. 199 f.

163 Paul Feyerabend, *Wissenschaft als Kunst*, Frankfurt am Main, 1984, pp. 77 f.
'Wahrheit ist, was der Denkstil sagt, daß Wahrheit sei. [...] Die Wahl eines Stils, einer Wirklichkeit, einer Wahrheitsform, Realitäts- und Rationalitätskriterien eingeschlossen, ist die Wahl von Menschenwerk. Sie ist ein *sozialer Akt*, sie hängt ab von der *historischen Situation*, sie ist gelegentlich ein relativ bewußter Vorgang – man überlegt sich verschiedene Möglichkeiten und entschließt sich dann für eine –, sie ist viel öfter direktes Handeln aufgrund starker Intuitionen. ,Objektiv' ist sie nur in dem durch die historische Situation vorgegebenen Sinn: auch Objektivität ist ein Stilmerkmal (man vergleiche etwa den Pointillismus mit dem Realismus oder dem Naturalismus). Man entscheidet sich also für oder gegen die Wissenschaften genauso, wie man sich für oder gegen punk rock entscheidet, mit dem Unterschied allerdings, daß die gegenwärtige soziale Einbettung der Wissenschaften die Entscheidung im ersten Fall mit viel mehr Gerede und auch sonst mit viel größerem Lärm umgibt.'

5. Home Movies and Super 8 Short Films

164   STUDIO BANKSIDE is documented on video in the version from the 1984 ICA projection: Compilation I, ICA, London, 1984. All of the Super 8 films from the years 1970 to 1983 shown in the context of the exhibition were recorded on a total of three tapes (Compilation I, II and III). In 1992 Jarman also used material from STUDIO BANKSIDE II in a music video for the song 'Being Boring', by the Pet Shop Boys.
Studio Bankside:
STUDIO BANKSIDE I (also: Home Movies Reel I): 1970, Super 8, blown up on 16 mm, colour and b/w, 3 min.; direction and camera: Derek Jarman.
STUDIO BANKSIDE II (also: Home Movies Reel I): 1972, Super 8, blown up on 16 mm, b/w, 3 min.; direction, camera and editing: Derek Jarman.
BEING BORING: 1972/1992, music video produced for the Pet Shop Boys, 5 min.; direction and camera: Derek Jarman. Excerpts from: STUDIO BANKSIDE II (1972).

165   Derek Jarman, *Dancing Ledge*, London, 1984, p. 204.

166   Roland Barthes, *Camera Lucida: Reflections on Photography*, London, 2000, p. 14.

167   Derek Jarman, *The Last of England*, London, 1987, p. 54.

168   'Talking Cinema: Derek Jarman in Conversation with Simon Field', Audio Tape No. 1496, Institute of Contemporary Arts (ICA), London, 1987.

169   'Discussion with Derek Jarman', in: Jonathan Hacker and David Price, *Take 10: Contemporary British Film Directors*, Oxford, 1991, p. 260.

170   Marnie Parrell, 'Repression; or, How to Make Good Movies', in: *Cineaction*, 30 (1992), Toronto, 1992, p. 22. Cited in: Laura Hudson, 'Promiscuous 8', in: <http://www.imaging.dundee.ac.uk/elevator/martin/prom.htm> [accessed May 1999].

171   Michael O'Pray, 'News from Home: Super-8, Video and Home Movies; Derek Jarman Discusses "Real" Film Making with Michael O'Pray', in: BFI, *Monthly Film Bulletin*, 51.605 (June 1984), London, 1984, pp. 189 f.

172   'Discussion with Derek Jarman', in: Jonathan Hacker and David Price, *Take 10: Contemporary British Film Directors*, Oxford, 1991, p. 249.

173   John Maybury in: Michael O'Pray, 'De Nieuwe Generatie in de Britse Experimentele Film', in: Stichting Ambassade (ed.), *De Jonge Romantici en Derek Jarman in de Britse Film*, catalogue of the festival 'The Romantic Aesthetics', Amsterdam, 1986, p. 21. 'Het experimenteren is op het dode spoor van het structuralisme terechtgekomen, waarmee de "underground"-film doeltreffend vermoord is. Ik zie mijn films als het alternatief van de amateur voor deze akademische dood. [...] Met de keuze voor een huis tuin en keukenmedium als Super 8 en het gebruik van de eenvoudigste camea-technieken, hoop ik de onschuld van het experiment weer in te voeren.'

174   In the secondary literature several more or less equivalent terms are used for these two techniques: single frame = stop frame, stop motion, time lapse; slow down = slow motion.

175   Derek Jarman, *The Last of England*, London, 1987, p. 145.

176   Ibid., pp. 145 f.

177   Michael O'Pray, 'News from Home: Super-8, Video and Home Hovies; Derek Jarman Discusses "Real" Film Making with Michael O'Pray', in: BFI, *Monthly Film Bulletin*, 51.605 (June 1984), London, 1984, p. 189.

178   'Talking Cinema: Derek Jarman in Conversation with Simon Field', Audio Tape No. 1496, Institute of Contemporary Arts (ICA), London, 1987.

179   Derek Jarman, *Modern Nature: The Journals of Derek Jarman*, London, 1991, p. 200.

180   Derek Jarman, *The Last of England*, London, 1987, p. 169.

181   Michael O'Pray, 'News from Home: Super-8, Video and Home Movies; Derek Jarman Discusses "Real" Film Making with Michael O'Pray', in: BFI, *Monthly Film Bulletin*, 51.605 (June 1984), London, 1984, p. 189.

182   Ibid., p. 189.

183   Derek Jarman, *Modern Nature: The Journals of Derek Jarman*, London, 1991, p. 200.

184   Derek Jarman, *Dancing Ledge*, London, 1984, p. 197.

185   'Discussion with Derek Jarman', in: Jonathan Hacker and David Price, *Take 10: Contemporary British Film Directors*, Oxford, 1991, p. 250.

186 'Talking Cinema: Derek Jarman in Conversation with Simon Field', Audio Tape No. 1496, Institute of Contemporary Arts (ICA), London, 1987.

187 Derek Jarman, *Dancing Ledge*, London, 1984, p. 197.

188 Simon Field and Michael O'Pray, 'Imaging October, Dr. Dee and Other Matters: An Interview with Derek Jarman', in: *Afterimage*, 12 (1985), *Derek Jarman ... of Angels & Apocalypse*, London, 1985, pp. 48 f.

189 IL MARE, dir. by Giuseppe Patroni Griffi, Italy, 1963. A love triangle between an actor, a young man and a woman on Capri.

190 Derek Jarman, *At Your Own Risk: A Saint's Testament*, London, 1992, p. 42.

191 Richard Dyer, *Now You See It: Studies on Lesbian and Gay Film*, London, 1991, pp. 102 f.

192 Laura Hudson, 'Promiscuous 8', in: <http://www.imaging.dundee.ac.uk/elevator/martin/prom.htm> [accessed May 1999].

193 Michael O'Pray, 'News from Home: Super-8, Video and Home Movies; Derek Jarman Discusses "Real" Film Making with Michael O'Pray', in: BFI, *Monthly Film Bulletin*, 51.605 (June 1984), London, 1984, p. 190; Derek Jarman, *Modern Nature: The Journals of Derek Jarman*, London, 1991, p. 137.

194 Richard Dyer, *Now You See It: Studies on Lesbian and Gay Film*, London, 1991, pp. 102 f.

195 Kenneth Anger cited in: Tony Rayns, 'Dedication to Create Make Believe', in: Jayne Pilling and Michael O'Pray, *Into the Pleasure Dome: The Films of Kenneth Anger*, London, 1989, p. 23.

196 Kenneth Anger cited in: Tony Rayns, 'Lucifer: A Kenneth Anger Compendium', in: ibid., p. 7.

197 Kenneth Anger, 'Modesty and the Art of Film', in: ibid., p. 21.

198 Recordings at 24 fps are also fragmentary documentations, however, the human eye no longer perceives the absent information as absent and disturbing.

199 Jon Savage, *England's Dreaming: Sex Pistols and Punk Rock*, London, 1991, p. 93.

200 Jarman had already met the Tunisian-born Gerald Incandela in 1973, during Ken Russell's Gargantua project in Rome, following which the two went back to London together. Incandela was involved in films including IN THE SHADOW OF THE SUN, THE ART OF MIRRORS and SEBASTIANE, and he made film stills for several of Jarman's films. The best known are the photographs related to SEBASTIANE and the series related to CARAVAGGIO, which were published in an illustrated volume created specifically for the film: Derek Jarman, *Caravaggio*, London, 1986.

201 Derek Jarman, *Dancing Ledge*, London, 1984, p. 165.

202 Commentary by Jarman on GERALD'S FILM on Compilation Tape 1, ICA London.

203 Derek Jarman, *The Last of England*, London, 1987, pp. 63–65. Further references to this period in New York can also be found in: Derek Jarman, *Dancing Ledge*, London, 1984, pp. 135 ff., and Derek Jarman, *At Your Own Risk: A Saint's Testament*, London, 1992, pp. 70 f.

204 *Spartacus International Gay Guide*, 29th edition, 2000/2001, Berlin, 2000, p. 1232.

205 Derek Jarman, *Chroma: A Book of Colour – June '93*, London, 1994, p. 95.

206 TAROT, CATALAN, DEPUIS LE JOUR, JUBILEE, CARAVAGGIO, THE LAST OF ENGLAND, THE GARDEN, EDWARD II.

207 Derek Jarman, *Dancing Ledge*, London, 1984, p. 124.

208 Derek Jarman, *Chroma: A Book of Colour – June '93*, London, 1994, p. 75.

209 Gaia Shaw, 'Queer Gravity: Alchemy and Sexuality in Derek Jarman's Films and Paintings', (master's thesis, Wimbledon School of Art, University of Surrey), 1994, p. 3.

210 Tony Rayns, 'Credo van een Voyeur', in: Stichting Ambassade (ed.), *De Jonge Romantici en Derek Jarman in de Britse Film*, catalogue of the festival 'The Romantic Aesthetics', Amsterdam, 1986, p. 50: 'Hij is niet geinteresseerd in de para-wetenschappelijke aspekten van de alchemie, maar gebruikt haar taal en symbolen voor zijn romantische retoriek.'

211 Derek Jarman, *Dancing Ledge*, London, 1984, p. 188. Later, in a talk with Simon Field, he referred to this once again, in: 'Talking Cinema: Derek Jarman in Conversation with Simon Field', Audio Tape No. 1496, Institute of Contemporary Arts (ICA), London, 1987.

212 Commentary of Derek Jarman on his film DUGGIE FIELDS: Video Compilation III, ICA, London, 1984.

213 Derek Jarman, *At Your Own Risk: A Saint's Testament*, London, 1992, p.67.

214 See: <http://www.altmissworld.org.uk/> [accessed July 2000]. On Andrew Logan and his Museum of Sculpture, see also: <http://www.andrewlogan.com/> [accessed July 2000].

215 Derek Jarman, *Dancing Ledge*, London, 1984, p. 138. On Alternative Miss World, see also: Derek Jarman, *Dancing Ledge*, London, 1984, pp. 119 and 133.

216 Derek Jarman, *Modern Nature: The Journals of Derek Jarman*, London, 1991, p. 193.

217 Derek Jarman, *Dancing Ledge*, London, 1984, p. 228.

218 Commentary of Derek Jarman on his film DUGGIE FIELDS: Video Compilation III, ICA, London, 1984.

219 Derek Jarman, *The Last of England*, London, 1987, p. 185. See also, e.g.: Michael O'Pray, 'News from Home: Super-8, Video and Home Movies; Derek Jarman Discusses "Real" Film Making with Michael O'Pray', in: BFI, *Monthly Film Bulletin*, 51.605 (June 1984), London, 1984, p. 189.

220 Derek Jarman, *Dancing Ledge*, London, 1984, p. 214.

221 Steve Jenkins, 'T.G.: Psychic Rally in Heaven', in: BFI, *Monthly Film Bulletin*, 48.569 (June 1981), London, 1981, p. 124.

222 Cynthia Rose, 'Broken English: Three Songs by Marianne Faithfull', in: BFI, *Monthly Film Bulletin*, 47.560 (September 1980), London, 1980, p. 182.

223 Derek Jarman, *Dancing Ledge*, London, 1984, p. 208.

6. 'Cinema of Small Gestures': Super 8 as Feature Film

224 Jean Cocteau, *The Art of Cinema*, ed. by André Bernard and Claude Gauteur, trans. by Robin Buss, London, 1994, pp. 67 f. Initial quotation cited in: Laura Hudson, 'Promiscuous 8', in: <http://www.imaging.dundee.ac.uk/elevator/martin/prom.htm> [accessed May 1999].

225 Ibid.

226 Derek Jarman, *The Last of England*, London, 1987, p. 146.

227 'The soundtrack is a palimpsest.' Derek Jarman, *The Last of England*, London, 1987, p. 166.

228 Derek Jarman, BFI-Special Collection, Item 99: unpublished typescript, London, n.d., p. 1.

229 Paul Verstraeten, 'Derek Jarman Interview', in: Stichting Ambassade (ed.), *De Jonge Romantici en Derek Jarman in de Britse Film*, catalogue of the festival 'The Romantic Aesthetics', Amsterdam, 1986, p. 45: 'Ik wil het liefst dat ze in een kleine zaal worden vertoond voor een klein, intiem publiek. Van een zonsondergang ga je toch ook niet genieten in begeleiding van een hele meute.'

230 Derek Jarman, *Dancing Ledge*, London, 1984, p. 13.

231 Ibid., p. 137.

232 Ibid., pp. 129 f.

233 Ibid., p. 128.

234 Ibid., p. 126.

235 See: *Afterimage*, 12 (1985), *Derek Jarman ... of Angels & Apocalypse*, London, 1985, pp. 26 ff.

236 Derek Jarman, *Silence*, 1986; oil, glass, light bulb, etc. on canvas, 51 × 40.5 cm, collection of Richard Salmon.

237 William Shakespeare, *The Sonnets and Narrative Poems: The Complete Non-Dramatic Poetry*, New York, 1986, Sonnet 151.

238 Simon Field and Michael O'Pray, 'Imaging October, Dr. Dee and Other Matters', in: *Afterimage*, 12 (1985), *Derek Jarman... of Angels & Apocalypse*, London, 1985, p. 58. See also: Derek Jarman, *The Last of England*, London, 1987, p. 134: 'I have seen very few films on male love which are gentle, they usually have a violent subtext – the violence you have to traverse before you make peace with yourself.'

239 Derek Jarman, *The Last of England*, London, 1987, p. 140.

240 Ibid., p. 142.

241 Paul Verstraeten, 'Derek Jarman Interview', in: Stichting Ambassade (ed.), *De Jonge*

Romantici en Derek Jarman in de Britse Film, catalogue of the festival 'The Romantic Aesthetics', Amsterdam, 1986, p. 42:
'Zoals altijd had ik mijn Super 8 camera bij me en daar speelden we mee. [...] De jongens werden tijdens de vakantie verliefd op elkaar en vroegen mij een liefdesscène met hen op te nemen. Om deze scènes heen kon ik een film konstrueren en eindelijk had ik een kapstok waaraan ik die prachtige sonnetten van Shakespeare, *The Angelic Conversations*, kon ophangen.'

242   See: Derek Jarman, *The Last of England*, London, 1987, pp. 142 f.
243   Simon Field and Michael O'Pray, 'Imaging October, Dr. Dee and Other Matters', in: *Afterimage*, 12 (1985), *Derek Jarman... of Angels & Apocalypse*, London, 1985, p. 52. See also: Derek Jarman, *The Last of England*, London, 1987, pp. 145 f.
244   Simon Field and Michael O'Pray, 'Imaging October, Dr. Dee and Other Matters', in: *Afterimage*, 12 (1985), *Derek Jarman... of Angels & Apocalypse*, London, 1985, p. 55
245   Derek Jarman, *The Last of England*, London, 1987, pp. 134 and 143.
246   Simon Field and Michael O'Pray, 'Imaging October, Dr. Dee and Other Matters', in: *Afterimage*, 12 (1985), *Derek Jarman... of Angels & Apocalypse*, London, 1985, p. 55.
247   William Shakespeare, *The Sonnets and Narrative Poems: The Complete Non-Dramatic Poetry*, New York, 1986
248   Mark Nash, 'Innocence and Experience', in: *Afterimage*, 12 (1985), *Derek Jarman... of Angels & Apocalypse*, London, 1985, p. 34.
249   In THE ANGELIC CONVERSATION and in the present book, Shakespeare's sonnets are cited from the edition: William Shakespeare, *The Sonnets and Narrative Poems: The Complete Non-Dramatic Poetry*, New York, 1986. The complete texts of all of the sonnets featured in the film as well as the times at which they begin can be found in Chapter 10 (see pp. 212 ff.).
250   Derek Jarman, *The Last of England*, London, 1987, p. 143.
      See also: Paul Verstraeten, 'Derek Jarman Interview', in: Stichting Ambassade (ed.), *De Jonge Romantici en Derek Jarman in de Britse Film*, catalogue of the festival 'The Romantic Aesthetics', Amsterdam, 1986, p. 41: 'By the way, it was a very conscious decision to have the sonnets spoken by a woman.' ('Overigens was het een zeer bewuste beslissing van mij om die sonnetten door een vrouw te laten inspreken.')
251   See: Derek Jarman, *The Last of England*, London, 1987, p. 143.
252   W.H. Auden, 'Introduction', in: William Shakespeare, *The Sonnets and Narrative Poems: The Complete Non-Dramatic Poetry*, New York, 1986, p. XX.
253   Ibid., pp. XXVIII f.
254   Kate Chedgzoy, *Shakespeare's Queer Children: Sexual Politics and Contemporary Culture*, Manchester and New York, 1995, p. 169.
255   Simon Field and Michael O'Pray, 'Imaging October, Dr. Dee and Other Matters', in: *Afterimage*, 12 (1985), *Derek Jarman... of Angels & Apocalypse*, London, 1985, p. 56.
256   See: Richard Davenport-Hines, *Sex, Death and Punishment: Attitudes to Sex and Sexuality in Britain Since the Renaissance*, London, 1991, pp. 330–383.
257   'Halsbury's Clause stated that a local authority shall not "(a) intentionally promote homosexuality or publish material with the intention of promoting homosexuality, (b) promote the teaching in any maintained school of the acceptability of homosexuality as a pretended family relationship".' See: Richard Davenport-Hines, *Sex, Death and Punishment: Attitudes to Sex and Sexuality in Britain Since the Renaissance*, London, 1991, p. 369.
258   Ibid., p. 370.
259   Ibid., pp. 371 f.
260   Ibid., p. 381.
261   Derek Jarman, *The Last of England*, London, 1987, p. 133.
262   Simon Field and Michael O'Pray, 'Imaging October, Dr. Dee and Other Matters', in: *Afterimage*, 12 (1985), *Derek Jarman... of Angels & Apocalypse*, London, 1985, p. 58.
263   All of the following sonnets are cited from: William Shakespeare, *The Sonnets and Narrative Poems: The Complete Non-Dramatic Poetry*, New York, 1986.
264   Derek Jarman, *The Last of England*, London, 1987, pp. 136 f.
265   Ibid., p. 133.

266 Ibid., p. 133.
267 Ibid., p. 143.
268 Ibid., p. 134.
269 Ibid., p. 143.
270 Ibid., p. 54
271 *Derek Jarman's Garden: With Photographs by Howard Sooley*, London, 1995, p. 40.

7. Farewell to Super 8

272 Derek Jarman, *Dancing Ledge*, 2nd ed., London, 1991, p. 7. Cited in: David Gardner, 'Perverse Law: Jarman as Gay Criminal Hero', in: Chris Lippard (ed.), *By Angels Driven: The Films of Derek Jarman*, London, 1996, p. 35.
273 THERE WE ARE JOHN ... DEREK JARMAN IN INTERVIEW, August 1993, UK, 1994, 16 mm and VHS, b/w, 31 min., dir. by Ken McMullen, interview by John Cartwright, prod. by Sarah Barry (The British Council).
274 Chris Lippard, 'Interview with Derek Jarman', in: Chris Lippard (ed.), *By Angels Driven: The Films of Derek Jarman*, London, 1996, p. 163.
275 Derek Jarman, *Modern Nature: The Journals of Derek Jarman*, London, 1991, p. 130.
276 John Maybury in: Karola Gramann, 'Tapetenwechsel: Interview mit John Maybury', in: *Sound & Vision – Musikvideo und Filmkunst*, exh. cat., Deutsches Filmmuseum Frankfurt am Main, 16 December 1993 – 3 April 1994, Frankfurt am Main, 1993, p. 34. Only a German translation of the interview was published in the catalogue; the English version here is a retranslation of that source: 'Die Ironie ist, daß so vieles, was wir in MTV sehen, direkt aus der Avantgarde kommt. Entweder der europäischen Filmavantgarde der zwanziger Jahre oder der amerikanischen Avantgarde der vierziger, fünfziger und sechziger Jahre. In jeder halben Stunde MTV wird in fünf Minuten ein Stück Avantgarde sichtbar. Das bleibt nicht ohne Wirkung auf das übrige Fernsehen, vor allem die Werbung. Neulich hat Malcolm Le Grice sich in einer Fernsehsendung zur Geschichte des abstrakten Films darüber beklagt, daß MTV der Avantgarde die Bilder klaut und sie damit entwertet. Sie hat es nicht anders verdient.'
277 Ibid., p. 31. Here the German translation, which served as the source of the retranslation into English: 'Ab 1982 habe ich bei der London Filmmakers' Coop meine Filme gezeigt und auch die Schneideräume genutzt. Später hatte ich ein paar Jahre Hausverbot, weil die Frauen, die die Coop zu dieser Zeit machten, meine Filme sexistisch fanden. Meine Schauspielerinnen trugen zu viel Make-up; daß es bei den Schauspielern genauso dick aufgetragen war, entkräftete ihren Vorwurf nicht. Ich fühlte mich wie Andy Warhol als Pop-Artist gegenüber dem Abstrakten Expressionismus. Für mich war Kunstmachen nicht so problembeladen. Ich saß nicht vor dem optischen Printer, sondern brachte meine Filme zu Boots, einer Drogeriekette. Das war für mich Filmemachen.'
278 Michael O'Pray, 'De nieuwe generatie in de experimentele Britse film', in: Stichting Ambassade (ed.), *De Jonge Romantici en Derek Jarman in de Britse Film*, catalogue of the festival 'The Romantic Aesthetics', Amsterdam, 1986, p. 26: 'Zij referen echter wel, vaak impliciet, aan een web van teksten, films, muziek en schilderwerk welke tot een traditie behoren, die het beeld centraal stelt. Associaties, citaten en suggesties hebben de plaats ingenomen van het purisme en de autonomie van de formalistische cinema.'
279 Ibid., p. 25: 'Theatraliteit, "amateuristische" home movie kwaliteit, speciale aandacht voor mise-en-scene en het thema seksualiteit, een radikale identifikatie met de homoseksuele ervaringswereld, deze karakteristieke elementen van Jarmans werk zijn voelbar in de nieuwe films.'

[10]

Shakespeare's Sonnets in
THE ANGELIC CONVERSATION

57 (in the film at 1'14")

Being your slave, what should I do but tend
Upon the hours and times of your desire?
I have no precious time at all to spend,
Nor services to do till you require.
Nor dare I chide the world-without-end hour
Whilst I, my sovereign, watch the clock for you,
Nor think the bitterness of absence sour
When you have bid your servant once adieu.
Nor dare I question with my jealous thought
Where you may be, or your affairs suppose,
But, like a sad slave, stay and think of naught
Save where you are how happy you make those.
   So true a fool is love that in your will,
   Though you do anything, he thinks no ill.

90 (7'11")

Then hate me when thou wilt; if ever, now;
Now, while the world is bent my deeds to cross,
Join with the spite of fortune, make me bow,
And do not drop in for an after-loss.
Ah, do not, when my heart hath 'scaped this sorrow,
Come in the rearward of a conquered woe;
Give not a windy night a rainy morrow,
To linger out a purposed overthrow.
If thou wilt leave me, do not leave me last,
When other petty griefs have done their spite,
But in the onset come: so shall I taste
At first the very worst of fortune's might,
   And other strains of woe, which now seem
   woe,
   Compared with loss of thee will not seem so.

43 (14'44")

When most I wink, then do mine eyes best see,
For all the day they view things unrespected,
But when I sleep, in dreams they look on thee
And, darkly bright, are bright in dark directed.
Then thou, whose shadow shadows doth make
bright,
How would thy shadow's form form happy show
To the clear day with thy much clearer light,
When to unseeing eyes thy shade shines so!
How would, I say, mine eyes be blessèd made,
By looking on thee in the living day,
When in dead night thy fair imperfect shade
Through heavy sleep on sightless eyes doth stay!
   All days are nights to see till I see thee,
   And nights bright days when dreams do show
   thee me.

53 (18'04")

What is your substance, whereof are you made,
That millions of strange shadows on you tend?
Since everyone hath, every one, one shade,
And you, but one, can every shadow lend.
Describe Adonis, and the counterfeit
Is poorly imitated after you;
On Helen's cheek all art of beauty set,
And you in Grecian tires are painted new.
Speak of the spring and foison of the year;
The one doth shadow of your beauty show,
The other as your bounty doth appear,
And you in every blessèd shape we know.
   In all external grace you have some part,
   But you like none, none you, for constant heart.

148 (26'53")

O me, what eyes hath Love put in my head,
Which have no correspondence with true sight!
Or, if they have, where is my judgment fled,
That censures falsely what they see aright?
If that be fair whereon my false eyes dote,
What means the world to say it is not so?
If it be not, then love doth well denote
Love's eye is not so true as all men's no.
How can it? O, how can Love's eye be true,
That is so vexed with watching and with tears?
No marvel then though I mistake my view;
The sun itself sees not till heaven clears.
    O cunning Love, with tears thou keep'st me
    blind,
    Lest eyes well-seeing thy foul faults should
    find.

126 (28'02")

O thou, my lovely boy, who in thy power
Dost hold Time's fickle glass, his sickle hour,
Who hast by waning grown, and therin show'st
Thy lovers withering as thy sweet self grow'st;
If Nature, sovereign mistress over wrack,
As thou goest onwards, still will pluck thee back,
She keeps thee to this purpose, that her skill
May Time disgrace and wretched minutes kill.
Yet fear her, O thou minion of her pleasure;
She may detain, but not still keep her treasure.
    Her audit, though delayed, answered must be,
    And her quietus is to render thee.

29 (34'06")

When, in disgrace with Fortune and men's eyes,
I all alone beweep my outcast state,
And trouble deaf heaven with my bootless cries,
And look upon myself, and curse my fate,
Wishing me like to one more rich in hope,
Featured like him, like him with friends possessed,
Desiring this man's art, and that man's scope,
With what I most enjoy contented least;
Yet in these thoughts myself almost despising,
Haply I think on thee, and then my state,
Like to the lark at break of day arising
From sullen earth, sings hymns at heaven's gate;
    For thy sweet love rememb'red such wealth
    brings,
    That then I scorn to change my state with
    kings.

94 (38'04")

They that have pow'r to hurt and will do none,
That do not do the thing they most do show,
Who, moving others, are themselves as stone,
Unmovèd, cold, and to temptation slow;
They rightly do inherit heaven's graces
And husband nature's riches from expense;
They are the lords and owners of their faces,
Others but stewards of their excellence.
The summer's flow'r is to the summer sweet,
Though to itself it only live and die;
But if that flow'r with base infection meet,
The basest weed outbraves his dignity:
    For sweetest things turn sourest by their deeds;
    Lilies that fester smell far worse than weeds.

30 (43'30")

When to the sessions of sweet silent thought
I summon up remembrance of things past,
I sigh the lack of many a thing I sought,
And with old woes new wail my dear Time's waste.
Then can I drown an eye, unused to flow,
For precious friends hid in death's dateless night,
And weep afresh love's long since canceled woe,
And moan th' expense of many a vanished sight;
Then can I grieve at grievances foregone,
And heavily from woe to woe tell o'er
The sad account of fore-bemoanèd moan,
Which I new pay as if not paid before.
    But if the while I think on thee, dear friend,
    All losses are restored and sorrows end.

55 (45'12")

Not marble, nor the gilded monuments
Of princes, shall outlive this pow'rful rhyme,
But you shall shine more bright in these contents
Than unswept stone, besmeared with sluttish time.
When wasteful war shall statues overturn,
And broils root out the work of masonry,
Nor Mars his sword no war's quick fire shall burn
The living record of your memory.
'Gainst death and all oblivious enmity
Shall you pace forth; your praise shall still find room
Even in the eyes of all posterity
That wear this world out to the ending doom.
    So, till the judgment that yourself arise,
    You live in this, and dwell in lovers' eyes.

27 (54'17")

Weary with toil, I haste me to my bed,
The dear repose for limbs with travel tired,
But then begins a journey in my head
To work my mind when body's work's expired;
For then my thoughts, from far where I abide,
Intend a zealous pilgrimage to thee,
And keep my drooping eyelids open wide,
Looking on darkness which the blind do see;
Save that my soul's imaginary sight
Presents thy shadow to my sightless view,
Which like a jewel hung in ghastly night,
Makes black night beauteous and her old face new.
　　Lo, thus, by day my limbs, by night my mind,
　　For thee, and for myself, no quiet find.

61 (62'00")

Is it thy will thy image should keep open
My heavy eyelids to the weary night?
Dost thou desire my slumbers should be broken
While shadows like to thee do mock my sight?
Is it thy spirit that thou send'st from thee
So far from home into my deeds to pry,
To find out shames and idle hours in me,
The scope and tenure of thy jealousy?
O no, thy love, though much, is not so great.
It is my love that keeps mine eye awake,
Mine own true love that doth my rest defeat,
To play the watchman ever for thy sake.
　　For thee watch I, whilst thou dost wake
　　　elsewhere,
　　From me far off, with others all too near.

56 (68'19")

Sweet love, renew thy force; be it not said
Thy edge should blunter be than appetite,
Which but today by feeding is allayed,
Tomorrow sharp'ned in his former might.
So, love, be thou; although today thou fill
Thy hungry eyes even till they wink with fullness,
Tomorrow see again, and do not kill
The spirit of love with a perpetual dullness.
Let this sad int'rim like the ocean be
Which parts the shore where two contracted new
Come daily to the banks, that, when they see
Return of love, more blest may be the view;
　　Or call it winter, which being full of care,
　　Makes summer's welcome thrice more wished,
　　　more rare.

104 (73'06")

To me, fair friend, you never can be old,
For as you were when first your eye I eyed.
Such seems your beauty still. Three winters cold
Have from the forests shook three summers' pride,
Three beauteous springs to yellow autumn turned
In process of the seasons have I seen,
Three April perfumes in three hot Junes burned,
Since first I saw you fresh, which yet are green.
Ah, yet doth beauty, like a dial hand,
Steal from his figure, and no pace perceived;
So your sweet hue, which methinks still doth stand,
Hath motion, and mine eye may be deceived;
　　For fear of which, hear this, thou age unbred:
　　Ere you were born was beauty's
　　　summer dead.

[11]

Bibliography

Most of the publications presented below have influenced my work on this theme, however, not all of them are cited by name in the text.

Titles marked with an asterisk (*) have been newly added for the English edition.

Primary Sources

Texts by DEREK JARMAN (in chronological order):

BFI-Special Collection, Item 69: 'Akhenatan – In the Shadow of the Sun', unpublished, London, n.d.
BFI-Special Collection, Item 99: unpublished typescript, London, n.d.
A Finger in the Fishes Mouth, Nr. Bridport, Dorset, 1972.
Dancing Ledge, London, 1984, 1991.
The Last of England, London, 1987.
The Last of England, Tokyo, 1988. *
Today and Tomorrow, London, 1991 (Derek Jarman, and Richard Salmon).
Modern Nature: The Journals of Derek Jarman, London, 1991, 1992.
At Your Own Risk: A Saint's Testament, London, 1992, 1993.
At Your Own Risk: A Saint's Testament, Tokyo, 1992. *
At Your Own Risk: A Saint's Testament, Woodstock, New York, 1993.
Chroma: A Book of Colour – June '93, London, 1994, 1995.
Chroma: Ein Buch der Farben, trans. by Almuth Carstens, Berlin, 1995.
Derek Jarman's Garden: With Photographs by Howard Sooley, London, 1995.
Derek Jarmans Garten: Mit Fotografien von Howard Sooley, trans. by Jörg von Stein, Berlin, 1996.
Kicking the Pricks, London, 1996 (reprint of *The Last of England*, 1987).
Smiling in Slow Motion, London, 2000.
Chroma: A Book of Colour, Tokyo, 2002. *
Ciò che resta dell'Inghilterra, trans. by Nicoletta Vallorani, Padua, 2007. *
A Finger in the Fishes Mouth, ed. by Testcentre, London, 2014 (facsimile edition). *

Screenplays and Books on Films and Works by DEREK JARMAN (in chronological order):

Caravaggio, London, 1986.
The Tempest, ed. by Takashi Asai, Tokyo, 1988. *
War Requiem: The Film, London, 1989.

The Garden, programme book, London, 1990.
The Garden: Sales Information, ed. by The Sales Co., London, 1990.
Queer Edward II, London, 1991.
Queer Edward II, Tokyo, 1992. *
Wittgenstein: The Terry Eagleton Script; The Derek Jarman Film, London, 1993.
Freeze Frame: Directed by Derek Jarman, ed. by Takashi Asai, Tokyo, 1993. *
Blue: Text of a Film by Derek Jarman, London, 1993. *
Blue: Text of a Film by Derek Jarman, Woodstock, New York, 1994.
Blue – Blauw: Tekst bij een film van Derek Jarman; Text of a Film by Derek Jarman, Rotterdam and Amsterdam, 1994.
Blue: Das Buch zum Film, Kassel, 1994.
Glitterbug: The Directors Cut, brochure with the VHS cassette *Glitterbug*, ed. by Dangerous To Know/Basilisk Communications, London, 1994.
Up in the Air: Collected Film Scripts, London, 1996.
Caravaggio, ed. by Leo Bersani and Ulysse Dutoit, London, 1999. *
Derek Jarman's Sketchbooks, ed. by Stephen Farthing and Ed Webb-Ingall, London, 2013. *
Derek Jarman: Die Skizzenbücher, ed. by Stephen Farthing and Ed Webb-Ingall, Berlin 2013. *
Derek Jarman Super 8, ed. by James Mackay, London, 2014. *

Exhibition Catalogues (in chronological order):

Derek Jarman: The Exhibition of Derek Jarman; Luminous Darkness, ed. by Takashi Asai, Tokyo, 1990.
Derek Jarman: Queer, ed. by Manchester City Art Galleries, Manchester, 1992.
Derek Jarman: Queer, ed. by Martin Baier and Cinemarstall e.V., Potsdam, 1993.
Derek Jarman: Queer, ed. by Palazzo delle Esposizione, Rome, 1992.
Blueprint: suoni e immagini dal cinema di Derek Jarman, ed. by Sabino Martiradonna, Palazzo delle esposizioni and British Council, Rome, 1993. *
Derek Jarman: Evil Queen; The Last Paintings, ed. by Whitworth Art Gallery, University of Manchester in collaboration with Richard Salmon Ltd., Manchester, n.d.
Derek Jarman: Brutal Beauty, ed. by Serpentine Gallery, London, 2008. *
Derek Jarman: Brutal Beauty, ed. by Kunsthalle Wien, Kunsthalle Zürich and Serpentine Gallery, Cologne, 2008. *
Derek Jarman, Jean Cocteau: Alchimie, ed. by Le Magic Cinema and La Ville de Bobigny, Bobigny, 2008. *
Derek Jarman: Super 8, ed. by Julia Stoschek Foundation e.V. and Philipp Fürnkäs, Düsseldorf, 2010. *

Audio Tapes:

'Talking Cinema: Derek Jarman in Conversation with Simon Field', Audio Tape No. 1496, Institute of Contemporary Arts (ICA), London, 1987.
'Pasolini Filmmaker: Sacred & Profane; Celebration and Consideration of Pasolini as a Film-Maker; With Tony Rayns, Geoffrey Nowell-Smith, Derek Jarman, Chris Burden, Simon Field', 29 September 1990, Audio Tape No. 577, Institute of Contemporary Arts (ICA), London, 1990.
'Talking Cinema: Wittgenstein; Jarman Discusses and Introduces His Film Wittgenstein', 26 March 1993, Audio Tape No. 871, Institute of Contemporary Arts (ICA), London, 1993.
'Jarman: Filmmaking for the Future; A Discussion of the Impact and Influence of the Late Derek Jarman and What Filmmakers Have to Learn from Derek; With Tony Rayns, John Maybury, Simon Watney', 29 May 1994, Audio Tape No. 1024, Institute of Contemporary Arts (ICA), London, 1994.

Secondary Literature

Secondary Literature on Derek Jarman:

Afterimage: 12 (1985), *Derek Jarman ... of Angels & Apocalypse*, London, 1985.

BAIER, Martin (ed.), *Derek Jarman Filmwerkschau*, on behalf of the Cinemarstall e.V. – Film-club am Filmmuseum Potsdam, Potsdam, 1993.

BALLENGER, Ruth, 'Musical Expression in Selected Texts from Benjamin Britten's War Requiem', in: <http://www.calstatela.edu/centers/wagner/requiem.htm> [accessed January 1998].

BERSANI, Leo, and Ulysse Dutoit, *Caravaggio*, London, 1999.

BIGA, Tracy, 'The Principle of Non-Narration in the Films of Derek Jarman', in: Chris Lippard (ed.), *By Angels Driven: The Films of Derek Jarman*, London, 1996, pp. 12–30.

CHARLESWORTH, Michael, *Derek Jarman*, London, 2011. *

Derek Jarman Retrospectieve, Kortrijk, 1988.

DILLON, Steve, *Derek Jarman and the Lyric Film: The Mirror and the Sea*, Austin, 2004. *

'Discussion with Derek Jarman', in: Jonathan Hacker and David Price, *Take 10: Contemporary British Film Directors*, Oxford, 1991, pp. 248–260.

DRISCOLL, Lawrence: '"The Rose Revived": Derek Jarman and the British Tradition', in: Chris Lippard (ed.), *By Angels Driven: The Films of Derek Jarman*, London, 1996, pp. 65–83.

EDSON, Barry (ed.), *Derek Jarman*, Turin, 1990.

ELLIS, Jim, *Derek Jarman's Angelic Conversations*, Minneapolis and London, 2009. *

FIELD, Simon, and Michael O'Pray, 'Imaging October, Dr. Dee and Other Matters: An Interview with Derek Jarman', in: *Afterimage*, 12 (1985), *Derek Jarman ... of Angels & Apocalypse*, London, 1985, pp. 40–59.

FREY, Martin, 'Derek Jarman: Einführung in Leben und Werk', lecture at the opening of the Derek Jarman retrospective in Vienna, April 1994, unpublished manuscript, Vienna, 1994.

FREY, Martin, 'Echoes of Past: Eine Rückschau auf das Leben und künstlerische Schaffen von Derek Jarman', in: *Filmkunst*, 46.143 (1994), Vienna, 1994. pp. 35–45.

FREY, Martin, 'Im endlosen Blau der Ferne: Derek Jarman; Filme eines Malers', in: *Media Biz*, 11 (February 1995), Vienna, 1995, pp. 18–20.

FREY, Martin, '"There's no place like the Home-Movie ...": Derek Jarman's Home-Movies und Super-8-Kurzfilme', in: *Fanzine*, 1 (2004), *Rohstoff,* Vienna, 2004, pp. 41–44.

FREY, Martin, '"It has snowed since you were here, and your tracks are covered." Eine Ausstellung in der Kunsthalle Wien würdigt den großen britischen Künstler und Filmemacher , in: *ray Filmmagazin*, 7/8 (2008), Vienna, 2008, pp. 108–113. *

HACKER, Jonathan, and David Price, 'Essay on Derek Jarman', 'Discussion with Derek Jarman', 'Filmography' and 'Bibliography', in: Jonathan Hacker, and David Price, *Take 10: Contemporary British Film Directors*, Oxford, 1991, pp. 229–269.

HAWKES, David, '"The Shadow of This Time": The Renaissance Cinema of Derek Jarman', in: Chris Lippard (ed.), *By Angels Driven: The Films of Derek Jarman*, London, 1996, pp. 103–116.

HOWER, Keith, *Outspoken: Gay News Interviews 1976–83*, London, 1995.

'Jubilee: Gay News Number 137', in: Keith Hower, *Outspoken: Gay News Interviews 1976–83*, London, 1995, pp. 65–66.

LIPPARD, Chris (ed.), *By Angels Driven: The Films of Derek Jarman*, London, 1996.

LIPPARD, Chris, 'Introduction', in: Chris Lippard (ed.), *By Angels Driven: The Films of Derek Jarman*, London, 1996, pp. 1–11.

LIPPARD, Chris, 'Interview with Derek Jarman', in: Chris Lippard (ed.), *By Angels Driven: The Films of Derek Jarman*, London, 1996, pp. 161–169.

LOBISSER, Verena, 'Caravaggio: Malerei im Film', unpublished thesis, University of Vienna, 1999.

NASH, Mark, 'Innocence and Experience', in: *Afterimage*, 12 (1985), *Derek Jarman ... of Angels & Apocalypse*, London, 1985, pp. 30–35.

O'PRAY, Michael, *Derek Jarman: Dreams of England*, London, 1996.

PEAKE, Tony, *Derek Jarman*, London, 1999.

PENCAK, William, *The Films of Derek Jarman*, Jefferson, NC, and London, 2002. *

PORTON, Richard, 'Language Games and Aesthetic Attitudes: Style and Ideology in Jarman's Late Films', in: Chris Lippard (ed.), *By Angels Driven: The Films of Derek Jarman*, London, 1996, pp. 135–160.

RAYNS, Tony, 'Credo van een Voyeur', in: Stichting Ambassade (ed.), *De Jonge Romantici en Derek Jarman in de Britse Film*, catalogue of the festival 'The Romantic Aesthetics', Amsterdam, 1986, pp. 46–50.

REED, Jeremy, *Just out of Reach: Elegies for Derek Jarman*, Birmingham and Clun, 1999. *

RICHARDSON, Niall, *The Queer Cinema of Derek Jarman*, London, New York, 2009. *

'Rough Magic: Gay News Number 178', in: Keith Hower, *Outspoken: Gay News Interviews 1976–83*, London, 1995, pp. 88–89.

SALMON, Richard (ed.), *Derek Jarman: Today and Tomorrow*, London, 1991.

SHAW, Gaia, 'Queer Gravity: Alchemy and Sexuality in Derek Jarman's Films and Paintings', unpublished MA thesis in Fine Art and Theatre, Wimbledon School of Art, University of Surrey, 1994.

Stichting Ambassade (ed.), *De Jonge Romantici en Derek Jarman in de Britse Film*, catalogue of the festival 'The Romantic Aesthetics', Amsterdam, 1986.

TAYLOR, Maggie, 'Jarman's Gentle Joke: An Examination of the Use of Irony in Derek Jarman's *The Tempest*', unpublished MA thesis, University of Auckland, New Zealand, 1995.

The Complete Derek Jarman, ed. by Arbeitsgemeinschaft Kommunales Kino e.V., Stuttgart, Stuttgart, 1988.

'The Making Of "Sebastiane": Gay News Number 104', in: Keith Hower, *Outspoken: Gay News Interviews 1976–83*, London, 1995, pp. 21–22.

VERSTRAETEN, Paul, 'Derek Jarman Interview', in: Stichting Ambassade (ed.), *De Jonge Romantici en Derek Jarman in de Britse Film*, catalogue of the festival 'The Romantic Aesthetics', Amsterdam, 1986, pp. 33–45.

WATSON, Gray, 'An Archaeology of Soul', in: Roger Wollen (ed.), *Derek Jarman: A Portrait*, London, 1996, pp. 33–48.

WOLLEN, Roger (ed.), *Derek Jarman: A Portrait*, London, 1996.

WOLLEN, Roger, 'Facets of Derek Jarman', in: Roger Wollen (ed.), *Derek Jarman: A Portrait*, London, 1996, pp. 15–32.

WYMER, Rowland, *Derek Jarman*, Manchester, 2005. *

Secondary Literature on Other Topics:

ADES, Dawn, 'Web of Images', in: The Tate Gallery (ed.), *Francis Bacon*, London, 1985, pp. 8–23.

Akademie der Künste (ed.), *Fernsehen alternativ: z.B. Channel Four*, Berlin, 1986.

The Andrew Logan Museum of Sculpture, at: <http://www.andrewlogan.com> [accessed July 2000].

AMMANN, Jean-Christophe, and Adam D. Weinberg, *View from Abroad: European Perspectives on American Art 2; Die Entdeckung des anderen: Ein europäischer Blick auf die amerikanische Kunst 2*, New York, 1996.

ANGER, Kenneth, 'Modesty and the Art of Film', in: Jayne Pilling and Michael O'Pray, *Into the Pleasure Dome: The Films of Kenneth Anger*, London, 1989, pp. 18–22.

ARCHIMBAUD, Michel, *Francis Bacon: In Conversation with Michel Archimbaud*, London, 1993.

AUDEN, W.H., 'Introduction', in: William Shakespeare, *The Sonnets and Narrative Poems: The Complete Non-Dramatic Poetry*, New York, 1986, pp. XVII–XXXVIII.

AUTY, Marty, and Nick Roddick, *British Cinema Now*, London, 1985.

BABUSCIO, Jack, 'Camp and the Gay Sensibility', in: *Gays & Film*, ed. by Richard Dyer, London, 1980, pp. 40–57.

Bad Object-Choices (ed.), *How Do I Look? Queer Film and Video*, Seattle, 1991.

BARTHES, Roland, *Camera Lucida: Reflections on Photography*, London, 2000.

BENVENISTE, Emile, *Problems in General Linguistics*, Miami, 1971.

BIEDERBECK, Reinhard, and Bernd Kalusche, *Motiv Mann: Der männliche Körper in der modernen Kunst*, Giessen, 1987.

BOORMAN, John, and Walter Donohue (eds), *Projections 2* (1993), *A Forum for Film-Makers*, London, 1993.

BRAME, Gloria G., 'An Interview with Poet Allen Ginsberg, 1996', in: <http://gloria-brame.com/glory/ginsberg.htm> [accessed March 1998].

CAMPEN, Crétien van, 'Deceiving Photographs: Visual Experiments of Jan Dibbets' (edited version of the article in *Kunst & Wetenschap*, 4.3 (1995), pp. 35–36.), <http://home-1.worldonline.nl/~cretien/dibbets.htm> and <http://www.tate.org.uk/coll/biohtm/dibbetsj.htm> [accessed March 2000].

CHEDGZOY, Kate, *Shakespeare's Queer Children: Sexual Politics and Contemporary Culture*, Manchester and New York, 1995.

COCTEAU, Jean, *The Art of Cinema*, ed. by André Bernard and Claude Gauteur, trans. by Robin Buss, London, 1994.

COHEN, Marshall, Leo Braudy and Gerald Mast, *Film Theory and Criticism*, New York and Oxford, 1992.

The Complete Reprint of Physique Pictorial, 3 vols, Cologne, 1997.

COOPER, Emmanuel, *The Sexual Perspective: Homosexuality and Art in the Last 100 Years in the West*, London, 1987.

CURTIS, David (ed.), *The Elusive Sign: British Avant-Garde Film & Video 1977–1987*, London, 1987.

CURTIS, David, and Deke Dusinberre, *A Perspective on English Avant-Garde Film*, London, 1977, 1978.

DAVENPORT-HINES, Richard, *Sex, Death and Punishment: Attitudes to Sex and Sexuality in Britain Since the Renaissance*, London, 1991.

DWOSKIN, Stephen, *Film is: The international free cinema*, New York, 1985.

DYER, Richard, *Now You See It: Studies on Lesbian and Gay Film*, London, 1991.

DYER, Richard, 'Stereotyping', in: *Gays & Film*, ed. by Richard Dyer, London, 1980, pp. 27–39.

FAUST, Wolfgang Max, *Bilder werden Worte – Zum Verhältnis von bildender Kunst und Literatur*, Cologne, 1987.

FEYERABEND, Paul, *Wissenschaft als Kunst*, Frankfurt am Main, 1984.

FEYERABEND, Paul, *Against Method*, 3rd ed., London, 1993.

Gay Left Collective (ed.), *Homosexuality: Power and Politics*, London and New York, 1982.

GERCKE, Hans (ed.), *Blau: Farbe der Ferne*, Heidelberg, 1990.

GEVER, Martha, John Greyson and Pratibha Parmar (eds), *Queer Looks: Perspectives on Lesbian and Gay Film and Video*, New York, 1993.

GIDAL, Peter, *Materialist Film*, London and New York, 1989.

GINSBERG, Allen, *Howl and Other Poems*, San Francisco, 1997.

GINSBERG, Allen, *Kaddish and Other Poems, 1958–1960*, San Francisco, 1993.

GINSBERG, Allen, *Snapshot Poetics: A Photographic Memoir of the Beat Era*, San Francisco, 1993.

GORSEN, Peter, *Sexualästhetik: Grenzformen der Sinnlichkeit im 20. Jahrhundert*, Reinbek bei Hamburg 1987.

GOTT, Ted, *Don't Leave Me This Way: Art in the Age of AIDS*, Canberra, 1994.

GOUGH, Jamie, and Mike Macnair, *Gay Liberation in the Eighties*, London, 1985.

GRAMANN, Karola, 'Tapetenwechsel: Interview mit John Maybury', in: *Sound & Vision – Musikvideo und Filmkunst*, exh. cat., Deutsches Filmmuseum Frankfurt am Main, 16 December 1993 – 3 April 1994, Frankfurt am Main, 1993, pp. 28–35.

GROFF, David, and Richard Berman (eds), *Whitman's Men: Walt Whitman's Calamus Poems Celebrated by Contemporary Photographers*, New York, 1996.

HALL, Stuart, *The Hard Road to Renewal: Thatcherism and the Crisis of the Left*, London, 1990.

HEBDIGE, Dick, *Subculture: The Meaning of Style*, London and New York, 1991.

HEUSINGER VON WALDEGG, Joachim, *Der Künstler als Märtyrer: Sankt Sebastian in der Kunst des 20. Jahrhunderts*, Worms, 1989.

HOLMES, Colin, *A Tolerant Country? Immigrants, Refugees and Minorities in Britain*, London, 1991.

HONNETH, Axel (ed.), *Jugendkultur als Widerstand*, Frankfurt am Main, 1981.
HOOVEN, Valentine F., *Beefcake: The Muscle Magazines of America 1950–1970*, Cologne, 1995.
HOPPS, Walter, *Robert Rauschenberg: The Early 1950s*, Houston, 1991.
HUDSON, Laura: 'Promiscuous 8', in:
<http://www.imaging.dundee.ac.uk/elevator/martin/prom.htm> [accessed May 1999].
HUYSSEN, Andreas, and Klaus R. Scherpe (eds), *Postmoderne: Zeichen eines kulturellen Wandels*, Reinbek bei Hamburg, 1989.
JAMESON, Fredric, *Postmodernism; or, The Cultural Logic of Late Capitalism*, Durham, NC, 1991.
KALLWITZ, C., *Das Sexualleben des Mannes nach den Ergebnissen des Kinsey-Report*, special edition, *Liebe und Ehe*, 7, Regensburg and Vienna, [1951(?)].
KAPOS, Martha (ed.), *Impressionismus*, Cologne, 1994.
KERSTING, Rudolf, *Wie die Sinne auf Montage gehen*, Basel and Frankfurt am Main, 1989.
KINDER CARR, Carolyn, *Rebel Painters of the 1950s*, in:
<http://www.npg.si.edu/exh/rebels/painters.htm> [accessed May 1998].
KINSEY, Alfred C. et al., *Sexual Behavior in the Human Male*, Philadelphia, 1948, 1998.
KINSEY, Alfred C. et al., *Sexual Behavior in the Human Female*, Philadelphia, 1953, 1998.
KORNBLUTH, Jesse, *Notes from the New Underground*, New York, 1968.
KRISTEVA, Julia, and Nicolas Ruwet (ed.), *Langue, discours, société: Pour Emile Benveniste*, Paris, 1975.
LAUTMANN, Rüdiger (ed.), *Homosexualität: Handbuch der Theorie- und Forschungsgeschichte*, Frankfurt am Main and New York, 1993.
LAUTMANN, Rüdiger, *Seminar: Gesellschaft und Homosexualität*, Frankfurt am Main, 1977.
LEVINE, Les, 'Post-larmoyante Kunst', in: Eleonora Louis and Toni Stooss (eds), *Die Sprache der Kunst: Die Beziehung von Bild und Text in der Kunst des 20. Jahrhunderts*, Vienna, 1993, pp. 311–318.
LOUIS, Eleonora, and Toni STOOSS (eds), *Die Sprache der Kunst: Die Beziehung von Bild und Text in der Kunst des 20. Jahrhunderts*, Vienna, 1993.
MELIA, Paul, 'DH on Drawing', interview with David Hockney, London, 14 December 1994, cited from: <http://www.zen.co.uk/home/page/paul.m/dhchat.html> [accessed June 1998].
METZ, Christian, *Semiologie des Films*, Munich, 1972.
MITCHELL, Jason Paul, 'Constructing Walt Whitman: The Critics Contend with the Good G(r)ay Poet', in: <http://sunset.backbone.olemiss.edu/~jmitchel/walt.htm> [accessed March 1998].
MÜLLER, Axel, 'James Turrell: Twilight Arch', informational sheet of the Museum für Moderne Kunst, Frankfurt am Main, 1991.
MURRAY, Timothy, *Like a Film: Ideological Fantasy on Screen, Camera and Canvas*, London, 1993.
NOEVER, Peter, and MAK (eds), *James Turrell: The Other Horizon*, Vienna, 1999.
O'PRAY, Michael (ed.), *Andy Warhol: Film Factory*, London, 1989.
O'PRAY, Michael, 'De Nieuwe Generatie in de Britse Experimentele Film', in: Stichting Ambassade (ed.), *De Jonge Romantici en Derek Jarman in de Britse Film*, catalogue of the festival 'The Romantic Aesthetics', Amsterdam, 1986, pp. 20–26.
PARK, James, *Learning to Dream: The New British Cinema*, London, 1984.
PARRELL, Marnie, 'Repression; or, How to Make Good Movies', in: *Cineaction*, 30 (1992), Toronto, 1992.
Performance Magazine: The Review of Live Art, 28 (February/March 1984), London, 1984.
PERRÉE, Rob, *Into Video Art: The Characteristics of a Medium*, Rotterdam and Amsterdam, 1988.
PETRIE, Duncan (ed.), *Screening Europe: Image and Identity in Contemporary European Cinema*, London, 1992.
PETRIE, Duncan (ed.), *New Questions of British Cinema*, London, 1992.
PETZKE, Ingo, *Das Experimentalfilm-Handbuch*, Schriftenreihe des Deutschen Filmmuseums, Frankfurt am Main, Frankfurt am Main, 1989.

PILLING, Jayne, and Michael O'Pray, *Into the Pleasure Dome: The Films of Kenneth Anger*, London, 1989.

Queer with Class: The First Book of Homocult, Manchester, 1992.

RAYNS, Tony, 'Dedication to Create Make Believe', in: Jayne Pilling and Michael O'Pray, *Into the Pleasure Dome: The Films of Kenneth Anger*, London, 1989, pp. 23–27.

RAYNS, Tony, 'Lucifer: A Kenneth Anger Kompendium', in: Jayne Pilling and Michael O'Pray, *Into the Pleasure Dome: The Films of Kenneth Anger*, London, 1989, pp. 5–17.

REICHERT, Holger, 'Film und Kino: Die Maschinerie des Sehens; Die Suche nach dem Ort des Betrachters in der filmtheoretischen Diskussion', unpublished thesis, University of Vienna, 1993.

RESTANY, Pierre, *Yves Klein: Fire at the Heart of the Void*, New York, 1992.

RUSSO, Vito, *The Celluloid Closet: Homosexuality in the Movies*, rev. ed., New York, 1987.

SAVAGE, Jon, *England's Dreaming: Sex Pistols and Punk Rock*, London, 1991.

The Sexual Subject: A Screen Reader in Sexuality, London, 1992.

SHAKESPEARE, William, *Die Sonette: Zweisprachige Ausgabe*, trans. by Christa Schuenke, Munich, 2000.

SHAKESPEARE, William, *The Sonnets and Narrative Poems: The Complete Non-Dramatic Poetry*, New York, 1986.

SHOWALTER, Elaine, *Sexual Anarchy: Gender and Culture at the Fin de Siècle*, London, 1991.

SITNEY, P. Adams, *Visionary Film: The American Avant-Garde 1943–1978*, New York, 1979.

SKED, Alan, and Chris Cook, *Post-War Britain*, London, 1990.

SLOTERDIJK, Peter, *Kopernikanische Mobilmachung und ptolemäische Abrüstung*, Frankfurt am Main, 1987.

SLOTERDIJK, Peter, *Eurotaoismus: Zur Kritik der politischen Kinetik*, Frankfurt am Main, 1989.

Sound & Vision – Musikvideo und Filmkunst, exh. cat., Deutsches Filmmuseum, Frankfurt am Main, 16 December 1993 – 3 April 1994, Frankfurt am Main, 1993.

Spartacus International Gay Guide, 29th ed., 2000/2001, Berlin, 2000.

STAM, Robert, Robert Burgoyne and Sandy Flitterman-Lewis, *New Vocabularies in Film Semiotics*, London, 1993.

STEWART, William, *Cassell's Queer Companion*, London and New York, 1995.

STICH, Sidra, *Yves Klein*, Stuttgart, 1994.

STOOSS, Toni, 'Am Anfang', in: Eleonora Louis and Toni Stooss (eds), *Die Sprache der Kunst: Die Beziehung von Bild und Text in der Kunst des 20. Jahrhunderts*, Vienna, 1993, pp. 1–48.

The Tate Gallery (ed.), *Francis Bacon*, London, 1985.

THOMAS, Karin, *Bis Heute: Stilgeschichte der bildenden Kunst im 20. Jahrhundert*, Cologne, 1981.

TSCHERKASSKY, Peter, *Film und Kunst – Zu einer kritischen Ästhetik der Kinematografie*, doctoral thesis, University of Vienna, Vienna, 1986.

Viennale Katalog 1988, Vienna, 1988.

VOLLHABER, Tomas, *Das Nichts, die Angst, die Erfahrung: Untersuchung zur zeitgenössischen schwulen Literatur*, Homosexualität und Literatur, vol. 1, Berlin, 1987.

WALKER, Alexander, *National Heroes: British Cinema in the Seventies and Eighties*, London, 1985.

WALTER, Aubrey (ed.), *Come Together – The Years of Gay Liberation 1970–73*, London, 1980.

WALTERS, Margaret, *Der männliche Akt: Ideal und Verdrängung in der europäischen Kunstgeschichte*, Vienna, 1986.

WEBB, Peter, *Portrait of David Hockney*, London, 1988.

WEEKS, Jeffrey, 'Capitalism and the Organisation of Sex', in: Gay Left Collective (ed.), *Homosexuality: Power and Politics*, London and New York, 1982, pp. 11–21.

WEES, William C., *Light Moving in Time: Studies in the Visual Aesthetics of Avant-Garde Film*, Berkeley, Los Angeles and Oxford, 1992.

WEITEMEIER, Hannah, *Yves Klein 1928–1962: International Klein Blue*, Cologne, 1994.

WEMBER, Paul, *Yves Klein*, Cologne, 1972.

'What is Alternative Miss World?', at: <http://www.altmissworld.org.uk/comp/index.html> [accessed July 2000].

WILHELM, Wolfgang, 'Die Regenbogenfahne als "Schande" – Auf dem Weg zu einem Anti-
diskriminierungsgesetz?' in: Wolfgang Förster, Tobias G. Natter and Ines Rieder (eds), *Der
andere Blick: Lesbischwules Leben in Österreich; Eine Kulturgeschichte*, Vienna, 2001.
WITTGENSTEIN, Ludwig, *On Certainty*, ed. by G. E. M. Anscombe and G. H. von Wright,
trans. by Denis Paul and G. E. M. Anscombe, Oxford, 1969.
WOOD, Linda, *British Films 1971–1981*, London, 1983.
YOUNGBLOOD, Gene, *Expanded Cinema*, New York, 1970.
Yves Klein 1928–1962: A Retrospective, ed. by Institute for the Arts, Rice University, Houston, in
association with The Arts Publisher, Inc., New York, Houston, 1982.
ZWEITE, Armin (ed.), *Robert Rauschenberg*, Cologne, 1994.
ZWEITE, Armin: '"Kunst sollte kein Konzept haben." Anmerkungen zu Rauschenbergs Werk
in den 50er und 60er Jahren', in: Armin Zweite (ed.), *Robert Rauschenberg*, Cologne, 1994,
pp. 17–60.

Articles in Periodicals:

ALCORN, Keith, 'Queer and Now (The Politics of Queer)' In: *Gay Times*, May 1992, London,
1992, pp. 20–24.
ARROYO, José, 'Angelic Compositions: The Legacy of an English Queer', in: *Gay Times*, April
1994, London, 1994, pp. 11–12.
'Arts Minister in Bid to Calm Fears', in: *Capital Gay*, 359 (9 September 1988), London, 1988,
p. 3.
AUTY, Martyn, 'The Tempest', in: BFI, *Monthly Film Bulletin*, 47.555 (April 1980), London,
1980, pp. 78–79.
'Battle of the Censors over Jarman Organ', in: *Capital Gay*, 493 (10 May 1991), London, 1991.
BAUER, Edgar J., 'Kunst in Zeiten von AIDS: Zu Derek Jarmans Film "Blue"', in: *Zeitschrift für
Sexualforschung*, 9.1 (March 1996), Stuttgart, 1996, pp. 22–43.
BECK, Alan, 'Screening Queen', in: *The Pink Paper*, 25 February 1994, London, 1994, p. 13.
BEVAN, Richard, 'Derek Jarman Speaks His Mind', in: *The Pink Paper*, 23 December 1989,
London, 1989, p. 16.
BLOUNT, Marcellus, Gregg Bordowitz, Holly Hughes, Jeff Nunokawa, Eve Sedgwick and Alisa
Solomon, 'Identity Crisis: Queer Politics in the Age of Possibilities', in: *The Village Voice*,
37.26 (30 June 1992), *Queer Issue*, New York, 1992, pp. 27–33.
BOURNE, Stephen, 'Brief Encounters: What Can the Lesbian and Gay Spectator Discover in
Popular British Cinema of the 1930s and 1940s?', in: *Gay Times*, March 1992, London,
1992, pp. 33–36.
'Boycott Threat Lifted as Guardian Talks Open', in: *Capital Gay*, 513 (27 September 1991),
London, 1991, p. 12.
BURSTON, Paul, 'The Last of Jarman', in: *Attitude*, 1.1 (1994), London, 1994, pp. 36–37.
BURSTON, Paul, 'The Death of Queer Politics', in: *Gay Times*, August 1992, London, 1992,
pp. 22–23.
CAREY, Alice, 'Pilgrimage Leads to a Garden without Walls', in: *The Washington Blade*, 16 June
1995, Washington, 1995, p. 61.
COLLIS, Rose, 'So Dish! Interview with Christine Vachon', in: *Gay Times*, May 1994, London,
1994, pp. 66–67.
CONIJN, Frits, Derek Jarman, 'Af en toe verlang ik naar een snelle en fatale longontsteking', in:
De Groene Amsterdammer, 23 February 1994, pp. 8–9.
COOPER, Emmanuel, 'The World's Most Famous Living Artist: Life and Work of David
Hockney', in: *Gay Times*, December 1988, London, 1988, pp. 28–30.
D'ARCY, Susan, 'In the Frame: Blue', in: *Fact*, n.p., n.d.
DE JONGH, Nicholas, 'Derek Jarman 1942–94', in: *Phase*, 2 (April 1994), pp. 84–87.
'Derek at Dungeness: The Filmmaker Wrests Life and Beauty from a Wasteland', in: *POZ*, 12
(February/March 1996), New York, 1996, pp. 60–65.
FINCH, Mark, 'Caravaggio', in: BFI, *Monthly Film Bulletin*, 53.627 (April 1986), London,
1986, pp. 99–100.

FRASER, Simon, 'The Jarman Collage', in: *Rouge*, 6 (April–June 1991), London, 1991, pp. 28–30.

FRICKE, Harald, 'Mit Haut, so dünn wie Zigarettenpapier', in: *die tageszeitung*, 14 February 1994, Berlin, 1994.

FULLER, Peter, 'Queer Saint: Derek Jarman', in: *Rites Magazine*, January/February 1992, Toronto, 1992, pp. 16–17.

GEKELER, Corinna, 'Clause 25 verabschiedet', in: *Magnus*, 3.7 (July 1991), Berlin, 1991, p. 33.

GRAHAM, Sarah, Derek Jarman and Isaac Julien, 'Out with the Bath Water?', in: *The Pink Paper*, 13 September 1992, London, 1992, p. 10.

GREUNER, Suzanne, 'Vom Glück der Erinnerung: Ein Gespräch mit dem Filmregisseur Terence Davies über Kindheit, Kino und Homosexualität', in: *Frankfurter Rundschau*, 17 December 1992, Frankfurt am Main, 1992.

HAKERT, Ulmann-Matthias, 'Queer – Bilder gegen Bilder: Bilder von Derek Jarman im Filmmuseum Potsdam', in: *Aktuell: Magazin der deutschen Aids Hilfe*, November 1993, Berlin, 1993, pp. 38–39.

'Halbherzige Reform', in: *A/K*, April–May 1994, Zurich, 1994.

HASKELL, Lisa, 'Video Scene: Gay Connoisseur Home Videos', in: *Rouge*, 9 (1992), London, 1992, pp. 38–39.

HENGELEIN, Hans, and Ewald Kentgens, 'Dereks England: Exclusiv Interview mit Derek Jarman', in: *Siegessäule*, 5.4 (April 1988), pp. 38–39 (Part 1); *Siegessäule*, 5.5 (May 1988), Berlin, 1988, pp. 40–41 (Part 2).

'A History of Aversion', in: *Gay Times*, August 1996, London, 1996, p. 38.

HÖFNER, Michael, 'Die Schönheit im blauen Nichts: Derek Jarmans "Blue"', in: *Siegessäule*, 5.2 (February 1994), Berlin, 1994.

HOLLINGS, Ken, 'The Dead Rose: Anger and After', in: *Performance Magazine*, 28 (February/March 1984), London, 1984, pp. 23–28.

HOLMES, John Clellon, 'This Is the Beat Generation', in: *New York Times Magazine*, 16 November 1952, New York, 1952, cited from: <http://www.charm.net/~brooklyn/Texts/ThisIsBeatGen.html> [accessed March 1998].

'Jarman Video Dropped from TV Screening', in: *Gay Times*, July 1988, London, 1988, p. 11.

JARMAN, Derek, 'On Britten's War Requiem: Some Notes on Making a Film', in: *Gay Times*, April 1989, London, 1989, pp. 36–38.

JARMAN, Derek: 'Aids and Prejudice', in: *Evening Standard*, 5 November 1991, London, 1991.

JARMAN, Derek, 'Jarman on Hockney', in: *Gay Life*, 29 (October 1988), Manchester, 1988, pp. 29–31.

JENKINS, Steve, 'In the Shadow of the Sun', in: BFI, *Monthly Film Bulletin*, 48.569 (June 1981), London, 1981, p. 115.

JENKINS, Steve, 'T.G.: Psychic Rally in Heaven', in: BFI, *Monthly Film Bulletin*, 48.569 (June 1981), London, 1981, p. 124.

JENKINS, Steve, 'The Angelic Conversation', in: BFI, *Monthly Film Bulletin*, 52.619 (August 1985), London, 1985, pp. 241–242.

JENKINS, Steve, 'The Last of England', in: BFI, *Monthly Film Bulletin*, 54.645 (October 1987), London, 1987, pp. 307–308.

JENKINS, Steve, 'Aria', in: BFI, *Monthly Film Bulletin*, 54.646 (November 1987), London, 1987, pp. 328–329.

KATHREIN, Rolf, 'Aufruhr im Königreich: Gesetze gegen Englands Schwule und Lesben', in: *Rosa Flieder*, 58 (April/May 1988), Nuremberg, 1988, p. 6.

KEATES, Jonathan, 'The Art of War: War Requiem', in: *Sight and Sound*, Spring 1989, London, 1989, pp. 133–134.

LA FRENAIS, Rob, 'Assault of Enjoyment: Out on the Ledge with Derek Jarman', in: *Performance Magazine*, 28 (February/March 1984), London, 1984, pp. 16–22.

LEWIS, Vicki, 'The Word Made Flesh: Aids and the Visual Arts', in: *perversions*, no. 5 (Summer 1995), pp. 6–41.

LITTMANN, Corny, '"Ich bin glücklich – sogar in diesem hinfälligen Zustand." Interview mit Derek Jarman', in: *magnus*, 6.3 (March 1994), Berlin, 1994, pp. 52–54.

LOMBARDO, Patrizia, 'Cruellement Bleu', in: *Critical Quaterly*, 36 (Spring 1994), pp. 131–133.

LUCAS, Klaus, 'Queer Nation', in: *Magnus*, 3.8 (August 1991), Berlin, 1991, pp. 40–41.

MACCABE, Colin, 'Derek Jarman – Obituary', in: *Critical Quaterly*, 36 (Spring 1994), pp. V–IX.

MACCABE, Colin, 'Edward II: Throne of Blood', in: *Sight and Sound*, October 1991, London, 1991, pp. 12–14.

'Major Offers Gay Talks', in: *Capital Gay*, 512 (20 September 1991), London, 1991, pp. 1 and 3.

MANNING, Toby, 'Jaded Days: Queer Culture Is Losing Its Radical Edge', in: *Gay Times*, March 1994, pp. 60–61.

MANNING, Toby, 'Flying the Flag', in: *Gay Times*, June 1994, London, 1994, pp. 14–19.

'McKellen Equality Plea', in: *Capital Gay*, 513 (27 September 1991), London, 1991, pp. 1 and 7.

MCKENNA, Neil, 'Queer Battle Royal', in: *Gay Times*, August 1991, London, 1991, pp. 22–24.

MEEK, Scott, 'Jubilee', in: BFI, *Monthly Film Bulletin*, 45.531 (April 1978), London, 1978, p. 66.

MILLER, Peter, 'Terence Davies: An Interview with a Shy Autobiographer', in: *New York Native*, 330 (14 August 1989), New York, 1989, pp. 34–35.

MORRISON, Richard, 'Derek Jarman: The Final Interview; Thursday, November 18, 1993', in: *Art & Understanding*, 3.1 (April 1994), New York, 1994, pp. 17–22.

NIGGEMEIER, Stefan, '"Wir werden wiederkommen."', in: *magnus*, 6.4 (1994), Berlin, 1994, pp. 10 and 11.

O'HAGAN, Sean, 'Derek Jarman: Laughing in the Face ...', in: *The Face*, January 1991, London, 1991, pp. 60–63.

O'PRAY, Michael, 'Edward II: Damning Desire', in: *Sight and Sound*, October 1991, London, 1991, pp. 8–11.

O'PRAY, Michael, 'News from Home: Super-8, Video and Home Movies; Derek Jarman Discusses "Real" Film Making with Michael O'Pray', in: BFI, *Monthly Film Bulletin*, 51.605 (June 1984), London, 1984, pp. 189–190.

O'PRAY, Michael, 'Britannia on Trial: Michael O'Pray Talks to Derek Jarman about Caravaggio, Obscenity & Xenophobia', in: BFI, *Monthly Film Bulletin*, 53.627 (April 1986), London, 1986, pp. 100–101.

PARKES, James Cary, 'A Painterly Gaze', in: *The Pink Paper*, 25 February 1994, London, 1994, p. 16.

PARKES, James Cary, 'Blues for Mister Jarman', in: *The Pink Paper*, 27 August 1993, London, 1993.

PESCHEK, David, 'Pleasure in Protest', in: *The Pink Paper*, 25 February 1994, London, 1994, p. 14.

PESCHEK, David, 'Jarman and Wittgenstein', in: *The Pink Paper*, 21 March 1993, London, 1993.

PETLEY, Julian, 'War Requiem', in: BFI, *Monthly Film Bulletin*, 56.661 (February 1989), London, 1989, pp. 60–61.

PHILIPP, Claus, '"Irgendwie bin ich wohl ein isoliertes Kind": Interview mit dem britischen Filmemacher Derek Jarman', in: *Die Bühne*, 5 (May 1992), Vienna, 1992, pp. 76–79.

POWELL, Vicky, and Colin Richardson, 'Psychiatrist, Heal Thyself', in: *Gay Times*, August 1996, London, 1996, pp. 37–38.

'"Queer Artist" Paddles', in: *Capital Gay*, 513 (27 September 1991), London, 1991.

RAYNS, Tony, 'Sebastiane', in: BFI, *Monthly Film Bulletin*, 43.514 (November 1976), London, 1976, pp. 235–236.

'A Renaissance Man', in: *The Pink Paper*, 25 February 1994, London, 1994, p. 15.

REYNOLDS, Dale, 'Philadelphia', in: *Gay Times*, February 1994, London, 1994, pp. 34–37.

RICHARDSON, Colin, 'Raising a Glass to Antony Grey', in: *Gay Times*, June 1992, London, 1992, pp. 33–35.

'The Romantic Aesthetics: Young English Filmmakers', *Ambassade II, Festivalkrant*, Amsterdam, 1986.

ROMNEY, Jonathan, 'Edward II', in: *Sight and Sound*, November 1991, London, 1991, pp. 154–155.

ROSE, Cynthia, 'Broken English: Three Songs by Marianne Faithfull', in: BFI, *Monthly Film Bulletin*, 47.560 (September 1980), London, 1980, p. 182.

SAGER, Peter, 'Der letzte Garten', in: *Zeitmagazin*, 37 (8 September 1995), Hamburg, 1995, pp. 12–19.

SCHÜTTE, Wolfram, 'Nachruf zu Lebzeiten: Derek Jarmans neuer Film "Blue"', in: *magnus*, 6.3 (March 1994), Berlin, 1994, pp. 54–55.

'Sebastiane: Boys and Arrows,' in: *Films and Filming*, 23.2 (November 1976), London, 1976.

SINFIELD, Alan, 'What's in a Name? (The Politics of Queer)', in: *Gay Times*, May 1992, London, 1992, pp. 25–27.

SMITH, Richard, 'And the Beat Goes On ... Richard Smith Remembers Allen Ginsberg', in: *Gay Times*, May 1997, London, 1997, p. 37.

SMITH, Richard, 'Papering over the Cracks', in: *Gay Times*, May 1992, London, 1992, pp. 28–29.

'Somerville, Jarman arrested in London, AIDS demo', in: *Outlines*, 5.11 (April 1992), Chicago, 1992, p. 9.

SOOLEY, Howard, 'Blue, an Open Door to the Soul', in: *The Guardian*, 15 September 1993, London, 1993, pp. 4–5.

TATCHELL, Peter, 'Private Exchanges', in: *Gay Times*, May 1997, London, 1997, pp. 38–40.

THIELE, Jens, 'Blue: Aids und die Bilder', in: *Rundbrief Film*, 3 (December 1995), pp. 175–179.

TREUT, Monika, 'A True Adventurer', in: *Gay Times*, April 1994, London, 1994, p. 12.

WALDER, Martin, '"Darkness Made Visible": Derek Jarmans kühner, bildloser Film "Blue"', in: *Neue Zürcher Zeitung*, 7 June 1994, Zurich, 1994, p. 45.

WATNEY, Simon, 'Derek Jarman 1942–1994', in: *The Pink Paper*, 25 February 1994, London, 1994, p. 15.

WEIR, John, 'Bent out of Shape', in: *Details*, February 1994, New York, 1994, pp. 131–133.

WERTHEIMER, Fay, 'Aversion Therapy: Kill or Cure?', in: *Gay Times*, August 1996, London, 1996, pp. 30–34.

WINKLER, Will, 'Blue: Der blaue Tod', in: *Zeitmagazin*, 38 (17 September 1993), Hamburg, 1993, pp. 29–33.

[12]

Filmography

This filmography contains all of the feature films and a selection of short films and music videos. The feature films (films with a running time of over 60 minutes) are listed in chronological order and the short films and music videos in alphabetical order. Short films are films with a running time of 60 minutes or less. These were primarily shot on Super 8 film, but several were also shot on 16 mm and 35 mm.

The information provided about the individual films varies among different sources and cannot be definitively determined in some cases. This is particularly true with regard to the years indicated and the running times. The year given is the year in which the film was created. Where the year of the film's creation and the year of its completion are not identical, both years are indicated (if they are known). The same applies to films consisting of footage that was shot in different years.

Some Super 8 films exist in versions that vary in length (depending, among other things, on the projection speed), and strongly diverging running times are sometimes also given for them. The running times listed here are thus to be seen as approximate points of orientation, and I have rounded them to whole minutes. In the case of the Super 8 films and music videos, individuals involved in their production have also been documented (if known).

Very comprehensive filmographies can be found in:
James Mackay (ed.), *Derek Jarman – Super 8*, London, 2014.
Tony Peake, *Derek Jarman*, London, 1999.
IMDb – Internet Movie Database: http://www.imdb.com.

A large number of Super 8 films can be found in the Derek Jarman film archive of James Mackay, London.

Feature Films

SEBASTIANE: 1976, 16 mm, blown up to 35 mm, colour, 86 min., Latin with English subtitles. Location: Sardinia and England. Directed by: Derek Jarman, Paul Humfress. Screenplay: Derek Jarman, James Whaley. Camera: Peter Middleton. Asst camera: Bob McShane. Editing: Paul Humfress. Asst Director: Guy Ford. Music: Brian Eno. Dance music: Andrew Wilson. Sound: John Hayes. Art director: Derek Jarman. Props: Daniel Egan. Choreography: Lindsay Kemp & Troupe. Translation: Jack Welch. Titles: Barney Wan, José Aguon. Illustrations: Christopher Hobbs. Production company: Megalovision. Produced by: James Whaley, Howard Malin. Cast: Graham Cracker, Michael Davis, Donald Dunham, Philip Fayer, Daevid Finbar, Ken Hicks, Peter Hinwood, Christopher Hobbs, Gerald Incandela, Barney James, Nicholas de Jongh, Jordan, Lindsay Kemp & Troupe, Neil Kennedy, Peter Logan, James Malin, Luciana Martinez, Staffano Massari, Robert Medley, Oula, Eric Roberts, Janusz Romanov, Norman Rosenthal, Leonard Treviglio, Richard Warwick.

JUBILEE: 1978, 16 mm and Super 8, blown up to 35 mm, colour, 104 min. Directed by: Derek Jarman. Camera: Peter Middleton. Asst camera: Bob McShane. Editing: Nick Barnard. Asst editor: Annette D. Alton. Asst director: Guy Ford. Music: Brian Eno. Songs: 'Plastic Surgery' (Adam and the Ants), 'Right to Work' (Chelsea), 'Paranoia Paradise' (Wayne County and the Electric Chairs), 'Love in a Void' (Siouxsie and the Banshees), 'Jerusalem' and 'Rule Britannia' (Suzi Pinns), arranged by Danny Beckermann, Will Malone. 'Wargasm in Pornotopia' arranged by Amilcar, Guy Ford. Sound: John Hayes. Sound asst: Trevor Rutherford. Art director: Kenny Morris (von Siouxsie and the Banshees) and John Maybury. Production and costume design: Christopher Hobbs. Hair: Keith of 'Smile'. Special Effects: Martin Gutteridge. Lighting: John Rogers. Production company: Megalovision/Whaley-Malin-Productions. Produced by: Howard Malin, James Whaley. Production manager: Mordecai Schreiber. Production asst: Lee Drysdale, Luciana Martinez. Cast: Adam Ant, Ian Charleson, Wayne County, Claire Davenport, Hermine Demoriane, Donald Dunham, Iris Fry, David Haughton, Quinn Hawkins, Barney James, Karl Johnson, Jordan, Lindsay Kemp & Troupe, Neil Kennedy, Howard Malin, Luciana Martinez, William Merrow, Little Nell, Richard O Brien, Gene October, Orlando, Jenny Runacre, Linda Spurrier, Ulla Larson-Styles, The Slits, Prudence Walters, Helen Wellington-Lloyd, Toyah Willcox, Joyce Windsor.

THE TEMPEST: 1979, 16 mm, blown up to 35 mm, colour, 95 min. Locations: Stoneleigh Abbey and Bamburgh, England. Directed by: Derek Jarman. Screenplay: Derek Jarman, based on *The Tempest*, by William Shakespeare. Camera: Peter Middleton. Asst camera: Robert McShane. Editing: Lesley Walker. Asst editor: Annette D. Alton. Music: Wavemaker (Brian Hodgson, John Lewis). Music for the dance: Gheorge Zamfir and his orchestra. Song: 'Stormy Weather', arranged by Steve Pruslin, played by Steve Pruslin, Dave Campbell, sung by Elisabeth Welch, produced by Guy Ford. Sound: John Hayes. Art director: Ian Whittaker. Design: Yolanda Sonnabend. Design (Prospero's cell): Simon Read. Costumes: Nicolas Ede. Make-up: Rosalind McCorquidale. Hair: Keith of 'Smile'. Location organisation: Simon Turner, Tim Deutsch. Choreography: Stuart Hopps. Lighting: John Rogers. Production company: Boyd's Company. Produced by: Guy Ford, Mordecai Schreiber. Executive producer: Don Boyd. Production asst: Sarah Radclyffe. Cast: Christopher Biggins, Jack Birkett, Peter Bull, Ken Campbell, Neil Cunningham, Claire Davenport, Karl Johnson, David Meyer, Kate Temple, Peter Turner, Richard Warwick, Elisabeth Welch, Helen Wellington-Lloyd, Angela Whittingham, Toyah Willcox, Heathcote Williams.

THE ANGELIC CONVERSATION: 1985, Super 8, transferred to video and blown up to 35 mm, colour, 78 min. Directed by: Derek Jarman. Screenplay: Derek Jarman (based on the sonnets of Shakespeare). Camera: Derek Jarman. 2nd camera: James Mackay. Editing: Cerith Wyn Evans, Peter Cartwright. Music: 'How to Destroy Angels' played by Coil, 'Sea Interludes' (*Peter Grimes*) by Benjamin Britten played by the Chorus and Orchestra of the Royal Opera House, Covent Garden. Conducted by: Colin Davies. Original music: Coil, John Balance, Peter Christopherson, Steven E. Thrower. Sound: Videosonics. Sound editing: Richard Anstead, Peter

Christopherson. Sound effects: Adrian Fogarty. Video transfer: Colour Video Services. Video post production: Research Recordings. Titles: Sally Yeadon, Dave King. Crew: Kenneth Bolton, Steve Radnall, Alice Stepanek, Andy Wilson. Production company: BFI in association with Channel 4. Produced by: James Mackay. Production manager: Stuart Dolin. Production asst: Christopher Hughes. Sonnets read by: Judi Dench. Cast: Dave Baby, Timothy Burke, Simon Costin, Christopher Hobbs, Philip MacDonald, Toby Mott, Steve Radnall, Paul Reynolds, Robert Sharp, Phillip Williamson, Tony Wood.

CARAVAGGIO: 1986, 35 mm, colour, 93 min. Location: Western Half Warehouse of Limehouse Studios, London E14. Directed by: Derek Jarman. Screenplay: Derek Jarman, based on an idea by Nicholas Ward-Jackson. 1st camera: Gabriel Beristain. 2nd camera: Steve Tickner. 2nd camera asst: Phil Bough. Editing: George Akers. Original music: Simon Fisher Turner assisted by Mary Phillips. Musicians: Bill Badley, Steart Butterfield, Lol Coxhill, Charlie Duncan, Brian Gulland, Stuart Hall, Julia Hodgson, Timothy Hugh, Neil Kelly, Chi Chi Nwanoku, Jocelyn Pook, Rodney Skeaping, El Tito, Veryan Weston. Singers: John Douglas-Williams, Charles Gibbs, Mary Phillips, Nicolas Robertson, Angus Smith. Music recorded at: Berry Street Studios. Music: 'Missa Lux et origo', 'Sicilian Work Songs', 'El Nino'. Sound: Billy McCarthy. Music engineer: Richard Preston. Art director: Mike Buchanan. Design: Christopher Hobbs, Mike Buchanan. Construction: Constructivist (Alistair Gow, Susan McLenachan, Robin Thistlethwaite). Paintings: Christopher Hobbs. Scenic artists: Annie La Paz, Lucy Morahan. Costumes: Sandy Powell. Make-up: Morag Ross. Project development: James Mackay. Lighting: Larry Prinz. Titles: Frameline. Production company: BFI in association with Nicholas Ward-Jackson for Channel 4. Produced by: Sarah Radclyffe. Executive producer: Colin MacCabe (BFI). Production manager: Sarah Wilson. Cast: Noam Almaz, Dawn Archibald, Sean Bean, Jack Birkett, Una Brandon-Jones, Imogen Claire, Robbie Coltrane, Garry Cooper, Sadie Corre, Lol Coxhill, Nigel Davenport, Vernon Dobtcheff, Terry Downes, Dexter Fletcher, Michael Gough, Jonathon Hyde, Spencer Leigh, Emil Nicolaou, Gene October, Cindy Oswin, John Rogan, Zohra Segal, Tilda Swinton, Lucien Taylor, Nigel Terry, Simon Turner.

THE LAST OF ENGLAND: 1987, Super 8, transferred to video and blown up to 35 mm, colour and b/w, 87 min. Locations: London, Liverpool, New York. Directed by: Derek Jarman. Camera: Derek Jarman, Christopher Hughes, Cerith Wyn Evans, Richard Heslop. Riot filmed by: Tim Burke, Richard Heslop. Editing: Peter Cartwright, Angus Cook, John Maybury, Sally Yeadon. Music/music arranged by: Simon Turner. Music played by: Brian Gulland, El Tito, Simon Turner. Singers: Claudine Coule, Martyn Bates. Harp: David Snell. Strings: Sally Herbert, Audrey Riley, Jocelyn Pool, Annie Stephenson, Bill McGee. Additional music: 'Refugee Theme' (Barry Adamson), played by Barry Adamson, Martin Micarrick; 'Terrorists' (Andy Gill), played by Andy Gill, Dean Garcia; 'Disco Death' (Mayo Thompson, Albert Oehlen); 'The Skye Boat Song', sung by Marianne Faithfull; 'Pomp and Circumstance' (Edward Elgar), played by the Scottish National Orchestra; 'La Treizième Revient', 'Deliver Me' (Diamanda Galas). Sound design: Simon Turner. Sound: Mathew Evans, Chris Gurney, Richard Anstead (musical mixing). Sound editing: Budge Tremlett. Sound effects: Bill Garlick, Felicity Cottrell. Mixing: Peter Maxwell. Design: Christopher Hobbs. Costumes: Sandy Powell. Wardrobe: Paul Treacy, Pam Downe. Make-up: Thelma Mathews, Wendy Selway. Hair: John Egan. Hair asst: Cleo Mathews. Research: Jo Comino. Special effects: Tony Neale. Lighting: Christopher Hughes. Footage from the twenties by: Harry Puttock. Footage from the forties by: Lance Jarman. Production company: Anglo International Films for British Screen, Channel 4, ZDF. Produced by: James Mackay, Don Boyd. Co-produced by: Yvonne Little, Mayo Thompson. Production asst: Elizabeth Burn. Cast: Gerrard McCarthur, Gay Gaynor, Matthew Hawkins, Spencer Leigh, John Phillips, Spring, Tilda Swinton, Nigel Terry (voice).

WAR REQUIEM: 1989, Super 8 and 35 mm, colour, 93 min. Directed by: Derek Jarman. Screenplay: Derek Jarman. Camera: Richard Greatrex. Editing: Rick Elgood. Asst directors: Julian Cole, Keith Collins. Music: *War Requiem*, opus 66, by Benjamin Britten. Soprano: Galina Vishnevskaya, Tenor: Peter Pears, Baritone: Dietrich Fischer-Dieskau. Accompanied by: Bach Choir, Melos Ensemble, Highgate School Choir and the London Symphony Orchestra and

Choir (choir directed by: David Willcocks). Original recording: The Decca Record Company Ltd., England. Sound recording: Garth Marshall. Art director: Michael Carter. Asst art director: Vicky Burton. Design: Lucy Morahan. Costumes: Linda Alderson. Hair and make-up: Peter King, Peter Owen. Lighting: Billy Pochetti. Video editing: John Maybury. On-line video editing: Steve Crouch. Asst video editor: Keith Collins. Steadicam operators: Peter Cavaciuti, John Ward. Marketing and advertising: Matthew Freud. Production company: Anglo International Films Ltd. for the BBC in association with Liberty Film Sales. Produced by: Don Boyd. Co-produced by: Christopher Harrison. Executive producers: John Kelleher, Herbert Chappell (Decca), Alan Yentob, Eben Foggitt (BBC). Production coordinator: Elizabeth Burn. Production manager: Sarah Swords. Super 8 unit: 1st camera: Christopher Hughes. Camera: Paul Bettell. Co-ordinators war footage: Lynn Hanke, Nick Hadcock, Sarah Swords, Richard Stirling. Okinawa sequence: Martin Friedmann. Camera war footage: Tim Cooper, Nick Downie, Ken Guest. Cast: Joe Baxter, Sean Bean, Milo Bell, Clancy Chassy, Rohan McCullough, Claire Davenport, Lucinda Gane, Jody Graber, Patricia Hayes, John Jagger, Alex Jennings, Kim Kindersley, Alicia Ligenza, Spencer Leigh, David Meyer, Laurence Olivier, Nathaniel Parker, Leo Ross, Liberty Ross, Beverly Seymour, Linda Spurrier, Richard Stirling, Tilda Swinton, Owen Teale, Nigel Terry, Stuart Turton.

THE GARDEN: 1990, Super 8, 16 mm and video, blown up to 35 mm, colour, 92 min. Locations: Dungeness, London, James Electrical Studios. Directed by: Derek Jarman. 1st camera: Christopher Hughes. Camera: Steve Farrer, Richard Heslop, Christopher Hughes, Derek Jarman. Additional footage: David Lewis, James Mackay, Nick Searle. Asst camera: Seamus McGarvey. Editing: Peter Cartwright. Original music: Simon Fisher Turner. Music recording: Marvin Black, Richard Preston. Musicians: Martyn Bates, Dean Broderick, Glen Fox, Paul Jayasinma, Andrew Okrezeja, Melanie Pappenheim, Ian Shaw, David Sinclair, Brian Springbacrou, Tito, Hugh Webb, the Balenescu Quartet (Alexander Balenescu, Tony Hinnigan, Jonathan Carney, Kate Musker, Mark Horn). 'Think Pink' (1957), composed by Roger Edens, arranged by Dean Broderick. Singers: Jessica Martin, Russian Orthodox Church Choir. Sound recording: Gary Desmond. Sound editing: Nigel Holland. Mixing: Peter Maxwell. Design: Derek Brown, Christopher Hobbs. Construction: Robin Thistlethwaite. Costumes: Annie Symons. Make-up: Thelma Mathews. Hair: John Egan. Lighting: Keith Osborne, Richard Holborow, Chris Bailey. Production company: Basilisk for Channel 4, British Screen, ZDF and Uplink, Japan, in association with Sohbi Corporation and Space Shower T.V. Produced by: James Mackay. Executive producer: Takashi Asai (Uplink). Production advisor: Simon Goldberg. Production manager: Chris Harrison. Production: Nick Searle. Studio production: Sarah Swords. Cast: Dawn Archibald, Milo Bell, Kevin Collins, Roger Cook, Vernon Dobtcheff, Michael Gough, Jody Graber, Mirabelle La Manchega, Spencer Lee, Philip Macdonald, Jessica Martin, Johnny Mills, Orlando, Leslie Randall, Tilda Swinton, Mike Tezcan, Matthew Wild, Pete Lee-Wilson. Voices: Michael Gough, Stephen McBride, Tilda Swinton.

EDWARD II: 1991, 35 mm, colour, 90 min. Directed by: Derek Jarman. Screenplay: Derek Jarman, Stephen McBride, Ken Butler, based on the play Edward II, by Christopher Marlowe. Camera: Ian Wilson. Editing: George Akers. Asst editor: Laura Evans. 2nd asst editor: Hermione Byrt. Assoc. director: Ken Butler. Production coordinator: Mairi Bett. Music: Simon Fisher Turner, Dean Brodrick, Richard Preston, Melanie Pappenheim, Glen Fox. Elektra Quartet: Jocelyn Pook (viola), Abigail Brown (violin), Sonia Slany (violin), Dinah Beamish (cello). Songs: 'Every Time We Say Goodbye' (Cole Porter), sung by Annie Lennox; 'Divertimento in F Major K138' (W.A. Mozart), played by Elektra Quartet; 'Dance of the Sugar Plum Fairy' (Tchaikovsky), played by Dean Broderick; 'Jingle Bells' (James Pierpont), arranged and played by Simon Fisher Turner. Sound: George Richards. Sound recording: Bill McCarthy. Art director: Rick Eyres. Design: Christopher Hobbs. Costumes: Sandy Powell. Make-up: Morag Ross. Asst make-up: Miri Ben-Shlomo. Choreography: Lloyd Newson, Nigel Charnock. Screenplay support: Pearl Morrison. Lighting: Norman Smith. Production company: Working Title Productions Ltd. for British Screen and BBC Films in association with Uplink, Japan. Produced by: Steve Clark-Hall, Antony Root. Executive producer: Sarah Radclyffe, Simon Curtis, Takashi Asai (Uplink). Production coordinator: Mairi Bett. Production manager: Sarah Swords. Cast: Chris Adamson,

Jill Balcon, Daniel Bevan, Andrew Lee Bolton, Andrew Charleson, Nigel Charnock, Barry John Clarke, Kevin Collins, Tristam Cones, Allan Corduner, Kim Dare, Mark Davis, Robb Dennis, John Henry Duncan, Thomas Duncan, Danny Earl, Renee Eyre, Jerome Flynn, Tony Forsyth, Ian Francis, David Glover, Jody Graber, Roger Hammond, Christopher Hobbs, Andy Jeffrey, Annie Lennox, John Lynch, Chris McHallem, Andrea Miller, Brian Mitchell, Giles de Montigny, Sharon Munro, Barbara New, Lloyd Newson, James Norton, David Oliver, Kristina Overton, Sandy Powell, John Quentin, Liz Ranken, Trevor Skingle, Jonathon Stables, Dudley Sutton, Tilda Swinton, Kate Temple, Nigel Terry, Andrew Tiernan, Steven Waddington, Michael Watkins.

WITTGENSTEIN: 1993, 35 mm, 75 min. Directed by: Derek Jarman. Screenplay: Derek Jarman, Terry Eagleton, Ken Butler. Camera: James Welland. Asst camera: Araf Khan. Editing: Budge Tremlett. Assoc. director: Ken Butler. Music: Jan Latham-Koenig. Featured music: Johannes Brahms, 'Intermezzo', opus 119, no. 1; 'Concerto for Piano and Orchestra', opus 83, in B flat major; César Franck: 'Sonata for Violin and Piano in A Major'; Gilbert & Sullivan: 'I Am Alone and Unobserved' from *Patience*; Leos Janacek: 'In the Mist'; Wolfgang Amadeus Mozart: 'Rondo in A Minor', K511; Modest Mussorgsky: 'Pictures at an Exhibition'; Francis Poulenc: 'Sonata for Flute and Piano', 1957; Maurice Ravel: 'Concerto pour La Main Gauche'; Erik Satie: 'Ogives', 'Gnossiennes'; Robert Schumann: 'Carnaval'. Sound: George Richards. Instruments: Jan Latham-Koenig (piano), Paul Barritt (violin), Judith Hall (flute). Sound: George Richards. Art director: Annie Lapaz. Design: Annie Lapaz. Make-up and hair: Morag Ross. Costumes: Sandy Powell. Screenplay support: Pearl Morrison. Lighting: John Turley. Production company: Bandung Ltd. for Channel 4 and BFI, in association with Uplink, Japan. Produced by: Tariq Ali. Executive producer: Eliza Mellor, Ben Gibson (BFI), Takashi Asai (Uplink). Production managers: Anna Campeau, Gina Marsh. Cast: Jill Balcon, Stuart Bennett, Anna Campeau, Clancy Chassay, Kevon Collins, Samantha Cones, Roger Cook, Vania del Borgo, Sally Dexter, Steven Downes, Peter Fillingham, Layla Alexander Garrett, Michael Gough, Sarah Graham, Chris Hughes, Karl Johnson, Jan Latham-Koenig, Perry Kadir, Aisling Magill, David Mansell, Gina Marsh, Hussein McGraw, Donald McInnes, Mike O Pray, Tony Peake, John Quentin, David Radzinowicz, Ashley Russell, Fayez Samara, Ben Scantlebury, Lynn Seymour, Nabil Shaban, Howard Sooley, Tilda Swinton, Kate Temple, Budge Tremlett, Michelle Wade, Tanya Wade.

BLUE: 1993, 35 mm, colour, 79 min. Screenplay and directed by: Derek Jarman. Assoc. director: David Lewis. Music composed by: Simon Fisher Turner. Music: John Balance, Gini Ball, Marvin Black, Peter Christopherson, Markus Dravius, Brian Eno, Tony Hinnigan, Danny Hyde, Jan Latham Koenig, Marden Hill and the King of Luxembourg, Miranda Sex Garden, Momus, Vini Reilly, Kate St. John, Simon Fisher Turner, Richard Watson, Hugh Webb. Additional music: 'Triennale', written and played by Brian Eno; 'Scheherazade', from *The Masques* by Szymanowski, played by Jan Latham Koenig; 'Summertime', by Marden Hill and The King of Luxembourg, courtesy of Mo Music; 'Disco Hospital', written and played by Coil & Danny Hyde; 'Fermina', written and played by Vini Reilly; 'Gnossiennes', by Erik Satie, played by Jan Latham Koenig. Music recording: Brian Eno's Wilderness Studio. Music recording engineer: Markus Dravius. Music rerecord: De Lane Lea Sound Centre, London. Rerecord mixer: Paul Hamblin. Sound: Marvin Black. Sound post production: The Sound Suite. Production company: Basilisk Communications/Uplink for Channel 4, in association with the Arts Council of Great Britain, Opal and BBC Radio 3. Produced by: James Mackay, Takashi Asai. Co-produced by: David Lewis. Production coordinator: Angela Connealy. Voices: Derek Jarman, John Quentin, Tilda Swinton, Nigel Terry.

Short Films

ANDREW LOGAN KISSES THE GLITTERATI: 1973, Super 8, colour, sound, *c.*8 min. Camera: Derek Jarman. Featuring: Duggie Fields, Andrew Logan, Gerlinda von Regensburg, Peter Schlesinger et al. Music: Lou Reed. *

ARIA: see DEPUIS LE JOUR.

ART AND THE POSE: 1977, Super 8, b/w, *c.*8 min. Camera: Derek Jarman. Music: Maurice Ravel. Featuring: Jean-Marc Prouveur, Gerald Incandela. Later blown up to 16 mm in: THE DREAM MACHINE (1986).

THE ART OF MIRRORS (also: BURNING THE PYRAMIDS, BURNING OF PYRAMIDS): 1973, Super 8, colour, sound, *c.*10 min. Camera: Derek Jarman. Music: Maurice Ravel. Featuring: Christopher Hobbs, Gerald Incandela, Luciana Martinez, Kevin Whitney. *

B2 TAPE/FILM: 1981/82, Super 8 transferred to video, colour and b/w, silent, with sound played during screening, *c.*30 min. (at projection speed of 3 fps). Camera: Derek Jarman. Music: Bessie Smith, Hoagie Carmichael et al. Featuring: Dave Baby, Judy Blame, Gerald Incandela, Jordan, Hussain McGaw, James Mackay, Padeluun, John Scarlett-Davies, Volker Stokes.

BARCELONA MAN: 1984, Super 8, colour and b/w, *c.*20 min. Camera: Derek Jarman. Featuring: Christopher Hobbs, Genesis P-Orridge.

BROKEN ENGLISH (THREE SONGS BY MARIANNE FAITHFULL): 1979, Super 8 and 16 mm, blown up to 35 mm, colour and b/w, sound, *c.*12 min. Directed by: Derek Jarman. Camera: Derek Jarman, Peter Middleton, Bob McShane. Editing: Dennis Firminger. Songs: 'Witches Song', 'Broken English', 'The Ballad of Lucy Jordan'. Mixing: Lou Hawks. Video: Nick Fry, Two Boroughs Video. Produced by: Guy Ford, in association with Marc Miller Mundy (Island Records). Featuring: Marianne Faithfull.

BURNING OF PYRAMIDS (also: BURNING THE PYRAMIDS, THE ART OF MIRRORS): 1973, Super 8, colour, *c.*32 min. Camera: Derek Jarman. Music: Maurice Ravel. Featuring: Kevin Whitney, Christopher Hobbs, Luciana Martinez, Gerald Incandela.

CAFE IN TOOLEY STREET: 1973, Super 8, b/w, *c.*3 min. Camera: Derek Jarman.

CATALAN: 1984, 16 mm, colour, *c.*7 min. Camera: Derek Jarman. Design: Christopher Hobbs. Featuring: Psychic TV.

DEPUIS LE JOUR (also: LOUISE, ARIA): 1987, segment for ARIA by Don Boyd, Super 8 and 35 mm, blown up to 35 mm, colour, sound, 5 min. Locations: Scotland, Cornwall and studios in London. Screenplay and directed by: Derek Jarman. Camera: Mike Southon, Christopher Hughes. Asst camera: Philip Sindel. Editing: Peter Cartwright, Angus Cook. Music: Gustave Charpentier. Aria: 'Depuis Le Jour' from the opera *Louise*. Sung by: Leontyne Price. Played by: RCA Italiana Orchestra, conducted by Francesco Molinari-Pradelli. Sound/playback: Matthew Evans. Design: Christopher Hobbs. Set design: Malcolm Sheehan. Set painter: Raymond Harris. Costumes: Sandy Powell. Make-up: Morag Ross. Hair: John Egan. Lighting: Tommy Moran. video post production: Air TV Facilities, London. Production company: LightYear Entertainment and Virgin Vision. Produced by: Don Boyd. Co-produced by: James Mackay, Al Clark, Mike Watts. Coordination of co-producers: David Barber, Michael Hamlyn, Paul Spencer. Executive producers: Jim Mervis (LightYear Entertainment), Tom Kuhn, Charles Mitchell (Virgin Vision). Cast: Amy Johnson, Spencer Leigh, Tilda Swinton.

THE DEVILS AT THE ELGIN (also: REWORKING THE DEVILS): 1974, Super 8, b/w, *c.*15 min. Camera: Derek Jarman.

232 | Derek Jarman

DIESE MASCHINE IST MEIN ANTIHUMANISTISCHES KUNSTWERK: 1982 (?), Super 8, b/w, c.5 min. Camera: Derek Jarman. Film for Psychic TV.

THE DREAM MACHINE: 1984, Super 8, blown up to 16 mm, colour, 35 min. Camera: Derek Jarman. Contains works by Cerith Wyn Evans, Derek Jarman (ART AND THE POSE, 1977), Michael Kostiff and John Maybury.

DUGGIE FIELDS (also: DUGGIE FIELDS AT HOME) 1974 (1975?), Super 8, colour, sound, c.10 min. Camera: Derek Jarman. Featuring: Duggie Fields. *

EVERY WOMAN FOR HERSELF AND ALL FOR ART (also: HOME MOVIES REEL I): 1978, Super 8, blown up to 16 mm, c.2 min. Camera: Derek Jarman. Featuring: Jordan.

FIRE ISLAND: 1974, Super 8, colour, sound, c.6 min. Camera: Derek Jarman. *

THE FOUNTAIN: 1978, Super 8, colour, sound, c.3 min. Camera: Derek Jarman. Featuring: Christopher Hobbs, Jean-Marc Prouveur. *

FRED ASHTON FASHION SHOW: 1974, Super 8, colour, c.68 min. Camera: Derek Jarman.

GARDEN OF LUXOR (also: BURNING THE PYRAMIDS or A GARDEN IN LUXOR): 1972, Super 8, colour, sound, 8 min. Camera: Derek Jarman. Design: Christopher Hobbs. Music: Nico. *

GERALD'S FILM: 1975, Super 8, colour, silent, with sound played during screening, c.12 min. (at projection speed of 3 fps). Camera: Derek Jarman. Music: Gustav Mahler. Featuring: Gerald Incandela. *

GLITTERBUG: 1994. Super 8 blown up to 35 mm, colour and b/w, sound, c.54 min. Camera: Derek Jarman. Editing: Andy Crabb, Nigel Finch & Anthony Wall (BBC). Assoc. director: David Lewis. Music: Brian Eno. Production company: Basilisk Communications and BBC. Produced by: James Mackay. 22 excerpts from Super 8 films from 1971 to 1986 (as listed on the sheet accompanying the video): Bankside London (1971), Andrew Logans Alternative Miss World (1975), Ulla's Fete, a garden party in Hammersmith (1974), A Journey to Avebury Stone Circle (1973), Sardinia, Sebastiane (1974), The Flat, Sloane Square (1975), At Home with Duggie Fields (1975), Eviction party, Sloane Square (1976), Filming of Jublilee (1978), Rome, research for Caravaggio (1978), Broken English shoot (1979), William Burroughs, The Final Academy (1983), Lots Road Party (1983), Early Summer, Hampstead Heath (1983), Jordans Wedding (1983), Florence, Punk concert at Santa Croce (1982), Spanish Arts Programme (1984), Barcelona with Genesis P-Orridge (1984), Sienna, Tilda Swinton and Spencer Leigh (1985), ICA Multi-media Event (1984), Summer Deptford (1986), Bankside, London (1971).

HERBERT IN NYC (also: NEW YORK WALK DON'T WALK): 1974, Super 8, colour and b/w, c.26 min. Camera: Derek Jarman. Music: Lou Reed. Featuring: Herbert Muschamp.

HOME MOVIES: 1981, Super 8, blown up to 16 mm, colour, 12 min. (9 min.?). Camera: Derek Jarman.

HOME MOVIES REEL I: see EVERY WOMAN FOR HERSELF AND ALL FOR ART, SEBASTIANE WRAP, STUDIO BANKSIDE I, STUDIO BANKSIDE II

HOME MOVIES REEL II: see SLOANE SQUARE, A ROOM OF ONE'S OWN.

HOUSTON, TEXAS: 1976, Super 8, c.1 min. Camera: Derek Jarman.

IMAGINING OCTOBER: 1984, Super 8 and video, blown up to 16 mm, colour and b/w, sound, 27 min. Locations: USSR and UK. Directed by: Derek Jarman. Screenplay: Derek Jarman, Shaun Allen. Camera: Derek Jarman, Cerith Wyn Evans, Richard Heslop, Carl Johnson, Sally Potter. Editing: Derek Jarman, Peter Cartwright, Cerith Wyn Evans, Richard Heslop. Sound collage/music: Genesis P-Orridge and David Ball. Paintings by John Watkiss. Production company: Dark Pictures. Produced by: James Mackay. Executive producers: Francesca Forbes-Moffat. Production manager: Stuart Dolin. Cast: Angus Cook, Peter Doig, Toby Mott, Steve Thrower, Keir Wahid, John Watkiss.

IN THE SHADOW OF THE SUN: 1972–74/80, Super 8, blown up to 16 mm, colour, sound, 50 min. Director, camera, editing: Derek Jarman. Music: Throbbing Gristle (based on Berlioz's *Grand Messe des Morts*). 16 mm blow up: John Hall. Graphics: Mark Robertson. Titles: Marek Budzynski. Production company: Dark Pictures. Produced by: James Mackay. Cast: Karl Bowen, Graham Dowie, Christopher Hobbs, Gerald Incandela, Andrew Logan, Luciano Martinez, Lucy Su, Kevin Whitney, Francis Wishart.

JORDAN'S DANCE: 1977, Super 8, colour, sound, *c.*6 min. Camera: Derek Jarman. Featuring: Jordan, Steve Treatment, Jean-Marc Prouveur, Howard Malin. *

JORDAN'S WEDDING: 1981, Super 8, colour, sound, *c.*5 min. Camera: Derek Jarman. Music: The Kinks, The Small Faces. Featuring: Jordan, Kevin Mooney et al. *

JOURNEY TO AVEBURY: 1973 (or 1972?), Super 8, colour, sound, 10 min. (5 min.?). Camera: Derek Jarman. Music: Maurice Ravel. *

KARL AT HOME: 1975, Super 8, b/w, *c.*18 min. Camera: Derek Jarman. Featuring: Karl Bowen.

KEN'S FIRST FILM: 1982, Super 8, colour, sound, 5 min. Camera: Ken Butler. (This film is normally included in Jarman's filmography.) *

L'ISPIRAZIONE: 1988, Super 8, edited on video, blown up to 35 mm, colour, sound, 3 min. Director and camera: Derek Jarman. Editing: John Maybury. Music: 'L'Ispirazione', by Silvano Bussotti. Produced by: James Mackay. Cast: Tilda Swinton, Spencer Leigh.

LOUISE: see DEPUIS LE JOUR.

THE MAGICIAN: see TAROT.

MISS GABY (also: MISS GABY GETS IT TOGETHER, ALL YOUR YESTERDAYS): 1972 (1973), Super 8, colour, sound, *c.*5 min. Camera: Derek Jarman, Marc Balet. Music: Roberta Flack. Featuring: Gaby Chautin. *

MISS WORLD: 1973, Super 8, b/w, *c.*28 min. Camera: Derek Jarman. Featuring: Gerald Incandela, Andrew Logan, Patrik Steede et al.

NEW YORK CITY (also: NYC): 1974, Super 8, colour. Camera: Derek Jarman.

THE PANTHEON: 1978, Super 8, colour and b/w, sound, *c.*8 min. Camera: Derek Jarman. Featuring: Christopher Hobbs, Jean-Marc Prouveur. *

PICNIC AT RAE'S (also: PICNIC AT RAY'S): 1974, Super 8, colour, sound, *c.*18 min. Camera: Derek Jarman. Featuring: Rae Spencer-Cullen (Miss Mouse), Gaby Chautin, Duggie Fields, Andrew Logan, Jenny Runacre et al. *

PIRATE TAPE (W. S. BURROUGHS): 1982, Super 8, later transferred to video and then to

16 mm, colour, sound, *c.*16 min. Director, Camera, Editing: Derek Jarman. Sound: 'Pirate Tape' by Psychic TV. Featuring: William S. Burroughs, Tim Burke, Peter Christopherson, John Giorno, James Grauerholz, Brian Gysin.

PONTORMO AND PUNKS AT SANTA CROCE: 1982, Super 8, colour, silent, with sound played during screening, *c.*14 min. (at projection speed of 3 fps). Camera: Derek Jarman. *

RED HOT AND BLUE: 1990, Super 8, colour, sound. Directed by: Ed Lachman. Video with Cole Porter Songs performed by various artists. Home movie fragments from Derek Jarman's video archive set to 'Every Time We Say Goodbye', sung by Annie Lennox.

REMOVAL PARTY: see SLOANE SQUARE.

REWORKING THE DEVILS: see THE DEVILS AT THE ELGIN.

SEBASTIANE WRAP (also: HOME MOVIES REEL I): 1975, Super 8, blown up to 16 mm, colour, sound, *c.*6 min. Camera: Derek Jarman. Featuring: Guy Ford and other members of the cast and crew of SEBASTIANE. *

SEX PISTOLS IN CONCERT: 1976, Super 8, b/w, *c.*5 min. Camera: Derek Jarman.

SHOWREEL: 1982, Super 8, video, colour, sound, 30 min. Camera: Derek Jarman. Contains the following music videos: DANCE WITH ME, 1983, for The Lords of the New Church; DANCE HALL DAZE, 1983, for Wang Chung; WILLOW WEEP FOR ME, 1983, for Carmel.

SLOANE SQUARE, A ROOM OF ONE'S OWN (also: SLOANE SQUARE, REMOVAL PARTY or HOME MOVIES REEL II): 1974–76/1981, Super 8, blown up to 16 mm, colour and b/w, sound, 9 min. Camera: Derek Jarman, Guy Ford. Music: Kraftwerk, Simon Turner (1981). Production company: Dark Pictures. Produced by: James Mackay. Featuring: Graham Cracker, Guy Ford, Alasdair McGaw, Gerald Incandela, Derek Jarman, Malcolm Leigh. *

STOLEN APPLES FOR KAREN BLIXEN: 1973, Super 8, b/w, *c.*3 min. Camera: Derek Jarman. Music: Claude Debussy. Featuring: Gerald Incandela.

STUDIO BANKSIDE I (also: BANKSIDE, HOME MOVIES REEL I): 1970, Super 8, blown up to 16 mm, colour and b/w, *c.*3 min. Camera: Derek Jarman. *

STUDIO BANKSIDE II (also: ONE LAST WALK ONE LAST LOOK BANKSIDE, HOME MOVIES REEL I): 1972, Super 8, blown up to 16 mm, b/w, *c.*3 min. Camera: Derek Jarman. *

SULPHUR: 1974, Super 8, colour, *c.*16 min. Camera: Derek Jarman. Featuring: Graham Dowie, Gerald Incandela, Derek Jarman, Penny Jenkins, Andrew Logan, Luciana Martinez, Kevin Whitney et al.

TAROT (also: THE MAGICIAN): 1972/73, Super 8, colour, sound, *c.*10 min. Camera: Derek Jarman. Design: Christopher Hobbs. Featuring: Christopher Hobbs, Gerald Incandela. *

T.G.: PSYCHIC RALLY IN HEAVEN (also: PSYCHIC RALLY IN HEAVEN): 1981, Super 8, blown up to 16 mm, colour, sound, *c.*8 min. Camera, Editing: Derek Jarman. Music: Throbbing Gristle (Chris Carter, Peter Christopherson, Genesis P-Orridge, Cosey Fanni Tutti). Songs: 'Slug Bait-Brighton', 'Maggot Death-Studio', 'Maggot Death-Rat Club', from *Second Annual Report*. Sound: Peter Christopherson. Production company: Dark Pictures. Produced by: James Mackay. Featuring: Throbbing Gristle. *

ULLA'S CHANDELIER: see ULLA'S FETE.

ULLA'S FETE (also: ULLA'S CHANDELIER): 1976 (1975?): Super 8, b/w, sound, *c.*10 min. Camera: Derek Jarman. Music: Mike Oldfield. Featuring: Liliana Cavani, Duggie Fields, Andrew Logan, Ulla Larscn-Styles, Luciana Martinez, Rae Mouse, James Whaley et al. *

WAITING FOR WAITING FOR GODOT: 1982, Super 8 and video, colour and b/w, sound, *c.*18 min. Camera: Derek Jarman. Produced by: James Mackay. Featuring: Sean Bean, John Maybury, Gerard McArthur, Johnny Phillips. *

(* = Films contained on the ICA Compilation Tapes 1–3. These tapes provided the basis for the analyses in this book.)

Music Videos

1969: 1986, music video produced for Easterhouse, Super 8, transferred to video, colour and b/w, 4 min. Directed by: Derek Jarman. Produced by: James Mackay.

ASK: 1986, music video produced for the Smiths, Super 8, transferred to video, colour, 3 min. Directed by: Derek Jarman. Produced by: James Mackay.

BEING BORING: 1970/1992, music video produced for the Pet Shop Boys, 5 min. Director, Camera: Derek Jarman. Excerpts from: STUDIO BANKSIDE (1970).

DANCE HALL DAZE: 1983, music video produced for Wang Chung, colour, 4 min. Directed by: Derek Jarman. Produced by: Aldabra.

DANCE WITH ME: 1983, music video produced for the Lords of the New Church, colour, 4 min. Directed by: Derek Jarman. Produced by: Aldabra.

HIGHLIGHTS: PET SHOP BOYS ON TOUR: 1990, music videos produced for the Pet Shop Boys, Super 8 and 16 mm, transferred to video, colour and b/w, 33 min. Locations: James Electrical Studios, Benjy's Nightclub, London (backdrop projection film) Wembley Arena (video). Directed by: Derek Jarman. Set design: Derek Jarman. Camera: Chris Hughes. Asst camera: Steve Farrer (backdrop projection film), Stephen Ley (video), Seamus McGarvey (backdrop projection film, video), Frank Meyburgh (video), Bob Penderhughes (video), John Simmons (video). Editing: Peter Cartwright, Adam Watkins. Asst editor: Keith Collins (backdrop projection film). Music: Neil Tennant, Chris Lowe (Pet Shop Boys); Courtney Pine (saxophone); Danny Cummings (percussion); Dominic Clarke (keyboards); John Henry, Michael Henry, Juliet Roberts, Carol Thompson (backing vocals); Geron Casper Canidate, Hugo Huizar, Derek Cooley Jackson, Robia Lamorte, Tracey Langran, Marion Jill Robertson (dancers). Songs: 'The Sound of the Atom Splitting', 'It's a Sin', 'Shopping', 'Love Comes Quickly', 'Domino Dancing', 'Rent', 'King's Cross', 'It's Alright'. Sound: Neville Young, Daniel Clarke (video). Mixing: David Jacob. Post production: Keith Collins (video). Design: Christopher Hobbs. Costumes: Annie Symons. Make-up: Pierre Laroche, Lynn Easton (stage show); Thelma Mathews (backdrop projection film, video). Hair: Leonard Hughes (stage show); John Egan (backdrop projection film, video). Choreography: Geron Casper Canidate. Lighting: Patrick Woodroffe (stage show); Keith Osbourne (backdrop projection film). Production company: Basilisk for Picture Music International and Areagraph Ltd. Produced by: James Mackay. Executive producers: Martin Haxby, Martin Smith (video). Production manager: Yvonne Tucker (backdrop projection film and video), Lana Topham (video).

I CRY TOO: 1987, music video produced for Bob Geldorf, Super 8, transferred to video, colour, 5 min. Directed by: Derek Jarman. Produced by: James Mackay.

IT'S A SIN: 1987, music video produced for the Pet Shop Boys, 35 mm, transferred to video, colour, 5 min. Directed by: Derek Jarman. Production company: Anglo International Films. Produced by: James Mackay. Cast: Hector Chronos, Duggie Fields, Naomi Gryn, Chris Hughes, Stephen Linnard, Amanda Metro, Ron Moody, Paola Pieroni.

LITTLE EMERALD BIRD: 1993, music video produced for Patti Smith, Super 8, colour, *c.*2 min. Camera: Derek Jarman. Production company: Basilisk Communications. Produced by: James Mackay. Featuring: Graham Cracker, David Dipnall. Editing and compilation: Keith Collins, Andy Crabb.

PANIC: 1986, music video produced for the Smiths, colour, *c.*3 min. Directed by: Derek Jarman.

POURING RAIN: 1987, music video produced for Bob Geldorf, Super 8, transferred to video, colour and b/w, *c.*5 min. Directed by: Derek Jarman. Produced by: James Mackay.

PROJECTIONS: PET SHOP BOYS. 1993, music videos produced for the Pet Shop Boys, video, colour and b/w, 46 min. Directed by: Derek Jarman. Camera: Chris Hughes. Asst camera: Seamus McGarvey. Editing: Peter Cartwright, Adam Watkins, Keith Collins. Asst to the director: Keith Collins, Julian Cole. Music: Pet Shop Boys. Songs: 'Opportunities', 'Heart', 'Paninaro', 'It's a Sin', 'Domino Dancing' (alternative mix), 'King's Cross', 'Always on My Mind', 'Violence' (Hacienda version), 'Being Boring'. Design: Christopher Hobbs. Costumes: Annie Symons. Makeup: Thelma Mathews. Hair: John Egan. Video project manager: Michael Christie. Video editing: Peter Beswick. Production company: Basilisk Communications. Produced by: James Mackay. Production manager: Yvonne Tucker.

RENT: 1987, music video produced for the Pet Shop Boys, 35 mm and Super 8, transferred to video, colour and b/w, *c.*5 min. Directed by: Derek Jarman. Production company: Basilisk. Produced by: James Mackay. Cast: Margi Clarke et al.

STOP THE RADIO: 1983, music video produced for Steve Hale. Directed by: Derek Jarman. Camera: Peter Middleton. Produced by: Aldabra.

TENDERNESS IS A WEAKNESS: 1984, music video produced for Marc Almond, 16 mm and video, colour, 6 min. Directed by: Derek Jarman.

THE QUEEN IS DEAD: THREE SONGS BY THE SMITHS: 1986, music video produced for the Smiths. Super 8, blown up to 35 mm, colour, 13 min. Director, Camera, Editing: Derek Jarman, together with Richard Heslop, John Maybury, Christopher Hughes, Sally Yeadon. Songs: 'The Queen is Dead', 'There Is a Light that Never Goes Out', 'Panic'. Produced by: James Mackay.

VIOLENCE (Hacienda Version): 1972/1992, music video produced for the Pet Shop Boys, 5 min. Director, camera: Derek Jarman. Excerpts from: GARDEN OF LUXOR (1972).

WHISTLING IN THE DARK: 1986, music video produced for Easterhouse, Super 8, transferred to video, colour and b/w, 4 min. Directed by: Derek Jarman. Produced by: James Mackay.

WILLOW WEEP FOR ME: 1983, music video produced for Carmel, 16 mm, colour, *c.*3 min. Directed by: Derek Jarman. Produced by: Aldabra.

WINDSWEPT: 1985, music video produced for Bryan Ferry, 16 mm, colour, *c.*4 min. Directed by: Derek Jarman, Marc Almond. Camera: Gabriel Beristain. Produced by: Aldabra.

[13]

Photography Credits

Cover:
Derek Jarman, *Sightless*,
1993, oil on colour photocopies on canvas, 213.5 x 213.5 cm.
© Estate of Derek Jarman. Photo: Prudence Cuming Associates.

Stills from the film JOURNEY TO AVEBURY,
1973. Camera: Derek Jarman.
Derek Jarman 1992 courtesy. © LUMA Foundation.

Fig. 1: Derek Jarman, Berlin, 1988.
© Photo: Ekko von Schwichow.

Fig. 2: Ford Madox Brown, *The Last of England*,
1855, oil on panel, 75 x 82.5 cm.
© Birmingham Museums Trust.

Fig. 3: 'The royal baby' in the film THE LAST OF ENGLAND, Derek Jarman, 1987.
© Photographed by Mike Laye/www.image-access.net.

Fig. 4: Derek Jarman, *Letter to the Minister*,
1992, oil on photocopies on canvas, 251.5 x 149 cm.
'Copies sent to the arts minister. Dear William Shakespeare I am 14 years old and I'm queer like you. I'm learning art. I want to be a queer artist like Leonardo or Michelangelo. But I like Francis Bacon best. I read Allen Ginsber [*sic*], Rimbaud. I love Tchaikovsky. If I make films I will make them like Eisenstein, Murnau, Pasolini, Visconti. Love from Derek.'
© Estate of Derek Jarman. Photo: Prudence Cuming Associates.

Fig. 5: Robert Rauschenberg, *Untitled (Night Blooming)*,
*c.*1951, oil, asphaltum and gravel on canvas, 158.1 x 80 cm.
© Untitled Press Inc./ Bildrecht, Vienna, 2015. Photo: The Menil Collection, Houston.

Fig. 6: Derek Jarman, *Untitled* (keys),
1989, bitumen and keys on canvas, 46.5 x 25.5 cm.
© Estate of Derek Jarman. Photo: Prudence Cuming Associates.

Fig. 7: Robert Rauschenberg, *Untitled* (Gold Painting),
*c.*1953, gold leaf on fabric, newspaper, wood, paper and glue on canvas, 50 x 50 cm.
© Untitled Press Inc./ Bildrecht, Vienna, 2015. Photo: The Menil Collection, Houston.

Fig. 8: Derek Jarman, *Fine Balance*,
1986, oil, glass and mixed media on canvas with spirit level, 41 x 36 cm.
© Estate of Derek Jarman.

Fig. 9: Robert Rauschenberg, *Untitled*,
1954, oil, fabric and newspaper on canvas, 179.7 x 121.9 cm.
© Untitled Press Inc./ Bildrecht, Vienna, 2015. Photo: The Eli and Edythe L. Broad Collection.

Fig. 10: Derek Jarman, *Blood*,
1992, oil on photocopies on canvas, 251.5 x 179 cm.
© Estate of Derek Jarman. Photo: Prudence Cuming Associates.

Fig. 11: Robert Rauschenberg, *Untitled* (washboard assemblage),
*c.*1952, wall-hanging assemblage: wood washboard with tricycle wheel, square-headed iron spike,
metal parts, key, copper wire, ribbon, rope, nails, glass shard, seashell, walnut and feathers,
74 x 36 x 5 cm.
© Untitled Press Inc./ Bildrecht, Vienna, 2015.

Fig. 12: Derek Jarman, *A Plant*,
1989, plastic, metal, wood, bone and stone on canvas, 51 x 35.5 cm.
© Estate of Derek Jarman. Photo: Prudence Cuming Associates.

Fig. 13: Robert Rauschenberg, *Bed*,
1955, combine painting: oil and pencil on pillow, quilt and sheet on wood supports,
191.1 x 80 x 20.3 cm.
© Untitled Press Inc./ Bildrecht, Vienna, 2015. Photo: © 2015. The Museum of Modern Art
(MoMA), New York/ SCALA, Florence.

Fig. 14: Derek Jarman, *TB or not TB that is the question*,
1990, oil and mixed media on canvas, 46 x 40.75 cm.
© Estate of Derek Jarman. Photo: Prudence Cuming Associates.

Fig. 15: Robert Rauschenberg, *Untitled* (Elemental Sculpture),
*c.*1953, steel flange and stone; assemblage: hinged steel flange, bent steel strap, steel masonry bolt
and stone, 35 x 46 x 23 cm.
© Untitled Press Inc./ Bildrecht, Vienna, 2015. Photo: Dorothy Zeidman.

Fig. 16: Derek Jarman, Garden sculpture at Dungeness,
© Estate of Derek Jarman: Photo: Howard Sooley.

Fig. 17: David Hockney, *The Last of England?*,
1961, oil on canvas with gold mount, 50.8 x 50.8 cm.
© David Hockney.

Fig. 18: Ted Warren, in: *Phyisque Pictorial*,
January 1960, vol. 9, no. 3, p. 29.
© Film and images by Bob Mizer and Athletic Model Guild courtesy of Bob Mizer Foundation
and under license by Bob Mizer Foundation.

Fig. 19: Double Bath, in: *Phyisque Pictorial*,
January 1961, vol. 10, no. 3, p. 31.
© Film and images by Bob Mizer and Athletic Model Guild courtesy of Bob Mizer Foundation
and under license by Bob Mizer Foundation.

Fig. 20: David Hockney, *American Boys Showering*,
1963, pencil and crayon, 50.2 x 31.8 cm.
© David Hockney.

Fig. 21: Robert Rauschenberg, *Balance*,
*c.*1951, black and white photograph of full-scale original blueprint exposed on blueprint paper,
30.5 x 13.7 cm.
© Untitled Press Inc./ Bildrecht, Vienna, 2015. Photo: The Menil Collection, Houston.

Fig. 22: Yves Klein, *Anthropometrie, Untitled* (ANT 63),
1961, pigment and synthetic resin on paper on canvas, 153 x 209 cm.
© Bildrecht, Vienna, 2015.

Fig. 23: James Turrell, *Wide Out*,
1998, MAK exhibition hall, Vienna.
Photo: © Gerald Zugmann/ MAK.

Fig. 24: Yves Klein, *IKB 3*,
1960, pigment on cotton on board, 199 x 153 cm.
© Bildrecht, Vienna, 2015. Photo: bpk | CNAC-MNAM | Adam Rzepka.

Fig. 25: Yves Klein, *MG 18*.
1961, gold leaf, pigment and synthetic resin on cotton on wood,
78.5 x 55.5 cm.
© Bildrecht, Vienna, 2015.

Fig. 26: Yves Klein: *La Lune I* (RP 22),
1961, pigment in synthetic resin on plaster on wood, 95 x 65 cm.
© Bildrecht, Vienna, 2015.

Fig. 27, 28: Jan Dibbets, *Perspective Correction – My Studio II*,
1969, photographs.
© Bildrecht, Vienna, 2015.

Fig. 29: Derek Jarman, *Cool Waters*,
1966–67, oil on canvas with tap and towel rail, 183 x 254 cm).
© Estate of Derek Jarman. Photo: Ray Dean.

Figs. 30a, b: Derek Jarman, *Avebury Series No. 4*,
1973, oil on canvas, 120 x 120 cm.
© Estate of Derek Jarman. Photo: Roger Wollen.

Fig. 31: Stills from the film JOURNEY TO AVEBURY,
1973 (or 1972?). Camera: Derek Jarman.
Derek Jarman 1992 courtesy.
© LUMA Foundation.

Fig. 32: Derek Jarman, *Silence*,
1986, oil, glass, light bulb, etc. on canvas, 51 x 40.5 cm.
© Estate of Derek Jarman. Photo: Prudence Cuming Associates.

Fig. 33: Derek Jarman eulogy and advertisement for the film PHILADELPHIA.
Reproduction of a page from the magazine *magnus*, Berlin, April 1994, p. 42.

[14]

Name Index

[15]

Subject Index

[16]

Film Index